How to Write for Percussion

How to Write for

Percussion

A COMPREHENSIVE GUIDE
TO PERCUSSION COMPOSITION

Second Edition

SAMUEL Z. SOLOMON

OXFORD

UNIVERSITY PRESS

OXFORD
UNIVERSITY PRESS

Oxford University Press is a department of the University of Oxford. It furthers
the University's objective of excellence in research, scholarship, and education
by publishing worldwide. Oxford is a registered trade mark of Oxford University
Press in the UK and certain other countries.

Published in the United States of America by Oxford University Press
198 Madison Avenue, New York, NY 10016, United States of America.

Library of Congress Cataloging-in-Publication Data
Solomon, Samuel Z., author.
How to write for percussion : a comprehensive guide to percussion composition / Samuel Z. Solomon.-
Second edition.
pages cm
Includes index.
ISBN 978-0-19-992034-1 (hardback: alk. paper)—ISBN 978-0-19-992036-5 (pbk.: alk. paper)
1. Composition (Music)   2. Percussion instruments—Instruction and study.   I. Title.
MT40.S82 2016
786.8'13—dc23
2015018562

CONTENTS

Nothing about Sam Solomon is ordinary. I remember vividly my first encounter with a precocious, extremely talented eighteen-year-old, brimming with self-confidence and exuding a musical maturity way beyond his years. The next four years were revelatory, as he soaked up information like a sponge and showed an ability to learn and understand music at a rate I've seldom seen, before or since. Since then I've followed his blossoming career with pride and admiration. When he told me he was contemplating writing this book, my reaction was twofold: first, that it was presumptuous for anyone in his mid-twenties to attempt an authoritative text like this; and second, that if anyone could do it, it would be Sam.

And . . . the book does not disappoint. Composers who take the time to study this book will find a wealth of information and insight. A broad range of topics are covered, from basic timbral considerations like stick and instrument choices to subtle problem areas of logistics and notation. Perhaps most informative are the comprehensively anno-tated score excerpts and the extensive listening and study list. If I could stress one point above all others to composers, it would be the vital importance of studying expert per-cussion writing of past masters such as those listed here. No amount of sound modules, samplers, or midi "scratch pads" can substitute for this kind of knowledge.

For those of you who might find this amount of detail a little bit daunting, remember, this is what we do. Percussion is all about minutiae—choosing just the right cymbal for the climax of a piece, finding a snare drum that will blend effortlessly with the brass, choosing a mallet that will articulate well but still sound full, finding the spot on the crotale that bows the easiest, and so on. For percussionists, God truly is in the details, and this book will certainly get you a lot closer to that ideal. Enjoy!

Daniel Druckman (2003)
Associate Principal Percussion, New York Philharmonic
Chairman, Percussion Department, Juilliard School

In its first ten years, *How to Write for Percussion* has made its way across the world onto the desks of composers of all genres and experience levels. The response has been overwhelmingly positive as more and more composers use this book to help unlock their percussion voice. This new edition of *How to Write for Percussion* fulfills a promise made in the first edition with its online Video Companion, complete with demonstrations of instruments and techniques discussed in the book, plus performances and analysis of some of percussion's most important works.

In addition to the video materials, the text of the second edition contains more instruments, more analysis, and more insights, including a new first chapter with concepts that organize and contextualize the remainder of the book. The material for this first chapter came from observations I made after working with composers who had been using *How to Write for Percussion*. Many readers wrote me to share their compositions, and some caught my eye for their unique failings. These composers had written great music for other media and were clearly good composers with good taste, and yet, even while following the instructions in my book, they were not writing good percussion music. Obviously, this was my shortcoming! Through observation, experimentation, and collaboration on these issues, the material for the new first chapter took shape, and it is my belief that this new text with its Video Companion is many times more effective in priming composers for success in their percussion pursuits.

Missing here, of course, is the most important element of successful composition: collaboration. Composers who are in touch with their performers will almost always write many times better, more effective, and more often-performed music than those who are not. Percussion is tricky, and percussionists are by and large excellent and enthusiastic collaborators. Call, email, text, or, better yet, meet with us on your percussion music. The process will strengthen your music and make your performers better at effectively realizing it.

The many stories of successful collaborations found in the videos of appendix A recount this point, and in the spirit of the joy of collaboration, I would like to officially invite my readers to be in touch with me. Through your input and experimentation, this resource becomes better, and through your contributions to our young repertoire, the percussion community becomes more prosperous. My contact information is available online, and I am always accepting submissions.

Samuel Solomon

2015

ACKNOWLEDGMENTS

I am extremely grateful to all those who volunteered their time to help make this text and video collection possible. First and foremost, I must thank my extraordinary wife, Kristy Errera-Solomon, for her support and patience through the long process of assembling these materials. Thank you to my lead editors, Chris Thompson and Byron Solomon, as well as to Helen and Robbie Solomon, Kristy Errera-Solomon, Jon Bisesi, Doug Perkins, Ian Ding, and Judd Greenstein for their editorial feedback. Thank you to those who contributed to the video interviews and demonstrations: Steven Schick, Daniel Druckman, Doug Perkins, Matthew Duvall, Colin Currie, Nancy Zeltsman, Steven Mackey, Ryan Streber, Judd Greenstein, Nico Muhly, Marcos Balter, Josh Quillen, Eric Poland, Michael Caterisano, Keith Aleo, Brandon Ilaw; and members of the Boston Symphony: Daniel Bauch, Kyle Brightwell, and Matthew McKay. Thank you to the manufacturers contributing product photos: Vic Firth, Zildjian, Pearl/Adams, Latin Percussion (LP), Marimba One, Gover, Ludwig/Musser, Remo, Hubb, Frank Epstein, Black Swamp, Ron Vaughn, IZZO, RhythmTech, Majestic, and Panyard. And finally, thank you to the organizations who contributed funding for this project: New Music USA, Boston Conservatory, Oxford University Press, and Boston University.

ABOUT THE VIDEO COMPANION

www.oup.com/us/htwfp
Username: Music3
Password: Book3234

The Video Companion to *How to Write for Percussion* contains over nine hours of videos with demonstrations, performances, interviews, and analysis to flesh out the material found in the book. In many cases, the information in the video is necessary for full understanding of the discussions in the text. Conversely, the text is essential to the full understanding of what is found in the videos.

All of the video demonstrations are purposely simple and quickly paced. They are recorded in practice rooms, teaching studios, and rehearsal spaces—with no EQ, reverb, or other effects applied—and the instruments presented are of common quality. These recordings aim to present a realistic experience of being in a percussionist's space, listening to his or her instruments, rather than a curated recording-studio experience with the best instruments and conditions possible. The videos, however, are not a replacement for collaboration with percussionists. The material here is just a taste to give the composer an idea of what he or she might want to pursue further.

The reader can find related material on the companion website when prompted by this icon in the text: ◓

Introduction

The story of percussion in Western music is one of novelty, exoticism, and spectacle. Like the treasure hunters of the time, composers of the last century used instruments from all corners of the globe to play together in a new, revolutionary music. But sounds that once took months-long journeys to experience are now available online in mere seconds. Such access allows today's audiences to know percussion is valuable not just because it is "cool" but also because it is capable of sophisticated contributions, comparable to its string, wind, and keyboard counterparts. Crafting these contributions requires the modern composer to understand both the instruments and the people who play them—the way instruments sound and function in an ensemble, as well as the way percussionists operate and respond to notation. *How to Write for Percussion* provides the framework for this understanding. It is the map composers can follow to tread deep into this labyrinth of instruments, to uncloak its mysteries, and discover the skills that will transform each would-be curator of oddities into an expert of percussion design.

HOW THIS BOOK IS ORGANIZED

Most other orchestration books present percussion by first describing each instrument separately and then discussing the specifics of setup, mallets, notation, and special effects. Although there are many very different instruments in the percussion family, the techniques used often apply to many if not to all percussion instruments. For this reason, *How to Write for Percussion* approaches each instrument through its similarities with other instruments, making the process of understanding and retaining this enormous amount of information as easy as possible.

The online Video Companion contains demonstrations, performances, and analysis to both augment the material in the text and flesh out the details of sound and movement that written word cannot effectively describe. Video references are found throughout the text, and it is recommended the reader view each video where marked.

There are nine chapters. The first four consider issues that apply to all percussion:

1. General Framework proposes concepts for how to listen to and choose percussion instruments, and how to work with the people who play them. This chapter provides a foundation for the material in the rest of the book.
2. General Logistics explores the behind-the-scenes issues of movement, instrument choice, instrument setup, and concert production. These are often overlooked concerns that significantly influence the success of a composition.
3. General Notation details the key notational concepts for percussion writing, including guidelines for how to create parts and scores, how to set up notational systems for multi-percussion setups, and how to deal with articulation, phrasing, note length, and special effects.
4. Beaters describes each beater, its specific uses, special effects, and issues of changing beaters within a piece.

The following five chapters discuss specific types of instruments:[1]

5. Keyboard Percussion
6. Drums
7. Metal
8. Wood
9. Miscellaneous Instruments

These chapters discuss each individual instrument. Non-keyboard instruments of determinate pitch and those of indeterminate pitch are not separated from each other, because the techniques used are not necessarily different (e.g., timpani and tom-toms).

The eight appendices expand and reinforce the concepts detailed in the rest of the book:

A. Repertoire Analysis examines in detail the percussion writing of specific orchestra, wind ensemble, mixed chamber, percussion ensemble, concerto, and solo works. Much of the material for this appendix will be found online in the form of video performances and interviews.
B. Sample Setups is a collection of instrument lists with their corresponding setup diagrams and instrument keys.

---

1. Other books choose to classify instruments with respect to the way they produce sounds: idiophones (instruments that produce sound through vibration of their entire body, like cymbals and marimba bars), membranophones (instruments that produce sound through vibration of a stretched membrane, like tom-toms and timpani), and aerophones (instruments that produce sounds with a stream of blowing air, like whistles). These terms are used here only in appendix H, where the instruments are organized with regard to their acoustic function. This method of categorization, however, is not colloquially used in musical contexts—in scores or in conversation—so this book largely prefers to classify instruments with the terms listed above.

C. Extended Techniques is a catalogue of playing techniques that fall outside common practice.

D. Pitch Specification charts the appropriateness of requesting specific pitches for each of the instruments.

E. Dynamics charts the relative sounding dynamic of each instrument struck with various beaters.

F. Register charts the sounding range for each instrument.

G. Beaters charts the appropriateness of each beater.

H. Percussion Family Tree charts each instrument with respect to its pitch clarity, register, note length, and method of sound production to describe the relationships between the instruments and explain how, why, and to what degree they are different.

INSTRUMENTS COVERED

The list of instruments discussed in this book represents all the most common and most readily available instruments in Western composition. Some redundancies occur for instruments that can participate in multiple categories.

Keyboard Percussion

Marimba, vibraphone, xylophone, glockenspiel, crotales, and tubular bells

Drums

Timpani, tom-toms, snare drum, field drum, tenor drum, concert bass drum, pedal bass drum, bongos, congas, timbales, roto-toms, frame drums, tambourines, djembe, doumbek, boobams, and drumset

Metal

Cymbals, gongs, triangle, finger cymbals, cowbells, almglocken, temple bowls, mixing bowls, brake drums, metal pipes, anvil, bell plates, junk metal, tin cans, pots and pans, ribbon crasher, spring coil, church bells, hand bells, thundersheet, steel drums, flexatone, sleighbells, tambourine, metal wind chimes, mark tree, and bell tree

Wood

Woodblocks, templeblocks, log drums, wood planks, wood drums, wooden boxes, cajón, Mahler hammer, claves, castanets, rute, guiro, slapstick, ratchet, and bamboo wind chimes

Miscellaneous Instruments

Bottles, cabasa, conch shell, crystal glasses, maracas, shakers, wind chimes, rain-stick, rice bowls, flower pots, sandpaper blocks, sirens, string drum, cuica, stones, thumb piano, vibraslap, whistles, and wind machine

This list does not include many exotic and rare instruments. A list of all percussion instruments could fill hundreds of pages, but only a small percentage would be practical for a composer to request. The above list is most representative of what is available and what percussionists know how to use.

WORKING WITH PERCUSSIONISTS

It cannot be stressed enough that composers should work with percussionists as much as possible. Although this text and the accompanying videos are very informative, they cannot compare with the experience of collaborating and experimenting with performers on a composer's specific vision. Only a composer who knows how percussionists communicate can devise clear notations, make effective instrument choices, and design creative and successful compositions for percussion.

LOCATION SPECIFICS

This book is written with respect to conditions in the northeastern United States, but all of it will be useful regardless of locale. Slight discrepancies with respect to location are most likely to be found in the availability of certain instruments, instrument ranges, familiar playing techniques, and union rules. Again, it is always best to consult the percussionist or group for whom the composition is written.

THE VALUE OF NOT READING THIS BOOK

Some performers may argue that ignorance can encourage originality. Great notational, sonic, and logistic innovations have resulted from composers writing without any understanding of the reality of performance. That is, however, a rare case, and the author believes that great innovations are most often launched from a foundation of knowledge rather than from ignorance.

CHAPTER ONE

General Framework

"Percussion" is a loosely defined term that can include hundreds of instruments, sounds, and associations. Such interpretive freedom can be attractive and encourage creativity, but the lack of structure can lead to misconceptions and missed opportunities. This chapter proposes concepts for how to listen to percussion instruments and how to communicate with the people who play them. It provides a foundation for the material in the rest of this book and offers a clear perspective from which to compose percussion music.

A DYSFUNCTIONAL FAMILY

The categorization of a group of instruments into a "family" is intended to be a useful way of understanding the relationships between those instruments. These family designations—string, woodwind, brass, and percussion—indicate relationships of sound, construction, and playing techniques.

The primary members of the string family—violin, viola, cello, and double bass—are similarly constructed, similarly played, and are capable of a blended homogeneous ensemble sound. Instruments of the brass family, too, are similar and can function homogeneously. Woodwinds are more diverse—single reeds, double reeds, and flutes—yet the sounds and functions of these instruments are similar enough that they can blend well together. In these cases, the "family" moniker illuminates sound characteristics that allow composers to use the groups in functionally effective ways.

Not so with percussion. There are members of the percussion family that are as different, as non-blending, and as non-homogeneous as one can find among all acoustic musical instruments. For example:

    timpani and guiro
    string drum and glockenspiel
    crystal glasses and maracas

And these are just a few examples of instrument pairs that have completely different sounds, constructions, and playing techniques. Such instruments are grouped together in this family only because they can all be played by the same person. The so-called percussion family thus tells us more about percussion*ists* than it does about the percussion instruments.

The problem appears when composers assume equivalencies between these instruments, as one might between members of any other instrument family. For example, most composers would not write for a tuba as they would for a harp; these instruments sound entirely different and therefore have completely different compositional functions. There are instruments in the percussion family that are even more dissimilar than are tuba and harp, yet composers commonly use them together as if they were violin and cello.

The result is clunky, nonfunctional percussion music. An intended single voice played on a collection of unrelated sounds instead becomes two or more disjunct nonsensical voices. Multiple voices in an ensemble played on unrelated-sounding instruments have no chance of blending into a cohesive aggregate or effectively sharing motivic material.

There is no wonder these issues exist. The commonly used methods of categorization inside the percussion family—wood/metal/skin, idiophone/areophone/membranophone, hit/scrape/shake, pitched/unpitched, and so on—are overly simple and incapable of capturing the sophistication of the relationships in this very large collection of instruments and sounds. Composers, without extensive listening and experimentation, are essentially combining instruments in the dark.

The Percussion Family Tree, found in appendix H (page 280), will shed some light. The tree charts each instrument with respect to its pitch clarity, register, note length, and method of sound production. Like a traditional family tree, this document describes the relationships between the instruments and explains how, why, and to what degree they are different.

Comparison of Family Relationships

These assumed equivalencies are an artifact of composers' attempts to translate a compositional language built for string, wind, and keyboard instruments into the language of percussion. As an example of such an attempt at translation, an excerpt from Stravinsky's *Symphony of Winds* (1947 version) is treated to a series of adaptations (figure 1.1). This excerpt is exemplary of the type of functional blend achievable between two members of one instrument family.

◐ Video 1.a—Stravinsky Flute/Clarinet Original

Listen to the performance in video 1.a. The flute and clarinet create a blended ensemble sound while maintaining discrete, individual lines and a clarity of melodic shape.

Figure 1.1
Excerpt from
Igor Stravinsky's
*Symphony of
Winds* (1947)

"Stravinsky Original" Scorecard

√ ensemble blend
√ distinguishable individual lines
√ representation of melodic shape

First Adaptation—Accidental Polyphony

In the first adaptation of this Stravinsky excerpt (figures 1.2 and 1.3), the flute and clarinet lines have been adapted to two multi-percussion setups, each with the same instruments. Two primary changes are made to the notation to make the score easier to read: the pitches are spread out over the staff (notes are most often separated by a third) and "X" noteheads are used to differentiate groups of instruments. (Detailed information on notation for setups can be found in chapter 3.)

----Tom-toms----   Cowbell   Woodblocks   Brake Drums   Tambourine

Figure 1.2
First Stravinsky
adaptation
instruments

Figure 1.3
First Stravinsky
adaptation

🌀 Video 1.b—First Stravinsky Adaptation

Listen to the performance in video 1.b. The instruments in these setups fail to blend together into a coherent line. When a single line is written for a collection of disparate instruments such as this, groups of like-sounding instruments merge into discrete voices, and inadvertent polyphony is created. In this case, four new voices emerge:

tambourine
2 brake drums
cowbell and 2 woodblocks
3 drums

What was once a single flute voice is now four separate accidental voices, each representing a narrow slice of the original line. Moreover, because of the timbral similarities across the setups, player 1's toms merge with player 2's toms, player 1's brake drums merge with player 2's brake drums, and so on.

Here are the original voices:

flute
clarinet

And here are the new accidental voices in this adaptation:

2 tambourines
4 brake drums
2 cowbells and 4 woodblocks
6 drums

As a result, this adaptation sounds more like figure 1.4. Listen to video 1.b again while following this score.

Figure 1.4
First Stravinsky
adaptation divided

Video 1.b displays a common mistake. A linear idea written for a collection of disparate instruments will separate in the listener's ear and be replaced by inadvertent polyphony. This will happen even in cases where there are only one or two instruments separate from the rest. The situation is problematic, as musical lines created by accident may not make sense and will distract from the flow and message of the passage.

The composer must always be mindful of the nonlinear potential of certain instrument combinations and write for them accordingly.

"First Adaptation" Scorecard

- ✗ ensemble blend
- ✗ distinguishable individual lines
- ✗ representation of melodic shape

Second Adaptation—Individual Non-Blended Voices

In figure 1.5, the flute line is adapted to nine wooden planks and the clarinet to ten pots and pans. This notation is the same as the original with the accidentals removed, the treble clefs replaced by percussion clefs, and the pitches transposed to be more centered on the staff.

Figure 1.5
Second Stravinsky
adaptation

🔊 Video 1.c—Second Stravinsky Adaptation

Listen to the performance in video 1.c. The homogeneity of the individual voices maintains the clarity of line and the identity of voice, similar to that of the original instruments. The woods and pans, however, have quite different qualities from one another so an ensemble blend does not occur. Moreover, the pitches sounding from these instruments are clearly identifiable but random. Part of what makes the original duet special is the blend achieved by the sharing of register and pitch material. This adaptation's random pitches keep the instruments functionally at a distance from one another. (See The Problem of Pitch later in this chapter.)

"Second Adaptation" Scorecard

- ✗ ensemble blend
- ✓ distinguishable individual lines
- ✓ representation of melodic shape

Third Adaptation—Reinterpretation of Pitch Material

In figure 1.6, the flute line is adapted to a timbale and clarinet to a conga. Melodic shapes are reinterpreted as a variety of dynamics and articulations. Different beaters, different beating spots, and open/dampened notes are used to provide contour and function in place of the pitches. (Detailed clarification of this and similar notations will be found in The Written/Improv Divide later in this chapter.)

Figure 1.6
Third Stravinsky
adaptation

One hand holds a stick, the other hand should be bare.
X noteheads = with stick; Regular noteheads = with hand.
Top line = edge of drum; Bottom line = center of drum.
+ = muted with the bare hand in the center of the head.
——— continues a + indication.
T, F = thumb, fingers

🔊 Video 1.d—Third Stravinsky Adaptation

Listen to the performance in video 1.d. This version is decidedly a different kind of music from the original, but it maintains many of the same characteristics of instrument relationship and function. The two drums sound similar, so ensemble blend is easily achieved. The drums have different pitches and slightly different timbres, so each voice maintains its identity. The melody and pitch material are absent, but in their place is a sophisticated vocabulary of articulations and timbres. This version is truly percussionistic.

"Third Adaptation" Scorecard

√ ensemble blend
√ distinguishable individual lines
√ representation of melodic shape

Such an adaptation highlights the differences between percussion and non-percussion instruments. What a drum can do and what it does well is different from what a clarinet can do and does well. The composer who understands the strengths and weaknesses of each instrument will have far more success in composition and orchestration. A simple one-to-one translation of ideas from non-percussion to percussion will result in simple, clunky music.

It should be mentioned that adapting the flute and clarinet lines to vibraphone and marimba is far less complicated. The sounds of the vibraphone and marimba are compatible (the differences in timbre are actually similar to those of the flute and clarinet), and these instruments have the ability to accurately represent Stravinsky's pitch material. Although keyboard instruments have less control over articulation than do wind instruments, the difference between articulated and slurred notes can be translated into subtle dynamic shapes and vibraphone pedaling. These adjustments would be done intuitively by the performers in response to Stravinsky's notation.

🌑 Video 1.e—Additional Family Examples

THE PROBLEM OF PITCH

One element commonly used to manage the blending and interaction of instruments is *pitch*, a compositional ingredient with which percussion has typically had a strange relationship. Many of the instruments in the percussion family are commonly referred to as "unpitched." This is clearly inaccurate; all sound comprises pitches, even a stomp on the floor. The word *unpitched* thus promotes misunderstandings of the sounds these instruments produce and how to use them successfully in composition. The following section offers clarification of the function of pitch within the percussion family and techniques to manage its unpredictability.

To begin, let's discard the term "unpitched." A tom-tom, woodblock, or cymbal is not without pitch; rather, it produces random pitches that are not (or at least not often) prescribed by the composer. A more appropriate description of these instruments is that they are "indeterminately" pitched.[1] This book adopts this term and defines it as follows:

DETERMINATELY PITCHED: an instrument whose pitches are prescribed by the composer.

INDETERMINATELY PITCHED: an instrument whose pitches are not prescribed by the composer.

---

1. Percussion instruments may also be described as "tuned" or "untuned," referring not to the way they sound but, rather, to the way they are designed; these terms are not ideal, however, because percussionists will often spending time "tuning" a drum—not to a specific pitch but to a specific quality of sound. In isolated situations where there are no determinately pitched non-keyboard instruments (e.g., timpani), "keyboard" and "non-keyboard" may be useful replacement words for "pitched" and "unpitched."

The Pitches of Percussion

The term "unpitched" exists because the pitches sounding from some percussion instruments are unclear and difficult to identify. This pitch distortion is the result of one of three characteristics: *noise content, register,* or *pitch malleability.*

Noise Content

All sounds are constructed of many different pitches (or frequencies). With most instruments of determinate pitch, the higher frequencies are in tune with the lowest fundamental pitch. This intonation creates a perceived blend, gathering all the pitches together into one coherent sound. In a blended sound, the many additional pitches serve to clarify rather than cloud the identity of the intended pitch. However, with "noise" sounds—like crashing waves, highway traffic, or those of many percussion instruments—the overtones are disorganized and out of tune, so it is more difficult for any single pitch to be identified.

Technically, acoustic noise is the simultaneous sounding of many pitches that are unrelated to one another via a lower fundamental pitch. Many percussion instruments have considerable presence of noise as part of their sound. A snare drum, for example, produces clear pitches from the top drum head, but the rattle of the snares against the bottom head introduces a significant amount of noise into the overall sound. Instruments like shakers and closed hi-hat have such a high noise content that it can be quite difficult to identify any single pitch.

Register

Humans have more difficulty distinguishing pitches at frequencies far below the range of the human voice, so it is easier for the pitch of certain low-register percussion instruments to escape the ear's discriminating radar. The sound of a concert bass drum in particular survives comfortably toward the bottom of the human range of hearing; overtones sound higher, but they are varied and unclear enough to give little help to the identity of the pitches beneath. A similar effect is exhibited by other large drums and large tam-tams at soft dynamics.

Pitch Malleability

For some percussion instruments, pitch is a constant variable. Obvious examples include sirens, mark trees, and bell trees, where a considerable change in pitch is a basic part of the instrument's sound. Instruments with the most malleability are those that have a sound constructed primarily or entirely of overtones. With all acoustic sounds, as volume increases, timbre becomes brighter. This brightening is simply the accentuation of higher overtones. In the case of instruments like cymbals, tam-tam, guiro, and wind machine, the sound is almost entirely a wash of overtones; when volume (and therefore timbre) fluctuates, the spectrum of sounding pitches seems to glissando up and down.

Indeterminate yet Clear Pitch

There are many percussion instruments that produce clear and recognizable pitches, but they are still treated indeterminately. Sounding pitches from temple bowls, brake drums, cowbells, congas, templeblocks, and other such instruments are easily identifiable, yet when it comes to using these sounds in the context of an ensemble, composers rarely request specific pitches and percussionists will rarely make instrument choices based on pitch.[2]

◑ Video 1.f—The Pitches of Percussion

For further clarification of pitch in percussion instruments, turn to the Pitch Clarity chart (figure H.1) found in appendix H. This chart categorizes all the instruments discussed in this book with respect to their pitch clarity, from Group One, "Clear Pitch," to Group Five, "Unclear Pitch." Please note that Group Two, "Somewhat Clear Pitch," contains instruments of determinate pitch (e.g., timpani, nipple gongs, and steel drums) while Group One contains instruments of indeterminate pitch (e.g., temple bowls, finger cymbals, and brake drums). This means some instruments commonly referred to as "pitched" are actually *less clear* in pitch than instruments commonly thought of as "unpitched."

The Validations and Limitations of Novelty

These instruments of clear but indeterminate pitch are commonly allowed to participate in mixed ensembles, even in pieces with otherwise rigorously constructed pitch material. Why? Because these sounds are a *novelty*.[3] Even the most discriminating listener can be seduced by a new sound. If the sound is interesting enough, it does not matter how well it functions; it simply becomes an event on its own rather than a participant in the architecture of a composition or orchestration. A sound's novelty thus validates its use (or misuse).

This novelty, however, will not last. Upon repeated hearings, the "cool" and exotic can become dull and commonplace. Many works in the current percussion repertoire rely heavily on the novelty of sound—so much so that the sounds are actually the primary composition material. In such cases, when the novelty expires, the work fails. In most non-percussion music, the instrument sounds function primarily as *tools* with which the composer colors and clarifies the composition. When percussion sounds are treated as tools and not as the primary means of compositional discourse, the repertoire achieves both novel and lasting value.

---

2. It should be noted that requesting specific pitches from instruments normally treated indeterminately is usually not an effective solution. A brake drum, templeblock, or opera gong with the requested pitch can be very difficult, time consuming, and expensive to acquire (see appendix D).

3. For better or worse, one of the primary roles of percussion throughout its involvement in Western concert music has been the explicit introduction of novelty, either as sound effects or as references to exotic cultures.

Three Methods for Indeterminately Pitched Instruments

Most composers spend a large portion of their education learning to understand and control pitch. Incorporating indeterminately pitched sounds into this thinking can be a considerable challenge, and successful use of these sounds can sometimes require a complete paradigm shift for a pitch-minded composer. There are three effective methods of approach:

1. Avoidance

The first method is to avoid these instruments altogether—that is, to write only for instruments of determinate pitch. Pierre Boulez's *Sur Incises* (1996/1998), one very successful example, requires three pianos, three harps, and three percussionists playing vibraphones, marimba, tubular bells, crotales, glockenspiel, timpani, and steel drums. Because Boulez is able to control the pitch relationships of these instruments, he can design blended colors across the ensemble.

Even though this approach may allow the composer to work within a comfortable compositional language, one must still take care not to treat percussion like strings, winds, or even other keyboard instruments. It is always important to fully understand the particular strengths and weaknesses of a given instrument. (For example, writing for marimba exactly as one would for piano is not advised—see chapter 5.) Examples of successful uses of determinately pitched percussion instruments can be heard in video 1.g.

◑ Video 1.g—Determinately Pitched Percussion

2. Orchestrational Ornamentation

The second method is to use indeterminately pitched percussion as orchestrational ornamentation. This is a traditional eighteenth- and nineteenth-century orchestral usage, by which the composer makes careful instrumental choices so these alien sounds do not interfere with the meticulously designed pitched material elsewhere in the ensemble. In this context, percussion plays a minimal role, simply adding color here and there. Most useful to this method are those instruments that sound less identifiable pitches (those from Groups Four and Five of the Pitch Clarity chart [figure H.1] in appendix H).

If one looks at the repertoire before the twentieth century, the instruments commonly found in Western music are those of determinate pitch:

timpani
xylophone
glockenspiel
tubular bells

And those of indeterminate but unclear pitch:

snare drum
bass drum
cymbals
triangle
tambourine
tam-tam
rute
castanets
sleighbells
slapstick

These instruments were likely allowed to participate because they did so without introducing random pitch material in a disruptive fashion.[4] Examples of indeterminately pitched percussion instruments successfully used as orchestrational ornamentation can be heard in video 1.h.

⬤ Video 1.h—Orchestrational Ornamentation

3. Recontextualization of Pitch Function

The third method is to recontextualize the pitch function by shifting the means of compositional discourse to other elements: rhythm, timbre, gesture, and the like. In this music, percussion sounds are freed from the ghetto of pitch limitation and can fully participate. It is here, in the rhythmically, sonically, conceptually, and philosophically driven music of Edgard Varèse, Henry Cowell, John Cage, and Iannis Xenakis, that these indeterminate sounds flourish. And it is here where percussion has participated in ethnic musics for thousands of years, whether in dance, ritual, communication, or military functions. More traditional composers have also used this method in moments when percussion is heavily featured—the pitch material becomes sparse, repetitive, or slow moving, often favoring rhythmic function over melody.

A repositioning of pitch as an element of composition is key to successfully incorporating many of these instruments. This can be a considerable challenge to a composer with a pitch-centered compositional voice. There are two simple ways, however, of tapping this resource without completely abandoning one's comfort zone. The first is to isolate the non-pitch treatment to a single solo voice; the second is the use of drone.

---

4. Other early appearances of indeterminately pitched instruments can be found in opera (anvils, thundersheet, etc.) as sound effects for theatrical rather than musical reasons.

SOLO

When a percussion voice is treated as solo, with material rhythmically, texturally, and functionally independent from the orchestration and harmony of the other instruments, then it is possible for the listener to perceive the percussion pitches only in the context of themselves.

DRONE

When a single sound is repeated, the ear can tire of its pitch and instead listen to it only in terms of its rhythmic function. This is by and large how indeterminately pitched percussion operates in non-notated musics across the world—a single bell or drum may sound continuously, thus erasing the function that pitch might have on the surrounding harmony. If, however, even one more bell joins the first, the two pitches will begin to impose a new and random harmonic identity of their own.

🌑 Video 1.i—Solo and Drone
🌑 Video 1.j—Recontextualization of Pitch

THE WRITTEN/IMPROV DIVIDE

The Third Stravinsky Adaptation shown earlier in this chapter (figure 1.6) is an example of recontextualization of pitch. The pitches of the original are reinterpreted as dynamics and articulation, and the static pitch of each drum serves only to help distinguish the voices from one another. The notations required for this recontextualization may seem unusual and overly complex. It is true that scores of this type are rare, but the playing style it represents is actually commonplace in non-notated music. Thus, this passage is evidence of another percussion curiosity: the striking difference between percussion music that is notated and percussion music that is improvised.

An improvising violinist will likely use his or her instrument in much the same way a composer would ask it be played. The same is true of wind, brass, and keyboard instruments; there may be stylistic differences, but the function of the instrument itself is very similar from one genre to the next. This is not true of percussion, however. A composer's usage of percussion instruments tends to be simple, even in works with a complex compositional language, while an improviser's usage tends to be highly sophisticated, even in simple pieces of music.

For example, most composers would expect a single cowbell to produce a single sound. The cowbell voice is, therefore, quite limited, and if the composer needs it to do more, he or she must add more cowbells or more instruments. For this reason, notated music for percussion tends to require many instruments. An improvising percussionist could cull a wealth of colors and articulations from that same cowbell, using only a handful of simple techniques. It is still a relatively simple instrument, but this variety of articulation yields a versatility of function and thus pushes the cowbell far closer to being a viable voice on its own. For this reason, improvised and other non-notated music for percussion tends to require fewer instruments.

🌀 Video 1.k—The Composer's Cowbell/ The Improviser's Cowbell

Music for multi-percussion[5] is particularly illustrative of these instrumentation discrepancies. Composers tend to be attracted to large collections of instruments, like those used in Karlheinz Stockhausen's *Zyklus* or James Wood's *Rogosanti*.

Stockhausen, Zyklus *(1959)*

> marimba
> vibraphone
> tam-tam
> nipple gong
> 4 cowbells
> 4 tom-toms
> snare drum
> guiro (one or more)
> 2 suspended cymbals
> hi-hat
> 2 slit drums (4 pitches)
> triangles (at least 2)
> suspended bunch of bells

James Wood, Rogosanti *(1986)*

> 4 bongos
> 4 congas
> large tom-tom
> large bass drum
> pedal bass drum
> large timpano
> small suspended tambourine with small bells attached
> wooden simantra
> bamboo clapper
> 2 crotales
> maraca
> thundersheet
> temple bowl
> tubular chime
> glockenspiel with added quartertones pitches
> large nipple gong

---

5. "Multi-percussion" or "setup" pieces are ones in which a single percussionist is asked to play many instruments at the same time or in quick succession.

One can find composed works for small setups, like Brian Ferneyhough's *Bone Alphabet* (1991) (seven small instruments chosen by the performer) or Frederic Rzewski's *To The Earth* (1985) (four flower pots and spoken voice), but such setups can appear less capable and therefore less desirable to composers of solo percussion music.

There is one multi-percussion setup common among improvising percussionists: drumset (figure 1.7). Drumset has evolved over the last century to become far more standardized and ubiquitous than any other multi-percussion setup. Although instrumentation for drumset can vary drastically, the most common is:

snare drum
pedal bass drum
2 or 3 tom-toms
hi-hat
2 or 3 suspended cymbals

Not only is this a compact setup but it is also applicable to millions of pieces of music in countless styles. The large setups for *Zyklus* and *Rogosanti* are each built for only a single piece of music.

Figure 1.7
Drumset

Photo courtesy of
Pearl/Adams

Expanding the Color Palette (to Shrink the Setup)

The techniques used by improvising percussionists are invaluable for making an instrument or group of instruments more efficient and versatile. One may or may not decide to use these techniques to reduce the number of needed instruments, but it does behoove the composer to think in these terms.

The advantages of using a smaller instrumentation are countless. Fewer instruments will fit in more practice rooms, on more concert stages, and within more concert programs. Fewer instruments will be available in more personal instrument collections and music school inventories. Fewer instruments will yield fewer complications in terms of notation, setup, balance, and beater considerations. Perhaps most important, fewer instruments will allow the composer to focus his or her compositional attention on the available sounds instead of trying to musically accommodate a large and varied collection of instruments. (Detailed discussion of these points will be found in chapter 2.)

Regardless of the efficiency of instrumentation, tapping the resource of improvising percussionists uncovers many valuable compositional tools. This process may seem daunting—many improvised techniques originate from deep within instruments' native cultures and musical styles—but making use of these techniques does not require the composer know what they are.

Guided Improvisation

Some percussionists are more comfortable with improvisation than others, but it can be assumed all percussionists have some experience and are capable of simple improvisation. The composer can take advantage of these skills by employing notations that encourage extra creativity from the performers.

Ornamented Ostinato

A simple figure can be repeated and embellished. In figure 1.8, four bars provide enough information to allow the percussionist to effectively maintain the character of the passage for many more bars to follow.

Djembe

ad lib.

Figure 1.8
Ornamented
ostinato

Vague Notation

The notation can be ambiguous in specific ways to encourage creative choices by the performer. In figure 1.9, general guidelines for instrument choice are provided, but the specifics are left to the performer. This allows the performer to choose instruments or sounds that are more creative, effective, and available.

Figure 1.9
Vague notation

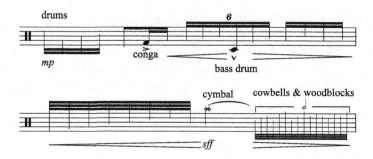

A drum chart, the music a drumset player might read, is probably the most common type of guided improvisation. Charts as shown in figure 1.10 contain information of what type of "time" the drummer should play (in this case "moderate swing"), indications where to play a drum fill, rhythms in the ensemble to embellish, structural information, and cues. Charts like these assume the performer already understands much about the particular style of music.

Figure 1.10
Drum chart

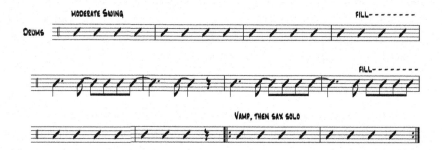

AMBITIOUS NOTATION

A notation can ask slightly more of an instrument than it is capable. These notations challenge the performer to find creative ways to effectively realize the music. It is important, however, that the composer not use a notation that is too far from what is possible; otherwise, the response from the performer will be more frustration than creativity. Consultation with a percussionist is recommended.

George Aperghis's *Le Corps à Corps* (1979) is a work for zarb (a Persian hand drum) and spoken voice. In the original publication, there was no indication of what any of the zarb notation meant. It is a single drum, and yet pitches are notated up and down the staff. This notation has some basis in traditional zarb playing, but it still requires the performer employ myriad techniques to effectively realize the score. The current publication shown in figure 1.11 includes some suggestions for how one might choose to execute the drum figuration, but much is still left to the performer's discretion.

Figure 1.11
Ambitious
notation

SOURCE: From
George Aperghis' *Le
Corps á Corp, www.
aperghis.com*

OUTSIDE REFERENCE

One can use a non-percussion reference as a guide to create a variety of sounds and articulations. John Bergamo's *Piru Bole* (1974) is a work for open instrumentation, usually played by a percussion ensemble featuring hand drums and other ethnic instruments. The notation includes only rhythms and vocal syllables (see figure 1.12). In the tradition of Indian classical music, the vocal syllables serve as guides to articulation, dynamics, and phrase structures that will be performed on the chosen instruments. Because the voice is a much more versatile instrument than most percussion instruments, the performer is forced to develop a vocabulary of sounds that matches that of the vocal part.

Figure 1.12
Outside reference

SOURCE: From John
Bergamo's *Piru Bole.*

Detailed Notation

If the composer does not wish to employ improvisation and instead chooses to have complete control over the score, an extensive knowledge of the idiosyncrasies of each instrument is still not required. Three simple variables on nearly all struck percussion instruments are available to the composer. They are:

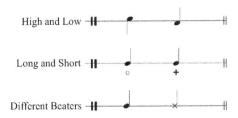

Figure 1.13
Timbral variables

HIGH AND LOW

All resonating bodies have nodal points at which they resonate less than at other points. For all struck percussion instruments, these nodal points, when struck, will sound a brighter color (a higher pitch) than the normal beating spots. Therefore, one can find at least two distinct pitches on every instrument. For example:

- On drums, striking toward the rim is brighter than striking on the center of the drum head.
- On cymbals, striking the bell is brighter than striking on the edge.
- On cowbell, striking the crown is brighter than striking on the lip.

LONG AND SHORT

For percussion instruments with any amount of sustain, the sustain can be manipulated with muting. That is, an instrument can be muted after it is struck to control the note length, or the instrument can be muted while it is struck to change both the note length and the timbre. (See Manipulations of Timbre in appendix C.)

DIFFERENT BEATERS

Percussionists can hold up to four beaters comfortably. Significantly different timbres can be achieved with a change in beater, and requesting the percussionist to play with even two different beaters on one instrument can double the perceived number of voices.

◐ Video 1.l—High/Low, Long/Short, Different Beaters

The Third Stravinsky Adaptation discussed earlier is one example of an extensive application of these techniques. For each drum there are two lines: the upper line indicates to strike near the edge of the head, and the lower line indicates striking at the center. One hand holds a stick and the other hand is bare; articulations with stick are indicated with "X" noteheads and those with bare hand have normal noteheads. "T" and "F" denote "thumb" and "fingers," adding two more beaters. The bare hand is sometimes left on the head to dampen, indicated by a plus sign. These techniques combine high and low pitches, different beaters, and long and short articulations (figure 1.14).

◐ Video 1.m—Third Stravinsky Adaptation Techniques

Effectively using all three of these variables together is challenging for the composer, and learning notated music with all three variables is challenging for the performer. Such projects should be reserved for instances when the composer has a

Figure 1.14
Third Stravinsky
adaptation

chance to work closely with a percussionist and is writing a solo work or solo passage in an ensemble work. However, usage of just one or even a simple combination of two of these variables is not difficult and can considerably expand the composer's options.

🌑 Video 1.n—Advanced Playing Techniques

The Value of Improvised and Non-Notated Music

Sophisticated use of instruments is just one thing composers can learn from non-notated percussion music. This is crowdsourced information gathered by thousands of people who have been experimenting, editing, and sharing all over the world for years. Such researchers will certainly discover perfectly functioning applications of these instrument sounds. To these people, percussion is not novelty—it is a tool. Some of these tools have been used for decades, some for millennia. Composers are encouraged to investigate the music native to a given percussion instrument to hear what solutions and applications that culture has discovered.

SOCIAL COMPOSITION

Lessons learned from non-notated music remind us that music is inherently social. Even composing by oneself in front of a computer or a piano is a social activity. The moment a single notation is made, the composer has entered into a relationship with his or her performers. Those performers will then have specific relationships with each other and with their audiences as a result of that notation. To care for the passage of information from the composer's imagination to the audience's ears is to honor these social interactions.

This is important to consider when writing for any instrument or ensemble, but it is especially so for percussion. Because of the inherent indeterminacies and the logistic and notational complexities of percussion music, composers must rely more heavily on percussionists than they do on other instrumentalists to be responsible for the success of their music. It is not enough to know how to write for percussion; one must also know how to write for percussion*ists*. Some examples follow, but the composer should apply this mindset to every page of this book and every interaction with his or her collaborators.

Write for People, Not Sounds

Because percussionists are able to play a dozen or more instruments from one standing position, it can be easy to think of the percussion sounds as disembodied from the people creating them. In some pieces with multi-percussion setups, music is notated for a large number of instruments, with little indication or care for how the instruments are set up in relationship to one another. In some ensemble scores, each non-percussion player or section of players will have one staff (one staff for violins, one for second trombone, one for third flute doubling piccolo, and so on), but the percussion staves in the same score indicate one *instrument* with no guidance as to which player is responsible for what staff, or even how many players are needed.

Notations like these are unfortunately all too common. Besides creating extra work for the performers, they can sabotage the composer's efforts, as logistic and notational difficulties will impede the performer's ability to make good music. The composer will certainly face limitations when holding a composition accountable for the reality of performance, but acknowledgment of these limitations will yield better and more accurate performances.

Specifically, when writing for a multi-percussion setup, the composer should start with a list of instruments that fulfills the musical requirements of the composition;[6] for example:

vibraphone
snare drum
low tom-tom
2 cowbells
2 woodblocks
2 cymbals

---

6. While a predetermined instrumentation will yield many compositional and logistical benefits, it may better suit a composer's process to choose instruments fluidly at the whim of his or her imagination. If so, it is still recommended the composer move in the direction of this example during the editing process.

The composer should then collaborate with a percussionist to determine a setup that makes physical, logistical, and musical sense (figure 1.15), determine a system of notation that relates to the setup (figure 1.16), and then write with these realities in mind.

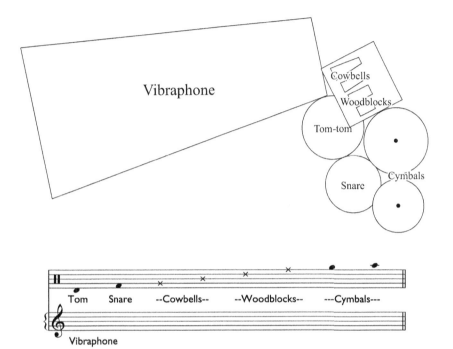

Figure 1.15
Example setup

Figure 1.16
Example Notation

When writing an ensemble piece, the composer should not write for a large list of instruments; for example, avoid:

four players

> timpani
> marimba
> vibraphone
> xylophone
> glockenspiel
> crotales
> 2 suspended cymbals
> tam-tam
> 3 tom-toms
> bass drum
> 5 templeblocks
> tambourine
> guiro
> triangle
> vibraslap

Instead, the composer should decide exactly who plays what, and write for those people standing in front of those specific setups:

player 1

   timpani

player 2

   marimba
   3 tom-toms
   bass drum
   2 suspended cymbals

player 3

   vibraphone
   5 templeblocks
   tambourine
   guiro
   tam-tam

player 4

   glockenspiel
   crotales
   xylophone
   triangle
   vibraslap

In both cases, these preparatory steps will reduce or eliminate unworkable and confusing notations, logistics, and setup/beater requirements. Moreover, these steps can considerably reduce the amount of non-musical work required of the performers, giving them more energy and time to devote to making the music sound good. (These points will be addressed further in the next two chapters.)

Write What Is Wanted, Not What to Do

The job of the performer, more or less, is to do what the composer says. There are many instances, however, when the details of percussion playing are best chosen based on elements that are beyond the composer's control—for example, the specific instruments, the performance venue, the specific ensemble, or even the weather. Therefore, it is often more effective if the composer indicates what he or she is hoping to hear rather than exactly what the percussionist should do to achieve it. The former more abstract notation allows percussionists to find solutions specific to their equipment and their environment. Such notations encourage the performers to make good decisions; more specific indications may limit their good sense.

The key to evoking these good decisions is to use prose descriptions that guide the performers' ears toward the conceptual musical material beyond the music notations on the page. Some examples:

Instrument Choice

temple bowl
temple bowl, medium almglocke, small gong, or similar

The second choice makes clear that the composer needs a ringing treble metal sound, not necessarily a temple bowl. This encourages the performer to listen to the sound of whatever instrument is chosen in context to make sure it is the best of the available options.

Dynamics

mp
mp, blend with the harp

The second indication makes clear not just the dynamic but also its orchestrational function. This can help determine both how loudly the performer plays and his or her dynamic phrasing, beaters, beating spots, and even instrument choice.

Beaters

hard mallet
brittle, articulated

The second indication makes clear the function of the instrument sound and allows the performer to make decisions not only about mallet choice but also about dynamic phrasing, beating spots, and instrument choice.

Beater indications are the most common place where composers exert control when they need not. Unless a specific unusual sound is desired (e.g., a triangle beater on a tam-tam or a brush on a snare drum), the composer should leave beater decisions up to the performers. Beater choices are particularly delicate and have everything to do with the unique situation of the specific performer and specific equipment in a specific venue.

Indications like those described above are not always appropriate or necessary, but it is in the composer's interest to ask for performers' help in these ways. It should always be the case that the performers are working on behalf of the success of the composition, but too often performers will just simply do what the composer tells them to do. If the composer tells them to use brass mallets, they will do that. If the composer asks them to listen and find the best sound, they will do that, too, with far better results. (More will be discussed on these points in chapters 3 and 4.)

Working with Percussionists

Composers writing percussion music should work with percussionists as often as possible—this is important. The point is stressed throughout this book, and for good reason. Percussion is amorphous, complex, and constantly evolving. Notation is communication, and a composer who speaks the language of percussion will be able to communicate most clearly.

Collaboration with percussionists is easy. Most performers who play new works are willing to meet or at least offer advice by email. Sending an instrument list, diagram setup, notational key, or few pages of music via email to a willing percussionist might return information that can significantly change for the better the course of a composition.

Once a composition is completed, it can be difficult to make changes. A single musical idea could be the seed for minutes of material. If this idea is problematic for any reason, it could interfere with large portions of the work. At the beginning of the compositional process, however, the choices made are relatively arbitrary. That musical seed, if recognized to be problematic, could easily be transformed into a more effective one.

It is at this early stage of the work when collaboration is most important. Problems that are identified early can be handled easily without disrupting the composition. This generates stronger compositions and happier percussionists. Happier percussionists tend to do a better job of preparing and performing music. One might think of it as an issue of respect: performers will more likely have respect for the score if the score has respect for its performers. Thus, it benefits the work of both composers and performers to be social, to collaborate, and to learn how to attain this mutual respect.

CHAPTER TWO

General Logistics

The logistic complexities inherent to percussion can often get in the way of the composer's musical intentions. This chapter discusses some of the general issues that percussionists and composers face with respect to instrument choice, instrument setup, physical movement, and concert production. These are mostly non-musical issues that have a significant effect on the final musical product.

Works that require a large number of instruments or instruments that are difficult to acquire will be performed less often. Works that require unnecessary virtuosity will be performed less well. In both cases, a little attention paid to potential logistic difficulties can go a long way in the life of a composition. Although it may not be the initial aim of composers to write music that is easy to produce and easy to play, these are some ways by which compositions will ultimately be measured, in both their value to performers and their musical effectiveness with audiences.

These recommendations should not be misunderstood to mean the composer should only write easy music for a small number of instruments; rather, the composer should take care that difficulties in his or her works be *artistically purposeful* and not artifacts of carelessness. The composer is encouraged to consult with percussionists often to be made aware of ways to simplify logistics.

INSTRUMENT CHOICE AND MANAGEMENT

Six Stories: Three Sad and Three Happy

I

Ludwig, a student composer, has a reading with his school orchestra. He was very excited to explore percussion in this piece, and he decided to request almost two dozen percussion instruments. He did not, however, plan ahead to indicate what player plays which instrument or how many players are needed. The three percussionists assigned to the reading receive the percussion score an hour ahead, along with the three other student pieces to be read that morning. With little time to divide the parts and gather and set up instruments, the percussionists simply each pick a handful of the requested instruments and cover as much as they can. As a result, many notes and passages are omitted and many are played on incorrect instruments. When Ludwig gets the recording of his reading, he finds it is largely misrepresentative because of the percussion cacophony throughout.

A week later, Ludwig consults with a percussionist to discover his piece would only have been possible with four percussionists, but six would be required to avoid excessively difficult instrument and beater switches.

II

Gustav is invited to help produce a piece of his for a concert series at a local gallery in New York City. He decides to program a "pierrot plus percussion" work (violin, cello, flute, clarinet, piano, and percussion). He has a $2,500 budget with which he intends to pay his friends $400 each for two rehearsals, a dress, and the concert, with $100 left to pay for time in a rehearsal space with a piano.[1] He books the performers and the rehearsal space a few months in advance.

A month before the concert, Gustav emails his percussionist the music with the instrument list: five-octave marimba, vibraphone, two octaves of crotales, three tom-toms, two cymbals, tam-tam, and tambourine.

"Where are we renting the instruments from?" the percussionist asks.

"Oh, I didn't realize we had to rent them. Can't you bring them yourself?"

"I have the toms, cymbals, and tambourine, but my marimba is only a 4.3 octave, and I don't have a car, so I can only really transport the tambourine and cymbals (without stands) on the subway. We'll have to rent the rest. You might also want to make sure we can leave this stuff overnight at the rehearsal space. Oh, and I'll need five or six music stands."

Oops. Gustav assumed all the players, with the exception of the pianist, would bring their own instruments and music stands. Luckily, both the rehearsal and concert spaces provide at least ten music stands, but the percussion instruments will be harder to come by. He looks into the rental and cartage for the rest of the equipment. He finds that it is $1,225 for a three-day rental of the following:

5-octave marimba
vibraphone
2 octaves of crotales with stands
3 tom-toms with stands
2 cymbals stands
tam-tam with stand

---

1. Costs are at 2013 price points.

Plus, $485 cartage for:

> delivery to rehearsal space
> pickup from rehearsal space
> delivery to performance space
> pickup from performance space

There's also an $80 fee for storage of equipment overnight in the rehearsal space.

Gustav decides to program a work for violin, cello, and piano instead. He still must compensate the flute, clarinet, and percussion players because they had reserved time for this gig and had even turned away other work that would have conflicted.

III

Igor tells a percussionist friend about his new piece for solo percussion. His friend is a big fan of Igor's music and is excited about possibly using the piece for an upcoming recital tour, including lecture-performances at three conservatories for the percussion students. Igor is excited about all the performances and exposure to other percussionists. He sends his friend the music. It requires vibraphone, bongos, three tom-toms, three cymbals, three large tuned nipple gongs, and seven tuned almglocken. Igor's friend does not have access to the large nipple gongs and almglocken, and they will not be available at the venues he is visiting. The setup for the piece ends up being too restrictive, and Igor's friend decides not to play the piece.

IV

Johannes, a student composer, has a reading with his school orchestra. Before he starts writing the percussion parts, he makes a modest list of instruments for each of the three players and writes only for those players playing those specific setups. He sends an email to a percussionist friend to double-check the school has all the instruments he plans to use. The morning of the reading, the players get their parts and have no trouble setting up. The reading goes off without a hitch.

V

Wolfgang is invited to help produce a piece of his on a concert series at a local gallery in New York City. He hopes to program a work for flute, piano, and percussion. He contacts a percussionist friend to find out which of the needed instruments (vibraphone, glockenspiel, snare drum, two cymbals, and two woodblocks) he would expect to be able to bring, where he would recommend renting the remainder of the equipment, and if he can recommend a rehearsal space that would have both a piano and the needed percussion. His friend says he will bring the snare drum and woodblocks, and recommends a rental company that has their own rehearsal spaces. Wolfgang gets a quote for the cost of six hours in the rehearsal space with use of the percussion ($330) and the rental and cartage of the vibraphone, glockenspiel, and cymbals for the concert ($550). These expenses fit neatly within his $2,500 budget, with enough to pay the three players each $500 (with an extra $120 left over for incidentals), so he books the musicians, rehearsal space, and instruments. Everything is set up to run smoothly, and Wolfgang is excited to start working with his players on the music itself.

VI

Alban tells a percussionist friend about his new piece for solo percussion. His friend is a big fan of Alban's music, and is excited about possibly using the piece for an upcoming recital tour. Alban sends his friend the music. It requires vibraphone, two bongos, low tom-tom, cymbal, hi-hat, and brake drum. The work fits perfectly into Alban's friend's repertoire. He takes it on tour, and posts a great video of one of the performances online. Students and professionals across the world start contacting Alban for the score, and the work becomes his most performed piece.

These six stories illustrate some of the frequent challenges composers and percussionists face with respect to instrument choice and management. In story I, Ludwig was careless and irresponsible with his scoring of percussion. In story II, Gustav was unaware and caught off-guard by the realities and expense of percussion availability and transport. In story III, Igor had done nothing wrong, but suffered the consequences of choosing unusual instruments. The composers in stories IV, V, and VI understood the needs of their performers, and thus enjoyed better, easier, and more numerous performances.

The lesson to pull from these scenarios is that composers benefit by making it easier for performers to play their works. It could be argued that when composers make it difficult, that advances the art and advances the skills of the performers. This may be true, but the composer should understand the consequences of such decisions and make them purposefully and with care.

Why Use Fewer Instruments?

As suggested, a large number of instruments will often introduce complications that make the music difficult to execute and produce.

Budget

Acquisition and use of a large number of percussion instruments, for the reasons listed below, will cost the player, ensemble, or presenter money. With unlimited funds, many of these issues disappear, but normally budget considerations are a significant factor.

Space

A large number of percussion instruments requires a large amount of space. This is commonly a problem in small chamber-music halls, on stages with different level risers, in opera or musical theater pits, and especially in rehearsal spaces. In small chamber-music halls, percussion setups must sometimes be placed on the floor in front of the stage instead of on the stage itself. On stages with different level risers, large percussion setups must sometimes be moved to awkward locations farther away from the other players. Percussionists with big setups in opera or musical theater pits are sometimes moved off stage or even into separate, isolated rooms to make space for the rest of the ensemble. A chamber group may need to rent additional space if the setup does not fit in their normal rehearsal space.

Instrument Availability

If the performer, ensemble, or institution does not already own an instrument, it must be bought, borrowed, or rented. This can cost money, take time, and may mean the instrument will not be available for some or all of the rehearsals. If the unavailable instrument is important enough, the piece may even need to be cut from a program.

Setup Time

A piece that takes a long time to set up can lead to considerable restrictions on the order of a program. The piece may have to be placed at the start of the concert or first after intermission so it can be preset; otherwise, a long pause must be added between pieces to accommodate the setup. Either way, performers and composers can face non-musical impositions to the flow and order of their programs.

Composers are often faced with a less than ideal amount of rehearsal time for their pieces. A piece with many instruments or with particularly complex setups can require 45 minutes or more to assemble. This can eat away at the piece's allotted rehearsal time, costing the players opportunities to work on the music itself.

A percussion part with many instruments will also tend to be practiced less. To do so, the percussionist must collect all the instruments and set them up. That alone may take up to an hour and will leave less time for practice. If, however, the instruments in the setup are used individually (for example, if a piece with a large setup has all the difficult passages on vibraphone alone), then the performer can practice just those parts without the entire setup. If the difficult passages use all the instruments in the setup, they must all be set up to be practiced.

Transportation

Transporting percussion instruments often becomes costly and time-consuming. Most soloists and touring ensembles must choose repertoire with careful consideration of instrument transportation. Only very small amounts of percussion can be transported reasonably on foot or by public transportation. Percussion equipment is generally large, heavy, and requires a cargo van or truck to get it from place to place.

A marimba or vibraphone can be broken down, but still will take up a lot of space in a large car or van. Tubular bells, large bass drums, and large gongs may fit by themselves into a minivan, but generally require a truck. Two timpani may fit into a minivan, but a set of four must be moved by truck. Even smaller instruments like drums and cymbals require heavy metal stands (called "hardware"), adding hundreds of pounds to the weight of the instruments themselves. Works using even a single percussionist often require a combination of keyboard instruments, drums, cymbals, and other instruments; this equipment would easily fill a minivan with the seats removed, leaving little or no room for the percussionist's ensemble mates.

In addition to a rented truck, a percussion move may require a few extra pairs of hands for the exhausting and time-consuming work of packing, unpacking, and transporting the equipment to and from the truck. Touring soloists and ensembles with the resources will hire people to help with load-ins, setups, breakdowns, and load-outs, but less fortunate groups must add these difficult jobs to their already packed concert-day schedule.

Logistic and Notational Difficulty

A single instrument or small setup of two or three instruments may be set up, notated, and played with little complication. With larger setups, it is more difficult for the composer to design a clear system of notation and more difficult for the performer to configure an effective setup. A large instrument collection will tend to be more diverse, introducing balance problems and requiring frequent beater switches. Instruments in a large setup may need to be placed farther away from each other, and then the performer will have a more difficult time maneuvering around the setup. As the setup grows, these issues become more numerous, more complicated, and more difficult to manage.

Common symptoms of a careless use of large instrument setups include awkward and unclear notation, unsolvable balance issues, the need to make concessions with beater choice (leading to unattractive sounds and further balance issues), and unnecessarily difficult passagework (limiting accuracy and musicianship). With manageable setups, performers are more likely to make better music.

Visuals

Percussion is an especially visual instrument, and visual musical gestures are very communicative. If a piece requires visuals that are different from the intended character of the piece because of numerous instruments or frequent beater changes, the piece can seem scrambled and disjointed. This is especially true of solo percussion music, in which the audience is sure to be looking directly at the percussionist. Excitement may be added if the performer must drop and pick up mallets quickly or run across the stage to get to an instrument, but this may not be the intended character; if the mood is slow and tranquil, fast motions will be a distraction. In a work with simple logistics, the performer is free to design visual gestures that are in tune with the identity of the piece.

Noise

The quick beater or instrument switches resulting from a large setup may create unwanted noise. If a percussionist has to drop and pick up mallets very quickly, some noise may result. Instruments that produce sound by shaking—tambourines, sleighbells, maracas, and shakers—will likely create unwanted noise during a hurried pickup or put-down. The sound of footsteps can also be a distraction if the player needs to walk quickly or run to another part of the stage. These issues are amplified during moments of quiet music or silence; a grand pause, for example, is the worst time for a percussionist to run to another setup. In all cases, noise will not be made if proper time is allotted.

Sonic Clutter

Percussion over-scoring can make a piece seem cluttered and awkward. Compositions often benefit from a controlled use of timbre. A string quartet, for example, is a very attractive ensemble for both composers and listeners because of, among other reasons, its balanced homogeneous sound. A wind quintet presents a much less homogeneous color palette, and if the repertoire is any indication, poses far more compositional challenges. Any large collection of percussion instruments will supply a tremendously heterogeneous sound palette, so issues of timbral control become that much more difficult. In the context of mixed ensembles like an orchestra, the excessive heterogeneity of an over-scored percussion section can disrupt any attempt at ensemble blend in the rest of the group. Additionally, overused percussion sounds will stick out far more than overused string or wind sounds, so a mature handling of percussion is all the more important.

Besides the potential negative effects on what the audience hears, a choice to use too many percussion instruments can cloud the composer's focus during the compositional process. A smaller percussion battery will encourage the composer to focus on using the available sounds in functionally effective and creative ways. He or she may then make use of playing techniques that expand the potential of individual instruments, reducing the heterogeneity and elevating each instrument's musical sophistication toward that of its string and wind counterparts. A composer working with a large list of percussion instruments may spend more time trying to compositionally justify these instruments than actually making meaningful use of them.

There exist many works in the repertoire that use a large number of percussion instruments with skill and purpose, and are worth whatever logistical hassle they require, but this does not discount these issues. In the interests of quality composition and quality and more frequent performances, the composer should try to consolidate his or her instrument needs wherever possible.

How to Consolidate

When choosing instruments, when is enough truly enough? With an enormous instrument list, some of the less important instruments can often be eliminated or easily and effectively substituted with something already on stage. Questions a composer must ask are:

- Is this sound significantly different in effect from something being used more prominently?
- Will it be heard?
- Is it necessary to have so many of the same type of instrument?
- Is it necessary to use as large a range?
- Does the player have time to get to the instrument, pick up the instrument, or get the appropriate beaters? Can the instrument be positioned closely enough for the performer to reach it?
- If the instrument has been used before, is it being used by the same person? If it is being used by a different person, does that person have time to get to the instrument that has been used, or does there need to be two of that same instrument on stage? If two are needed, is there room to have multiples of this instrument, and is the second person's part substantial enough to justify having two of these instruments?

Let us examine two hypothetical examples of effective instrument consolidation.

Consolidation Example 1

A composer is writing a piece for cello, clarinet, and percussion. She decides the percussionist will use a setup comprising the following instruments:

vibraphone
crotales
3 suspended cymbals
china cymbal
hi-hat
5 tom-toms
snare drum

pair of bongos
tam-tam
cowbell
maracas

The percussionist with whom she is working understands that such a large instrumentation will be difficult to set up, difficult to transport, and more difficult to execute passages and get quality sounds. He knows a smaller instrumentation would be less hassle, yield more performances, and encourage a more sophisticated usage of instruments.

The percussionist sets up the instruments for the composer as shown in figure 2.1. (Maracas rest on the trap table.) She agrees the setup is unnecessarily large, and together they start to trim it down to something more manageable, taking into account the musical needs of the piece she is about to start writing.

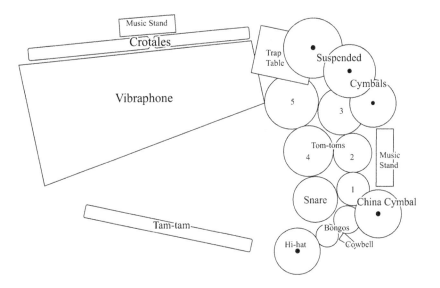

Figure 2.1
Unconsolidated setup

First, the setup has many drums. The five tom-toms, snare, and bongos take up a large portion of the setup. It is determined that five tom-toms could be reduced to two, and the setup would still maintain similar functionality (figure 2.2):

- When using the tom-toms, the snares of the snare drum would need to be turned off anyway so as to not buzz sympathetically with the other drums in a distracting way.
- The snare drum (without snares) and bongos can also function as tom-toms.
- Snare drum plus bongos plus two toms equals five drums, effectively replacing the five tom-toms while maintaining the added colors of the snare drum and bongos when needed.

Figure 2.2
Drum
consolidation

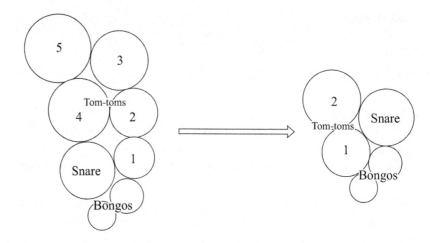

Removing three tom-toms does not sound like much, but it is a considerable space-saver and will bring the remaining instruments much closer to the performer. Moreover, the composer can use different beating spots (on the head and adding rim sounds), beaters, and degrees of muting to amplify the effectiveness of the remaining drums.

Second, they decide to reduce the three suspended cymbals to just one. The composer had imagined the hi-hat, china cymbal, and tam-tam as entities separate from the three suspended cymbals. With the percussionist's help, she realizes the hi-hat, china, and tam-tam can effectively take part in the suspended cymbal passages, making the extra cymbals unnecessary (figure 2.3). Moreover, she can manipulate beating spots, beaters, and degrees of muting to augment the colors already present.

Figure 2.3
Cymbal
consolidation

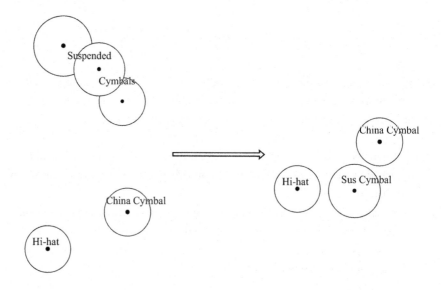

Finally, the vibraphone will be the primary voice of the percussion part with the crotales as a mostly ornamental color. Two octaves of crotales weigh heavily on the other side of the setup, and of the pitches in the low octaves of crotales, only six (F♯–B) are not already present in the vibraphone. The composer decides she can make do with just the high octave. The new setup, as shown in figure 2.4, is:

vibraphone
crotales (high octave only)
suspended cymbal
china cymbal
hi-hat
2 tom-toms
snare drum
pair of bongos
tam-tam
cowbell
maracas

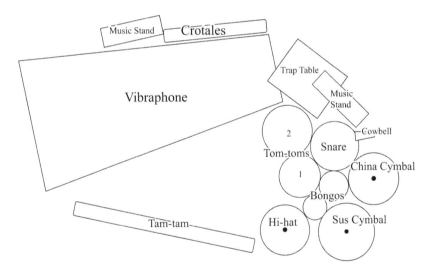

Figure 2.4
Consolidated setup

With just a few tweaks, the setup is made significantly more efficient with little to no limitations on the composer's vision.

◗ Video 2.a—Setup Consolidation Example

Consolidation Example 2

A composer emails the percussion score for a new orchestra piece to a percussionist friend for some notational advice. The work calls for timpanist plus three percussionists ("T+3"). Upon studying the score, the percussionist finds some errors and unnecessary redundancies in the instrument list. The original list is:

timpani
percussion 1: crotales, vibraphone, snare drum, crash cymbals, guiro, gong
percussion 2: xylophone, vibraphone, 4 tom-toms, hi-hat, slapstick
percussion 3: glockenspiel, crotales, marimba, 2 tenor drums, bass drum, 2
        suspended cymbals

Players 1 and 2 both need vibraphone. Could all the vibraphone material be covered by one person? If not, can that vibraphone be shared, or does the piece require two vibraphones? He investigates and determines that despite one quick switch from xylophone, player 2 can cover all the vibraphone material.

Players 1 and 3 both need crotales. He investigates and finds that both players need a full two octaves of crotales, and they cannot share because they play at the same time. While player 1 plays crotales several times in the piece, player 3's part has only one crotale measure. Since player 3 already has glockenspiel, is this one measure worth having two full sets of crotales on stage? The composer concedes that player 3 could play the passage on glockenspiel without issue and the extra crotales are unnecessary.

Player 3 needs a marimba, but how large? He finds the part fits on a 4.3 octave (low A) instrument with the exception of two low D's. The 5-octave instrument required for these low D's takes up a lot more room than a 4.3 octave instrument. These notes are doubled by the celli and bass clarinet, so the composer decides to notate an *ossia* octave-up transposition for those two notes in case the performers cannot fit a five-octave marimba on stage.

There is hardly a difference between a "tenor drum" and a concert "tom-tom." The percussionist checks to see if player 3's tenor drum music could possibly be played on player 2's tom-toms. It works logistically, but is the distinction between tenor drum and tom-tom really necessary? The composer agrees it is unnecessary, and player 3 can play the tenor drum music on the tom-toms. He recommends the composer specify this in the instrument list.

Looking further, the percussionist notices that although player 2's list requests four tom-toms, only two are ever used in the piece!

The indication "gong" in player 1's list is ambiguous. The word *gong* is like *drum* in that it requires further specification. Should this be a nipple gong? The composer clarifies he meant "tam-tam."

After the consultation, the clearer, more accurate, and tighter instrument list is:

timpani
percussion 1: crotales, snare drum, crash cymbals, guiro, tam-tam

percussion 2: xylophone, vibraphone, 2 tom-toms (shared with player 3), hi-hat, slapstick

percussion 3: glockenspiel, marimba (5-octave preferred), 2 tom-toms (shared with player 2), bass drum, 2 suspended cymbals

Inexpensive Instruments

Most percussion instruments must be manufactured by professional instrument makers, but some can be easily found or constructed by lay people. The following instruments cost little to no money to acquire and therefore may easily be requested in large numbers.

sandpaper blocks
stones
tin cans
bottles
rute
wooden planks
slapstick

Exotic Instruments

If an especially rare instrument is requested, it is possible that one will not be acquired in time for the concert. In this case, the composer should plan to provide the instrument or let the performers use a substitute instrument. A description of the sound of the instrument (written in the score) will help the performer find an appropriate substitute (e.g., "The Southwest Siberian xiboxia has a high, bright, and metallic sound with a metallic buzz and a short decay"). Or the composer could suggest a specific substitute for the instrument (e.g., "If a B♭ hubcap is not available, a B♭ nipple gong may be used").

Electronic Percussion

Synthesized and sampled percussion sounds are not an effective replacement for acoustic sounds—these tools are usually best used for invented or altered sounds. The equipment needed is often expensive or hard to find, and setup is time-consuming, with computer crashes, cable failures, and feedback as just a few of the many things that can go wrong.

When used with care and expertise, however, synthesized and sampled percussion can effectively be used alone or alongside acoustic percussion (see John Adams's *Death of Klinghoffer*). A percussionist may have an electronic MIDI controller, such as an Octapad, DrumKat, or MalletKat, within a setup of acoustic instruments. Regular keyboard synthesizers are oftentimes more practical than the percussion MIDI controllers listed above, however, because they are more widely available.

With MIDI percussion controllers, sound will be consistent no matter what beater strikes the pad, so mallet changes are unnecessary. These controllers take up very little space in a setup; an acoustic sound that could require a very large instrument or group of very large instruments can be replaced by a compact drum pad. The sounds produced can be changed during a piece, so one small MIDI drum pad or keyboard can produce hundreds of different sounds that would normally require a stage full of instruments and a stage full of percussionists. For this reason, MIDI controllers are popular in Broadway pits, where space is often tight.

Even in the best of circumstances, if electronics are involved, generous dress rehearsal time should be allotted to get everything set up and working correctly.

Multiple Options for a Specified Instrument

Just as different mallets are used to get different colors on the same instrument, percussionists often use more than one of the same instrument for different dynamics, pitches, or orchestrations. For example, for a suspended cymbal part, a percussionist may use two or three cymbals: a medium-size, thin, dark-sounding cymbal for soft notes; a smaller, thicker, bright-sounding instrument for loud choked notes; and a very large cymbal for loud sweeping rolls. Multiple snare drums are also sometimes used for involved parts: a bright, loud, dry metal shell drum for loud articulate passages with the brass and a smaller drum with wire snares for soft rolls.

Other times a percussionist will be forced to use multiple instruments because one instrument is incapable of meeting all the requirements for the part. If loud and soft passages are written for a ratchet, then two different ratchets might be used. If both very loud passages and very articulate *pianissimo* passages are written for shaker, then two shakers might be used.

The use of extra instruments will usually be determined by the performer, but indications in the part by the composer (after the part has been worked out by a performer) may be appropriate.

Instruments Percussionists May Not Play

There are an enormous number of instruments in the percussion family, many of which most percussionists do not study. Percussionists are frequently required to learn new instruments and can easily do so by applying techniques from commonly studied instruments. In some cases, however, it is not so easy.

Cimbalom

Few percussionists study cimbalom. A composer should only write for cimbalom if it is known that there is someone who plays and has access to this instrument.

Steel Drums (Steel Pans)

Steel drums are frequently found in percussion collections, although not all percussionists are proficient in pan technique. The pitches are not arranged like a keyboard, and the layout can be unfamiliar. Fast, notey passages will be difficult and will need to be memorized; slow lines, ostinati, and isolated notes can easily be executed. (See chapter 7 for more information.)

Tabla

Tabla is a highly specialized percussion instrument native to Indian classical music with which few Western percussionists are proficient. Many of its playing techniques are unique to this specific instrument, so even percussionists having expertise with other hand drums may not be able to play tabla convincingly.

Musical Saw

Musical saw is an instrument percussionists rarely play. Simple melodies can be executed with practice, but especially complicated parts should be reserved for musical saw specialists.

Non-Percussion Keyboards

Non-percussion keyboard instruments (piano, harpsichord, and celeste) are generally left to the professional keyboard players. There are many non-keyboardist musicians who are proficient in piano and can play these instruments well, but this should not be assumed. All percussionists will, however, have basic knowledge of the keyboard and can play a few chords or simple lines if necessary. (See Luciano Berio's *Circles*, Jacob Druckman's *Animus II,* and Henry Cowell's *Set of Five.*)

Multiple Percussionists

To avoid problems with multi-player logistics, the composer should always assign instruments to each player before the parts are written. For example, before starting a piece, the composer decides that there are four percussionists:

player 1: timpani
player 2: marimba, 3 tom-toms, bass drum, and 2 suspended cymbals
player 3: vibraphone, 5 templeblocks, tambourine, guiro, and tam-tam
player 4: xylophone, glockenspiel, triangle, and vibraslap

If those setups are maintained while writing, numerous problems are automatically avoided. Predetermining the player setups is *highly recommended*. In contrast, conceptualizing the previous arrangement is far easier than trying to organize like this:

four players

timpani
marimba
vibraphone
xylophone
glockenspiel
2 suspended cymbals
triangle
tam-tam
3 tom-toms
bass drum
5 templeblocks
tambourine
guiro
vibraslap

With the latter plan, it is easy to lose track of who is playing which instrument, what mallets they are holding, where they are on the stage, where the instrument is on stage, and so on.

Section Setup

Unless stage positions are used for spatial effects, the placement of each player does not need to be specified. The section setup is often out of the composer's hands for logistic or acoustic reasons specific to the piece or hall, or as a result of the preference of the players, conductor, or organization.

Orchestra

Professional orchestras usually have a timpanist plus three or four percussionists. The timpanist is hired to play timpani exclusively. If the timpanist plays any instrument other than timpani, he or she is paid a doubling fee. When writing works for orchestra, it is best to not give the timpanist anything else to do, even if there is plenty of extra time in his or her part; commissions from professional orchestras may require this. The other percussionists in an orchestra can play any instrument, but they may also receive a doubling if asked to play timpani.

Depending on the specific contract and union rules for the timpanist, writing for prepared timpani or for striking the timpani bowls (see Timpani in chapter 6) may not qualify as additional percussion and thus may be permissible. In this case, it is best to research the orchestra and union's rules.

A traditional orchestral setup will look as shown in figure 2.5.

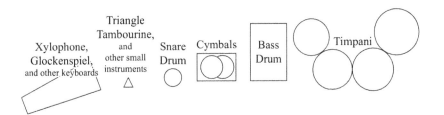

Figure 2.5
Orchestra setup

Wind Ensemble

Pieces written for contemporary wind ensembles often use excessive amounts of percussion. This is often less for musical reasons and more to accommodate the large number of percussion players in the school ensemble for which the piece is written. While giving everyone something to play may be musically workable when doubling clarinets, overused percussion sounds are far more distracting. As a result, there are many examples of poor percussion scoring and notations in this repertoire.

Wind ensembles commonly contain six or seven percussionists. The timpanist is not separate but, rather, may be fully incorporated into the rest of the section.

Broadway Pit

The percussion section in a score for a musical theater show often consists of a drumset player and a percussionist. The percussion part can include many instruments: vibraphone, marimba, glockenspiel, tubular bells, bongos, congas, many little instruments (a.k.a., the "toys"—wind chimes, shakers, triangles, woodblocks, cowbells, etc.), and timpani (often no more than two, owing to space constraints).

Drum Corps and Marching Bands

Music for drum corps is historically designed to be played outdoors, often on a football field or in parades. Composers and arrangers of music for college- and professional-level drum and bugle corps are usually deeply immersed in this world, and thus are comfortable with the playing styles unique to the medium. The drummers of pipe bands or drum and fife corps (like those common in police precincts) typically play traditional music learned by rote. In all cases, this drum music derives from a line of military and parade drumming traditions with their own unique styles, rhythmic inflections, and notation. Composers unfamiliar with this music should collaborate with drum corps specialists before attempting to write for these ensembles. The front ensemble (or *pit*) of a drum and bugle corps is where this medium most closely resembles concert percussion music and for which the advice in this book will be most applicable.

Specialists

Although percussionists tend to be proficient at all things hit, scraped, and shaken, many percussion players choose to focus their energies on a single instrument, a category of instruments, or a musical style. These percussion subcommunities create unique markets for works that feature their preferred instruments.

Drumset Players

More percussionists consider themselves drumset players than those in any other category of percussion. These players play drumset exclusively and specialize primarily in rock and jazz styles. Although drumset players are not always able to read music, many concert percussionists come from a drumset background and maintain an affinity for this instrument.

Timpanists

Many percussionists aspire to be orchestral timpanists and will focus on this instrument. The timpani repertoire is largely orchestral, and timpanists are particularly attracted to that medium. These players are therefore less likely to seek new solo or chamber works for timpani, but there is a small market for such works.

Marimbists

Marimba specialists are becoming more numerous, as marimba degree programs continue to pop up in conservatories around the world. Marimbists are particularly active in commissioning new works.

Vibraphonists

The vibraphone rose to fame as a jazz instrument in the early and mid-twentieth century. Vibraphone soloists are, therefore, often jazz players, but vibraphone-centric concert percussionists are not hard to find, either. These performers are also likely to be active in commissioning new works.

Hand Drummers

Hand drum players are often experts in the improvisatory styles from Latin American, African, Middle Eastern, or Indian traditions. Hand drummers active in commissioning concert works are not common, but there are some concert percussionists who will seek compositions that feature these instruments.

Non-Percussionists Playing Percussion

Simple percussion playing is sometimes asked of non-percussionists. Although creating a sound with percussion instruments is child's play, playing them in time (and musically) is not easy. Moreover, the appearance of a non-percussionist playing these instruments will look decidedly amateur.

Even though percussionists may not be playing these instruments, they will be expected to supply them. The instrument and person for whom the instrument is supplied should be listed in the percussionist's part of the instrument list.

Some non-percussionists, most notably wind players and vocalists, are not used to producing sounds with a large physical motion. String players, conductors, and keyboard players (especially pianists) will have a much easier time playing percussion instruments well than wind players or vocalists, because the former are used to moving their arms in time in relation to an object (i.e., a string or piano key).

Chairs and Stands

Often, composers organize their own rehearsals and are in charge of setting up the chairs and stands. Percussionists usually need far more than one stand—sometimes up to nine or ten. They may even need a few chairs for mounting a bass drum or placing crash cymbals. The composer should consult the percussionist involved to determine his or her exact needs.

ISSUES OF PLAYABILITY

Excessive Polyphony

Owing to the extreme variety of percussion instrument sounds, a solo percussion part can sometimes resemble an ensemble score. The instruments encourage this; dissimilar sounds have difficulty participating in a single line, so multiple lines must be maintained to involve multiple instruments. Percussionists are known for their one-man-band style of performance, but often these circus tricks are requested at the expense of compositional integrity and quality of execution. The same may be said of classic showpieces for violin or piano, where the performer's virtuosity is a central compositional feature; instances of polyphony involving numerous percussion instruments can easily become excessive, however.

The logistic demands imposed by an ensemble-style percussion part can make it largely unplayable. A playable version tends to be watered down, and beyond its value as a show of virtuosity, it may not be convincing music. The composer may ask, "Would it still be a good piece if this part were played by three or four percussionists instead of one?" If the answer is no, the piece may benefit from a reworking. Solo parts that are intended to be solo from conception can provide the composer with a better chance to design substantive and effectively playable material. (See The Written/Improv Divide in chapter 1.)

◉ Video 2.b—Excessive Polyphony

How Fast Percussionists Can Play

There are a number of conditions that affect the speed at which a percussionist can play.

Number of Surfaces and Distances Between Them

Passages on just one surface (such as one drum) are easiest to play quickly. If the writing requires maneuvering around a setup or large instrument (like marimba or timpani), however, speed is sacrificed. The farther apart the instruments or notes are, the more time it takes to get there.

Weight of the Beater

The weight of the beater significantly affects speed: the heavier the beater, the slower it is to move. For example, percussionists can play faster while holding two mallets than while holding four, and play faster with drumsticks than with large bass drum beaters.

Dynamics

At extreme dynamics, percussionists have to exert energy to maintain the dynamic that could otherwise be channeled into speed. This is especially true of soft dynamics, for which significant restraint may be necessary. The amount of energy required depends on how a particular instrument, played with a particular beater, speaks with respect to dynamics (see appendix E). For example, a percussionist can play very quickly at soft dynamics when playing with hands or soft mallets around a set of five drums; to produce an equivalent speed and dynamic with drumsticks would be extremely difficult.

Endurance

A percussionist can maintain a high speed if the passage does not continue for too long. Even a few very short rests placed periodically throughout a passage can make it easier and give the player's muscles a short opportunity to regain oxygen and discard built-up waste (lactic acid and carbon dioxide). Endurance will often come into play for very short bursts of very fast notes; for example, a quick series of up to five strokes can be squeezed out by one hand with the help of gravity and bounce. Quick figures that diminuendo are more easily executed than those that crescendo or stay constant. In figure 2.6, note that it would be far more difficult to play six beats of straight 16th notes in one hand at that speed.

Figure 2.6
One-handed figuration with breaks

Double Strokes

Under certain conditions, percussionists can use a double stroke or bounce stroke, by which the beater makes two articulations each time it strikes the instrument. Double strokes will be used for especially fast passages when both hands are on the same surface. The composer does *not* need to indicate the use of double strokes.

Double strokes are most common with drum sticks but can also work with hard plastic, hard rubber, or wood mallets. With softer sticks, the cushioning of the felt or yarn will reduce the bounciness of the beater and make it more difficult to perform a double stroke. Bounces can be more easily and quickly executed on tight drums (bongos, snare drum, high toms) than on other, less bouncy surfaces.

Physical Balance

It is easier to play fast alternating (hand-to-hand) strokes than fast strokes with both hands simultaneously. The hand-to-hand motion creates a balance, while using two hands together requires the performer's body to compensate. As an example, the reader may try this exercise: move your arms in the air as if drumming on an imaginary conga (right, left, right, left, etc.) as fast as you can. Now move both arms together as fast as you can so that both hands strike the imaginary conga simultaneously. Switch back and forth between the two motions and notice the difference in the way your head moves. As you can see, two hands at once requires much more energy.

Specific Tempi

When playing hand-to-hand for an extended period of time, an average percussionist can play 16th notes at ♩=144.[2] That means one hand can move at half that speed.

---

2. The tempi given throughout this section are comfortable and are for passages in which each hand or mallet stays on one surface. Faster playing is possible, but should be used with caution and with consideration of the issues discussed. "Hand-to-hand" playing means the hands simply alternate (right, left, right, left. . .) instead of using double strokes or more complicated four-mallet stickings.

When the percussionist is holding four mallets (figure 2.7),[3] the speed is slowed to 16th notes at ♩=120, because two mallets in a hand are more mass to move. This tempo applies to both hand-to-hand motion and mallet-to-mallet motion with each hand.

Figure 2.7
Four-mallet
figuration

Double strokes can be executed as 16ths at up to ♩=200 with snare drum sticks. With hard plastic, hard rubber, and wood mallets, that tempo is decreased slightly to ♩=170. If softer beaters and four mallets are used, double strokes cannot be made any faster than hand-to-hand single strokes. The double-stroke tempo (♩=200) does not mean that one hand can play half as fast, because steady articulations do not result when one hand is isolated (figure 2.8). When the percussionist is using hands and fingers without sticks or mallets, it can be assumed the speeds are slightly less than that of a pianist.

Figure 2.8
Double strokes

Sixteenth notes at ♩=100 can be expected when the percussionist is using both feet when seated (♪=100 for one foot). Just as a hand can squeeze out quick notes in small groups (see figure 2.6), a foot can perform two quick notes.

Unidiomatic Writing—Music That Often Requires Memorization

The following four situations often require memorization for accuracy:

quick beater or instrument switches
quick tuning on timpani
unidiomatic writing for keyboard instruments
quick passages that include many different instruments

---

3. Four-mallet stickings are often notated 1, 2, 3, and 4, with 1 being the left-most mallet.

While picking up mallets or switching instruments, the percussionist may need to look away from the music or conductor; this requires that the performer memorize exactly what to pick up, put down, or go to—and how much time each takes to execute. Quick timpani tuning often requires that the player put an ear down to the drum and listen to the pitch or look down at the tuning gauge; as a result, the player must memorize exactly which pitch to go to, on which drum, and how much time it takes to execute.

Keyboard percussion instruments are large and awkward, and during passages that are especially unidiomatic (see chapter 5) the player must often look down for accuracy. The layout of a multi-percussion setup will be relatively unfamiliar to the percussionist, and he or she will have to look down during passages that move quickly over many different instruments; this is especially true for setups that include both keyboard and non-keyboard instruments.

In all four cases, the performer's attention is momentarily away from the music and the conductor. Memorization thus will usually be required, and the performer will need more time to prepare the part.

Dynamics

◉ Video 2.c—Dynamics, Reaching Instruments, Pedals

Dynamics are often a function of velocity—that is, how fast the beater is moving when it strikes the instrument. For this reason, when a fast motion is required, a louder dynamic will be most natural. For example, if one hand is required to consecutively strike two instruments on opposite sides of a large setup, the stroke will need to be very quick and the resulting dynamic will tend to be loud.

Maintaining dynamic continuity around a setup of instruments that speak differently can be a considerable challenge. One common problem occurs when a snare drum is included with other drums; the bright, sharp sound of the snare drum sticks out. In certain playing situations, it may be impossible to compensate for this significant dynamic difference. (See A Dysfunctional Family in chapter 1.)

In a large ensemble such as an orchestra, especially soft sounds will not project enough to be heard. Some special effects described in this book are subtle and soft, and should therefore be reserved for chamber and solo contexts.

When the percussionist is holding four mallets, his or her control of dynamics is limited between the two mallets of one hand when simultaneously striking a surface. For example, if two mallets of one hand strike two notes of a marimba together, they will tend to sound the same dynamic. Slight dynamic differences are possible but difficult, and attempts to achieve extreme dynamic differences may result in the mallets not striking at the same time. In this case, the best way to achieve two different dynamics is by striking with two separate hands or by holding mallets of two different hardnesses.

Reaching the Instruments

◐ Video 2.c—Dynamics, Reaching Instruments, Pedals

Instruments far away from each other in a setup may not be able to be played at the same time. This can be a problem, especially with two mallets in one hand. The performer may be able to reach two instruments with two separate hands, but not with the two mallets of one hand (the mallet span is much smaller than the arm span). This commonly becomes a problem with stacked mallet instruments. (See Stacked Instruments in chapter 5.)

Instruments with Pedals

◐ Video 2.c—Dynamics, Reaching Instruments, Pedals

Vibraphone and tubular bells have sustain pedals, timpani have pedals that adjust the pitch, and hi-hats and pedal bass drums have pedals that strike the instrument. With especially large setups, it may be impossible for the performer to reach a pedal while playing another area of the setup; the sustain on a vibraphone may need to be cut short or a bass drum articulation may need to be substituted if the percussionist is positioned too far from the pedal.

Simultaneously operating multiple pedals is possible, but the percussionist may need to sit down to do so. Keyboard instruments often require that the player stand, so complicated passagework on multiple pedals in setups that include keyboard instruments should be avoided. Playing multiple pedals with just one foot can also be awkward and difficult. If a foot pushes a bass drum pedal, and then moves to another pedal, the bass drum pedal may swing back and forth and create unwanted noise. In some cases, the foot may need to rest on the pedal for a moment after it is depressed to ensure the proper sound (such as the choked clash or "sock" of the cymbals of a hi-hat). Performers commonly sit when complicated timpani tuning is required, but tuning with accuracy can be especially difficult if the foot must quickly leave the pedal.

Occasionally, composers request that instruments normally struck with a stick or mallet instead be articulated with a bass drum pedal. This can be advantageous, as it can free up the hands to play other things, but it can also create setup challenges. Mounting an instrument in the proper position to be played with a pedal often requires that the performer build or buy a special device. Devices exist for mounting cowbells and plastic woodblocks for pedal operation, which makes those the most probable candidates for adding pedal instruments. This, however, remains more difficult than playing these instruments with a hand-held beater. (A discussion of idiomatic pedal writing can be found in Idiomatic Writing for Drums in chapter 6.)

Physical Exertion and Shaking

Percussionists are commonly required to use physical force to execute a passage. Crash cymbals, loud rolls, and quick passages can tax the player's muscles and increase his or her heart rate. This will make the player's hands shake slightly, and for up to a minute afterward the execution of soft delicate passages may be difficult.

Working with Headphones or Headset Microphones

A percussionist may have to wear headphones or a headset microphone in pieces involving electronics. If the player has to move around a large setup, he or she can easily get tangled in the cord. The cord can also get caught on instruments, disturbing them or pulling the headphones or microphone from the performer's head. In these situations, it is best to keep motion to a minimum, if possible. Wireless headsets are preferable if a lot of moving around is involved.

Such pieces should always be practiced with the equipment before the performance; this can bring to light any problems that can be fixed before the dress rehearsal. These logistics are often the performer's issue, but composers are frequently involved in getting the equipment for such pieces and they should be aware that these problems may arise.

CHAPTER THREE

General Notation

Musical notation and music are both types of language. The process by which nota-tion becomes music is a translation, or series of translations, from one language to another language. The fewer and more intuitive these translations, the more success-ful the process will be. The language of percussion notation is especially abstract and must often be newly defined for each specific instance. By understanding the ways percussionists interpret notations and how they translate them into setup, sound, and music, the composer will be able to employ notations that make it easiest for the per-former to understand and execute the composer's intentions.

BASICS OF PERCUSSION PARTS AND SCORES

Instrument List

A complete list of instruments employed should *always* be included at the begin-ning of the score and the percussion part (see figure 3.1). This list should be complete for the entire piece, not just for an individual movement. Lists for movements are also useful, but only when they are in addition to a complete list. An instrument list makes it much easier for the percussionist to gather and set up the needed instruments and beaters. If the player must go through the percussion part to identify all the necessary instruments, there is a much greater chance one will be overlooked. An instrument list can also help clarify any ambiguous instrument indications in the score.

If the piece requires multiple percussionists and the parts are divided, then the instrument list should be divided by player. Any instrument shared by two or more players should appear in each player's lists, with an indication that it is to be shared and with whom it is to be shared. This information allows the percussionists to set up so the shared instrument is within reach of both players.

Ranges of keyboard instruments should be included if a nonstandard range is required. It is advisable to always include the ranges of marimbas, as a different size of marimba can mean a different instrument setup; a 5-octave marimba takes up much more space than a 4.3-octave instrument.

Figure 3.1
Example
instrument list

Player 1:
timpani

Player 2:
marimba 4.3 oct (shared with player 3)
two tom-toms
large bass drum
two suspended cymbals

three nipple gongs

one bass bow

Player 3:
vibraphone (with motor)
five temple blocks
tambourine
guiro
tam-tam (shared with player 4)
marimba 4.3 oct (shared with player 2)
two bass bows

Player 4:
glockenspiel
xylophone

four crotales

triangle
vibraslap
tam-tam (shared with player 3)

If instruments with only a small number of defined pitches are used (like nipple gongs, roto-toms, and tubular bells or crotales taken out of the set), then the instrument list should indicate the pitches. Need for the vibraphone motor should be listed so the players can obtain extension power cables. Any specified beater, especially bows, should also be included in the instrument list.

The composer should check the instrument list in the final copies of the score and parts, as instrumentation may change over the course of composition and preparation of the piece.

Instrument Key

An instrument key indicates where and how the instruments are notated on the staff (figure 3.2). (Details on how to make an instrument key are found later in this chapter.)

Figure 3.2
Example
instrument key

Bass   ----Timbales----   ----Bongos----   Cymbal Cymbal
Drum   Dome

An instrument key is usually unnecessary, used most often for complicated setups in solo and chamber works. If a piece uses multiple percussionists with complicated setups, multiple instrument keys are then appropriate.

Even with an instrument key, whenever possible and practical, the composer should write the name of the instrument above each of its entrances; it is best to not require the performer to memorize an instrument key (figure 3.3). If a group of instruments is used as one instrument (e.g., a snare drum, three tom-toms, and a bass drum are always played together), instead of writing each instrument as it enters, the composer may indicate entrance of that group (e.g., "drums").

Figure 3.3
Notated
instrument names

SOURCE: From
Elliott Carter's
Tintinnabulation.

It is especially important in a conductor's score to write the instrument name. If the conductor wishes to look down and see what instrument is being played, he or she should not have to refer back a few pages or look at an instrument key at the beginning of the score. (Details on percussion notation in conductors' scores are found later in this chapter.)

The composer should be sure to proof the instrument key in the final copies of the score and percussion parts, as instrumentation and notation may change over the course of the composition and preparation of the piece.

Setup Diagram

A setup diagram is a pictorial representation of the instrument setup for performance and may be included in the beginning of the percussion part. A setup diagram is usually unnecessary, most often used only for complicated setups in solo and chamber works. It is best to consult with a percussionist or even wait until the piece has been performed to settle on a diagram, as the setup may change during the performer's preparation of the piece. For example, figure 3.4 shows a diagram for a setup that includes:

2 cowbells
2 bongos
3 tom-toms
2 suspended cymbals
china cymbal
pedal bass drum
tam-tam

Figure 3.4
Example setup
diagram

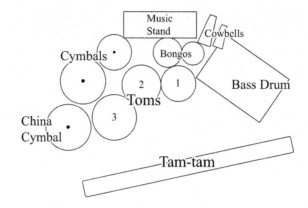

Language

Instrument names and performance instructions should be written in one language, preferably English. English-speaking composers sometimes use foreign terms for instruments (e.g., *gran cassa* instead of *bass drum*); this is not recommended except in the case of instruments that are commonly called by foreign names, like *timpani* or *glockenspiel*. Composers writing in other languages may want to include an English translation of any text in the percussion part.

The names of standard instruments written in other languages will usually not give performers some trouble (although an English translation, if only in the opening instrument list, is still much welcomed). Language can be a real barrier with more complex performance instructions and unusual beater or instrument specifications. In these cases, it is best to keep the vocabulary as clear and nonspecialized as possible so that Internet translating software can do an effective job.

Abbreviations

Poor use of abbreviations can make indications unclear. When abbreviating, the composer must include the entire unabbreviated name of the instrument earlier in the piece or in the instrument list. Ambiguous abbreviations like "T. Bls." (could be either templeblocks, tubular bells, or temple bowls) or "Mar." (could be marimba or maracas) should be avoided; the abbreviation used should apply to one instrument and one instrument only. It is also helpful to put the abbreviation in parentheses next to the full instrument name in the instrument list; this will leave little chance of confusion. For example:

marimba (Mba.)
snare drum (SD.)
bass drum (BD.)
cymbal (Cym.)

cowbells (CB.)
woodblock (WB.)
triangle (Tri.)

Standard abbreviations do not exist.

Parts

Parts for an ensemble piece with multiple percussionists can be designed one of three ways: as separate parts, as a divided score part, or as an undivided score part.

Separate Parts

Separate parts (one player's music per part) can reduce visual clutter and facilitate page turns. Separate parts *must* be divided correctly, however; otherwise, many more problems are created than are solved.

Divided Score Part

Parts can be divided but notated together in a score (figure 3.5). This allows the percussionists to see what others in the section are playing. Divided score parts are also useful when players are required to move around and share setups; a player moving to his or her neighbor's setup can just look at the music that is there and not have to bring along his or her music. Additionally, divided score parts allow percussionists to divide the music between them differently from how the composer has done it, without having to pencil in music from another part.

Parts may be partially divided (e.g., two parts—one with players 1 and 2 and the other with players 3 and 4).

Undivided Score Part

With an undivided score part, all the music appears on the same page, with no indication of what music is to be played by which player. This means that the performers have to determine how many are needed and then divide the parts among themselves. This is the least preferred method for making parts.

If the parts are rather simple and sparse, with only a few instances of more than one person playing at a time, then an undivided score part is acceptable. In this case, more than one player can read from the same music, and the players can follow each other's parts, as shown in figure 3.6.

On the other end of the spectrum, the composer may choose an undivided score part if he or she has made the mistake of writing complicated parts without previously determining each player's instruments. As described in chapter 2, writing for many instruments without predetermined player divisions is discouraged.

Figure 3.5
Divided score part

Figure 3.6
Simple undivided
score part

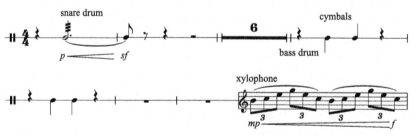

If the composer has a collection of parts with no clear way to divide them, then an undivided score part may be preferable, however. Figure 3.7, for example, is what figure 3.5 would look like without player divisions. In this case, the performers have to divide the parts themselves, and having each other's music in one place makes the process much easier.

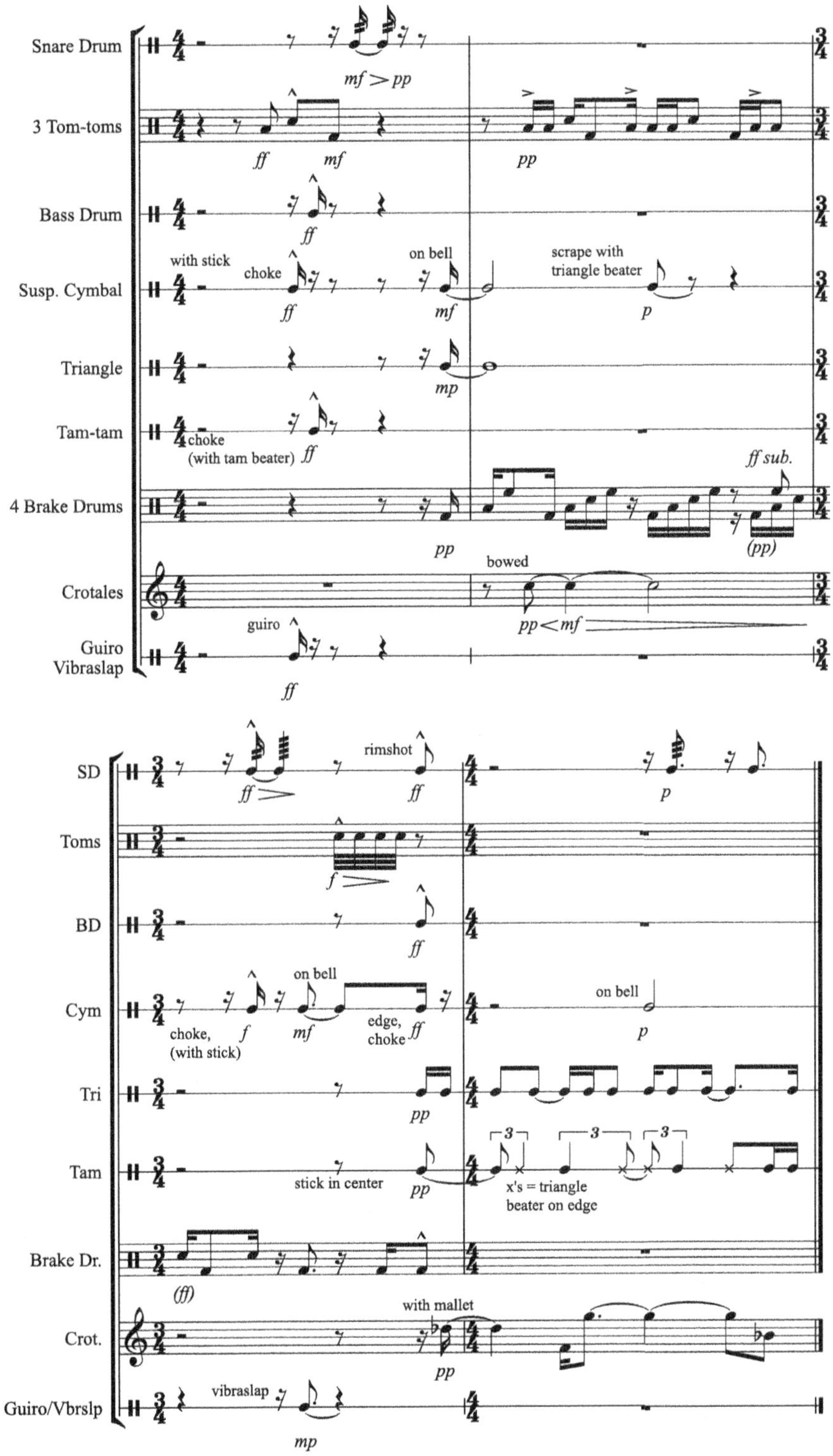

Figure 3.7 Complex undivided score part

Moreover, if the parts are indeed difficult to divide, then the composer *should not* try to divide the parts him or herself. Far worse than a poorly constructed undivided part is a poorly constructed part that has been improperly divided by the composer. If the composer does not want to or does not know how to divide the parts properly, a percussionist could help, or this task could be left for the percussionists who perform the piece. But, to reiterate, if the player divisions are determined before the parts are written, these problems will never arise.

Finally, involved score parts often create especially difficult page turns.

Handwritten versus Computer-Generated Parts

A beautifully handwritten part is always welcome, but for many reasons, a computer-generated part is usually clearer and easier to read. When using large instruments or setups, percussionists are often forced to play at a distance from their music. An eighth rest that looks a bit like a quarter rest, or an E♭ that is a little too close to the D line, will be a serious problem. Most of these problems are solved with a computer-generated part, however.

Multiple Copies of Parts

If large setups are involved, the composer should provide at least two copies of the parts. Percussionists will often need extra copies for different areas of a large setup. An extra copy eliminates the need for the performer to move the music around during the piece or to have to make last-minute photocopies.

Cues

Cues are always helpful. Exposed solo passages from any member of an ensemble are the best cues, but during thickly textured passages where there is no obvious cue, a cue from another percussionist is most useful. In this case, the person playing the cue is close by, heard very well, easily distinguishable from the rest of the ensemble, and often visible. More specifically, the best percussion cue is the entrance of a new instrument.

Next to percussion, the horns can be a good cue source in an orchestral setting. The horns are often situated directly in front of the percussion, with their bells pointed backward. The rest of the back row—trumpets and low brass—are easily heard and can be watched for entrances. Entrances and distinct rhythms in the strings can easily be seen from afar, if not heard. Unexposed and sustained passages are less helpful.

During a mallet switch, instrument switch, or timpani tuning change, the percussionist may momentarily shift his or her attention from counting rests, thus cues before entrances after these spots are especially appreciated. Cues, not just at the end but also in the middle of especially long rests, are helpful in orienting the performer before he or she must be ready to play.

Percussion in the Conductor's Score

In a conductor's score, the percussion section is traditionally found just beneath the trombones and tuba and above the harp, keyboard instruments (piano, celeste, etc.), soloists, chorus, and strings. The timpani is usually on top of the other percussion, with its own bracket. There is no guarantee that the percussionists will set up in the order notated in the score, so the labels "player 1" or "player 2" can be arbitrary.

For pieces with multiple percussionists playing multiple instruments, the player's number and the instrument name should appear on each page of the score (figure 3.8). The conductor should not have to flip back a few pages or look at an instrument key in the beginning of the score to see which instrument is being played.

Figure 3.8
Percussion in conductor's score

SOURCE: From Jefferson Friedman's *Sacred Heart: Explosion.*

Dynamics

When an instrument switch is made, a new dynamic specific to the new instrument should always be notated. Instruments can have a far different dynamic range from one another, even when struck with the same mallet at the same intensity. For example, a *fortissimo* maraca will not have a chance against a *fortissimo* brake drum with brass mallets, and a fast passage on four small tom-toms with snare sticks cannot get as soft as a similar vibraphone passage with yarn mallets. (See appendix E for a detailed explanation of dynamic discrepancies.)

DESIGNING A NOTATIONAL SYSTEM

Because of the infinite combinations of instruments and the infinite ways of setting them up, there is no standard, specific system of notation, so one must be devised for each new piece. The following are guidelines for forming an effective notation.

Clefs

For determinately pitched instruments, percussionists read either treble or bass clefs. Soprano, alto, and tenor clef should be avoided. Indeterminately pitched percussion is always notated in the percussion clef. Percussion clefs can be drawn a number of ways, as long as they do not specify pitch. Figure 3.9a displays the two most common percussion clefs.

Figure 3.9a
Common clefs

A clef can be created to map out the lines or spaces used for each specific instrument (figure 3.9b). For example, a piece for four toms may use a four-notehead clef that shows where each drum is notated. These noteheads should be in parentheses so they are not confused with the written music. The names of the instruments with brackets, lines, or arrows that show their placement on the staff is another common clef (figure 3.9c).

Figure 3.9b
Notehead clefs

Figure 3.9c
Instrument
name clefs

It is not required that clefs like those in figures 3.9b and 3.9c appear at the start of each system of a part; however, they should be re-notated where a reminder is appropriate.

For most scores, a regular percussion clef (figure 3.9a) is most appropriate when used in conjunction with written instructions or an instrument key. Otherwise, as the reader can see, there is a lot of leeway in clef construction.

In a lot of older music, indeterminately pitched percussion is notated in treble or bass clefs. This does not mean that the composer was indicating a specific pitch for those instruments; percussion clef simply had not yet been developed. In contemporary scores, treble and bass clefs should be used only for determinately pitched instruments.

Staves

Different lines and spaces on a staff can be used to denote different notes, different instruments, and even different playing techniques. In figure 3.10, instead of two or three instruments, the staff lines are used for different sounds on one instrument.

Figure 3.10
Sounds notated on
a staff

For a small number of instruments or sounds, only a one-line staff may be needed. One line can show up to three instruments or sounds: below the line, on the line, and above the line (figure 3.11). For clarity, however, it is often best to separate the instruments by a third or greater (see figure 3.10), so a one-line staff is best suited for one or two sounds.

Figure 3.11
One-line staff

Notations requiring more sounds should use a traditional five-line staff, augmented with ledger lines if necessary. Two bracketed five-line staves (like a grand staff) can be used for larger setups (figure 3.12). Anything larger should be avoided as it can make the part difficult to read.

Figure 3.12
Grand staff

SOURCE: From
Marcos Balter's
Descarga.

The use of many one-line staves is not ideal because it can result in excessive cross-beaming and notated rests. (See the percussion part in Stravinsky's *Histoire du Soldat* and the timpani part in *Rite of Spring.*) For example, figure 3.13a is much easier to read when noted as shown in figure 3.13b. Such a passage will, however, sound more like the former notation. (See A Dysfunctional Family in chapter 1.)

Figure 3.13a
Multiple
one-line staves

Figure 3.13b
Consolidated five-
line notation

One line with symbols or written instructions can also be used. The first example of figure 3.10 may also be notated as shown in figure 3.14. One line may even be appropriate for parts with multiple instruments. Stem direction should be used to further clarify instruments (figure 3.15).

Figure 3.14
One line with
symbols

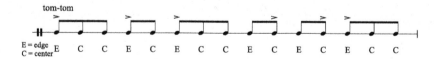

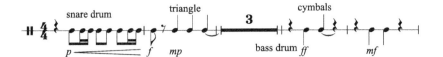

Figure 3.15
One line with
instructions

Noteheads

Differently shaped noteheads can be used to make the instruments immediately recognizable, easier to pick out at a glance. In a setup, the drums are usually regular noteheads and instruments like cymbals, cowbells, or woodblocks may be "X"s. Additional noteheads can be used, but should be reserved for a single instrument; for example, the triangles in a large setup may have triangle-shaped noteheads. Under normal playing conditions, instruments of determinate pitch should always be notated with regular noteheads.

Mixing Determinately and Indeterminately Pitched Instruments

When keyboard instruments are included among many indeterminately pitched instruments, it is best to add extra staves. More than one keyboard instrument can coexist on one staff, but only if the writing is sparse. In this case, the composer can make instruments distinguishable with note stem direction and by writing the instrument name above the music that belongs to it, as shown in figure 3.16.

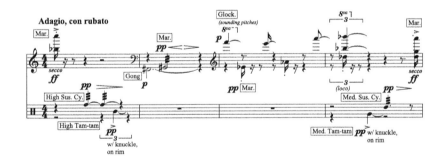

Figure 3.16
Mixing definitely
and indefinitely
pitched
instruments
SOURCE: From Ryan
Streber's *Rondel.*

Determinately pitched instruments that use only a few pitches (e.g., tuned gongs, crotale notes, chime notes, almglocken, roto-toms, or timpani) do not necessarily need to be notated on a separate pitched clef. The pitches can be specified at the beginning of the part and subsequently notated as for indeterminately pitched instruments (figure 3.17).

Figure 3.17
Definite pitch
notated as
indefinite

Key Signatures

If the clef of one staff frequently changes from pitched clef to percussion clef so as to accommodate both determinately and indeterminately pitched instruments, then a key signature would be confusing. In this case, accidentals should be notated next to the appropriate notes, as shown in figure 3.18. Other key signature rules are the same for percussion as for all other instruments.

Figure 3.18
Shared staff without key signature

What Goes Where on the Staff

If a piece of music requires a single player to play multiple instruments, but each instrument is always used alone, then the positions of the instruments on the staff may be chosen based on readability for the individual instruments. A setup of two tom-toms, two bongos, and five templeblocks, where the drums and blocks are used separately, may be notated as shown in figure 3.19.

Figure 3.19
Instrument groups notated separately

This is quite readable, as the instruments are centered on the staff, the notes are separated by thirds, and the instrument groups are clarified by noteheads and by spaces/lines. Such a notation, however, would make figuration between the drums and blocks difficult to read.

When different instruments are played simultaneously or in quick succession—as if they are different notes on one instrument—then a careful setup/notation relationship is necessary. In these cases, it is advantageous to maintain what percussionists already know about keyboard notation by relating the position of the instruments on the staff to the physical setup. Specifically:

left to right in a setup = low to high on the staff
back to front = low to high (i.e., instruments closer to the performer will be
    notated lower than instruments farther from the performer)
anything played by the feet is notated on the bottom

The setup with two tom-toms, two bongos, and five templeblocks might be set up in one of the two ways shown in figure 3.20 (the "X" indicates the position of the performer). If the composer requested figuration between the drums and blocks, it would be notated instead as shown in figure 3.21, representing the whole setup as one instrument.

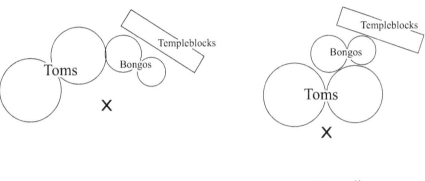

Figure 3.20
Instrument setup

--Tom-toms--   ---Bongos---   ----------------Templeblocks----------------

Figure 3.21
Instrument groups notated like one instrument

In addition to the physical setup, it is equally important for the notation to represent the relative pitch relationships among the instruments. It can be difficult to accurately notate pitch relationships when combining indeterminately pitched instruments (see appendix F), but even a close approximation will help the readability for the performer, as well as make it easier for the composer to understand the setup's function during the composition process.

If the notation disagrees with the setup or pitch relationships, however, it is not the end of the world. Percussionists are used to this and can adapt, but the music will be more difficult to read and learn. (More information and examples of this process can be found in appendix B). The composer's best option is to work directly with a percussionist on a specific example.

The Chicken or the Egg?

Which comes first—the notation or the setup? It could go either way. Most often, composers will compose without a specific setup in mind. In these cases, the performer designs a setup to fit the notation as closely as possible, but because of physical demands that the writing imposes or physical demands that the size or shape of the instruments impose, the setup may not fit the notation exactly. As stated earlier, this is not a significant problem—percussionists commonly read notations that do not exactly fit the setups—but a percussionist may ask the composer to re-notate especially complicated and difficult-to-read parts.

For a complicated setup or one on which very fast or very difficult figures will be played, it is advantageous for the composer to devise a setup before starting to write. With a preconceived setup, the composer is sure to use appropriate notation, thus making the piece easier to read and learn. Also, with a setup diagram to reference while writing, the composer can see how the performer will move about the instruments and can more easily avoid requiring uncomfortable or impossible choreography. This kind of preparatory work can yield significant benefits over the life of the composition. (See Social Composition in chapter 1.)

It is best to consult a percussionist to determine how the instruments may be set up. Setting up the instruments has a lot to do with personal preference, the writing in the piece, and the size and shape of the instruments. The composer can get an idea of instrument setups from appendix B, but should work with percussionists whenever possible.

Unspecified Instruments (Indeterminate Instrumentation)

Because of the enormous size of the percussion family, composers can sometimes afford to be vague with their instrument specifications. Such vagueness allows performers to be creative and/or practical with their choices; they may then use something that is of limited availability, an interesting combination of instruments, or an instrument they made or discovered (keep in mind that percussion "instruments" can be found in attics, basements, kitchens, living rooms, back yards, toy stores, etc.). Certain characteristics may be specified, such as material (wood, metal, skin [drum], glass, etc.), pitch register, and amount of resonance. For example, David Lang's *The Anvil Chorus* calls for three resonant metals, four non-resonant metals, four pedal-operated metals (with no additional specification), two woodblocks, and a pedal bass drum.

Drum choices are commonly left open. Instead of specifying two high tom-toms, two congas, two timbales, two timpani, and a bass drum, the composer may write "nine drums." This allows the performer to pick the instruments that are more creative, effective, and available. (See Nico Muhly's *Ta & Clap*, Iannis Xenakis's *Psappha*, and Morton Feldman's *King of Denmark*.)

How Much to Notate

Sometimes passages on indeterminately pitched instruments may be vaguely notated. Most percussionists are accustomed to improvising and can do so effectively. Instead of writing out a part completely, it may be better for the composer to write an outline of the rhythm or indicate the character of the part, and let the player fill in the rest. A completely written-out part might be more work for both the composer and player, and may end up sounding exactly like an improvisation. (See The Written/Improv Divide in chapter 1.)

Systems of Notation for Which There Is No Standard

Notations for many special effects are not standardized and should be explained at the beginning of the score and parts. If no specific notation is suggested in this book, the composer should create one or should write out the instructions. Remember, English is always standard notation.

Return to a "Normal" Method of Playing

When an unusual method of playing is indicated (e.g., using a prepared instrument or playing with unusual beaters), it should be indicated when the player should stop doing this (e.g., "remove paper clip" or "return to normal beaters").

NOTE LENGTH, ARTICULATION, AND PHRASING

Percussion instruments manage note length, articulation, and phrasing much differently from other instruments. Percussion note lengths are often chosen exclusively for rhythmic readability, and articulation markings must often be reinterpreted as dynamic phrasing. The pointy-ness of these instruments' sounds requires different expectations and different accommodations in playing and in notation.

Although real control over different articulations is not always possible or practical, either because of the nature of a given instrument or the context of a passage, articulation and phrasing markings are still helpful. Percussionists realize these notations through dynamic phrasing, mallet choice, and variations in muting or beating spot. A composer should not hesitate to write slurs into a glockenspiel or even a snare drum part; the slur sound can be achieved even though each note must be articulated. The effect will not be as apparent as it would be on a clarinet, but these notations will make a difference.

On resonant instruments with pitch bend capabilities, such as timpani or flexatone, a true legato can be executed by striking the instrument once and then changing the pitch, but this is not particularly effective. The success of this effect depends on the volume of the resonance—the further the slurred note is from the original articulation (in time and in interval), the softer it will be. A slur alone will not indicate a glissando; glissando must be notated separately.

Note-Length Chart

The following chart categorizes instruments with respect to the length of their ring or sustain. Arrows indicate the range of instruments with variable sustain. All Group 2, 3, and 4 instruments can be dampened to have minimal sustain (Group 1).

Mark tree can only be dampened to be as short as Group 2. All instruments can be "sustained" with tremolo to sound as long as Group 4.

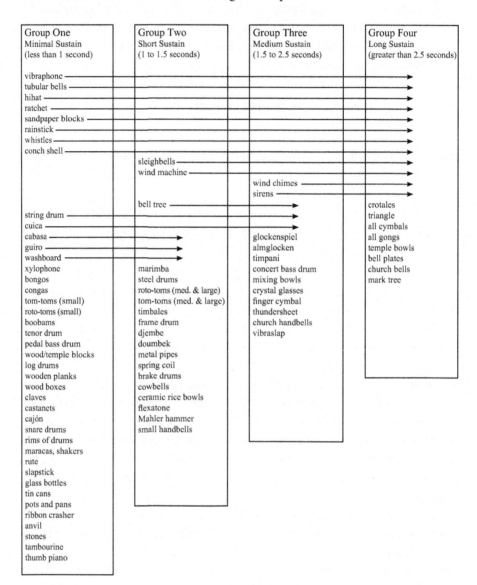

Exact or Inexact Note-Length Indications

Instruments in Group 1 of the Note-Length Chart (those without variable sustain) have little or no natural resonance. For these instruments, note length does not need to be notated exactly; a whole note will not ring any longer than a 16th note. The note length will not change unless the instrument is dampened while it is struck.

Instruments in Group 2 of the chart have a little resonance that can be controlled through dampening, but are generally left to sound for their full lengths. If accurate short durations are desired for special articulation effects, then dampening should be notated.

Under normal circumstances, the note lengths of these Group 1 and 2 instruments *need not be notated accurately* and should instead be chosen for rhythmic readability. Excessive rests can clutter a part and make it difficult to read (figure 3.22a). If inexact note lengths create phrasing problems, articulations can substitute (figure 3.22b).

Figure 3.22
Exact or inexact
note lengths

With the resonant instruments of Groups 3 and 4 in the chart on page 72, resonance should be considered and controlled either with accurate note lengths, dampening indications, or through the discretion of the performer. For the most control over note length, exact note lengths can be written (as one would for piano music) with an indication at the beginning of the part that note lengths should be accurately observed. For less specific notation, indications can be used only when necessary (for cymbals and other resonant instruments). An *l.v.* (*laissez vibrer,* "let vibrate") or an open slur indicates to let the instrument ring (figure 3.23), and a coda symbol, two slashes, or the word *cut, choke, damp,* or *secco* indicates dampening.

Figure 3.23
Muffle notation

Depending on the context, specification of note lengths and dampening may be best decided by the performer. Percussionists are accustomed to making decisions about when to stop an instrument from ringing and can often be expected to do so effectively.

The composer should be careful to not over-indicate note lengths and dampening. There may not be enough time for the player to execute these indications, and many long notes and ties can clutter the part without any realistic effect. Dampening may take just a fraction of a second, but that fraction of a second must still exist. If the player needs to play, turn a page, or change mallets, then dampening might not be possible. A performer can sometimes dampen with one hand (especially with small instruments), in which case the other hand is free to do other things.

Of course, with instruments sustained by being rolled on, bowed, scraped, shaken, cranked, or blown through, note length should always be notated exactly.

Muting (Muffling, Dampening)

🔊 Video 3.a—Note Length and Articulation

Instruments can be muted with a piece of cloth, tape, a mallet, a hand, or another body part. If an instrument is dampened directly after it is struck, it will simply shorten the note length. If the instrument is dampened while it is struck, it not only shortens the length but also changes the sound. Additionally, the sound of the resonance will change if the instrument is only somewhat dampened after the attack. (See Manipulations of Timbre in appendix C.)

Light dampening with a piece of cloth is often done to make drums drier and darker, and to clear up soft articulate passages on timpani and other large resonant drums. Heavy dampening is commonly done with pedal bass drums; towels, sheets, or something similar are often inserted into the drum, giving it a full but punchy sound. Muting can be used as a special effect on all instruments.

When a cloth mute is used, it takes some time to place it onto or remove it from the instrument. Other means of muting are more flexible; by muting with a mallet, finger, hand, leg, or torso, the percussionist can adjust the degree of muffling while playing. When complex muting is required, it is best if only one hand is required to play so the other hand is free to muffle.

Closed and open (dampened and free to ring) are commonly notated with +'s and o's, respectively. Passages like that shown in figure 3.24 are most effective on smaller instruments like the triangle, where dampening can be done quickly and easily; on instruments such as a large tam-tam, this is difficult to execute.

Figure 3.24
Open/closed
notation

Figure 3.25 is a more complex example in which the sustain of multiple instruments is manipulated simultaneously or in quick succession. The brake drums can be muted by the mallet that strikes them, making quick dampening possible. These instruments only ring a short time, so the dampening must happen soon after the strike (in this case, an eighth note afterward). The cymbals and triangle must be muted by hand, so there must be a little extra time provided to get the hand in position to stop the resonance. This is further complicated by the fact that the hands are each holding two mallets. These instruments ring for a few seconds after being struck, so longer durations are possible.

Percussionists often use various dampening techniques on resonant instruments to control the sound and note lengths, regardless of whether or not the dampening is

Figure 3.25
Advanced
muffling example

SOURCE: From Judd
Greenstein's *We Shall
Be Turned.*

indicated by the composer. For example, the resonance of a concert bass drum head is usually controlled with a leg, hand, or towel.

Dampening some wind chimes or a mark tree is somewhat difficult to execute effectively. These instruments are often left to exhaust themselves naturally, even though they ring for a rather long time. Some mark trees have damper bars that allow the percussionist to muffle the instrument in less time.

Dead Stroke

🔊 Video 3.a—Note Length and Articulation

A dead stroke is achieved by holding the mallet on the instrument after the attack, so as to dampen the vibration. Dead strokes are commonly notated with a plus sign (+) over the note. Ringing notes in a passage with dead strokes can be indicated with a circle (o) over them; this is not necessary but can help to clarify. "D.S." or staccato dots are other common indications for a dead stroke. These notations are not standard and should be explained at the top of the score and part.

Dead strokes take more time to execute than normal strokes because the mallet head needs to spend more time on the instrument. Dead-stroke passages will not be effective at fast tempos.

With drum sticks, wood mallets, plastic mallets, and hard rubber mallets, dead strokes create a buzz sound as the beater bounces quickly on the instrument (like the bounce of a buzz roll). Mallets wrapped with yarn, cord, and felt have a soft layer of material to cushion the attack and eliminate the bounce. This buzz can be avoided by using wrapped mallets (e.g., instead of plastic mallets, very hard yarn or cord mallets could be used) or by wrapping a layer of moleskin or tape around the mallet head.

Dead strokes can be used as short notes on a marimba or vibraphone to contrast with the resonating normal strokes (see Steven Mackey's *See Ya Thursday*). On drums they sound harsher and raise the pitch slightly as the drum head is stretched by the pressure of the dead stroke.

Damper Pedals

🔊 Video 3.a—Note Length and Articulation

The vibraphone and tubular bells have damper pedals, so note length is more easily observed. Some glockenspiels have pedals, but this is rare. Pedaling can be notated as one would for piano (mm. 2–7 in figure 3.26). Pedal indications are very clear but limited because all the notes are dampened and released at once; these instruments do not have the piano's ability to sustain individual notes while the damper is applied. If specific note lengths are written without pedal indications, percussionists can try to use the pedal while dampening individual notes with a mallet or hand. This would allow some notes to ring longer or shorter than other notes as necessary (mm. 20–27 in figure 3.26). Often, slurs are used to indicate pedal groupings (mm. 8–10). When using accurate lengths and slur marks following a passage that uses pedal indications, the composer may indicate "pedal ad lib." to avoid ambiguity. Within complicated passages, it should be expected that some concessions be made where notes must be slightly shortened or extended.

Figure 3.26
Pedal notation
SOURCE: From
Nico Muhly's
Sustained Music.

Flutter pedal is often used on the vibraphone, but rarely notated. Half pedal does not work well because the damper bar on most vibraphones is inconsistent. The use of such pedal techniques is best left to the performer's discretion. Effective realization of vibraphone passages often requires complex pedaling as the performer responds to the subtleties of his or her particular instrument. It is recommended that a composer not over-notate pedal usage so as to encourage the performer's sensitivity. Moreover, excessive pedal indications can clutter a part and leave little room for dynamics.

If necessary, a weight could be used to hold down the pedal of a vibraphone or a set of tubular bells to leave them free to sustain without the player's foot. Most tubular bells and some vibraphones have a mechanism that can be used to keep the damper open.

Rolls

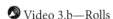 Video 3.b—Rolls

A roll is a tremolo. Percussionists and composers often use rolls to simulate sustain, but it only truly functions as sustain with soft mallets on especially resonant non-articulate instruments, like cymbals and gongs. Some instruments from Groups 2 and 3 of the Note-Length Chart on page 72 (such as large drums and the low register of a marimba or vibraphone) are also capable of producing seamless sustain, but only with soft mallets and at soft dynamics. In all other cases, a roll will be perceived as a tremolo and should be treated as such.

The character of tremolo is much different from that of a true sustain; it is a source of rhythmic intensity and often also provides audible rhythmic material. One might treat this material as ornamentation, the way a harpsichordist, guitarist, or harpist might use ornamentation or arpeggiation to replace longer note values. This is especially true with multiple-surface rolls—those executed by one player on more than one pitch or instrument (e.g., rolled four-note chords on marimba). In these cases, the tremolo on each pitch or instrument will be far slower because it will likely be played by just one hand. In such instances, percussionists must work extra hard to simulate sustain by varying the roll speed, roll type, and balance, as too much regularity will sound like an intended rhythm.

The composer may choose to have control over the material inside a roll by replacing a rolled passage with notated rhythms and figuration, or this may simply be left to the discretion of the performer. With the latter option, the performer will have a much easier time achieving success if the composer uses the rolls with acknowledgment of the activity they communicate.

Rolling on One Surface

Rolls can be notated a number of ways. The composer should use only one of these notations within a given piece, however, unless he or she is intending to notate different techniques. For example, in figure 3.27:

(a) The three-slash notation is most common but can be confused with abbreviated measured 32nd notes. If the three-slash notation is used for rolls, it should not also be used to indicate 32nd notes in the same piece. It is also advisable that four or even five slashes be used at slower tempi to avoid the suggestion of metered rhythm.

(b) The trill sign notation is also common but can be confused with a trill.

(c) This trill notation without the "tr," like an extended mordent, signifies a roll without the confusing double meaning.

(d) The "Z" notation is another clear option. It suggests an especially dense roll when used for snare drum and other small drums.

Figure 3.27
One surface rolls

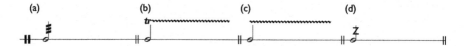

Unique to drum sticks is the *buzz* or *closed roll*, where the sticks bounce and make numerous articulations per stroke to create a very rapid tremolo. A *single-stroke roll* (no multiple bounce in each hand, just single strokes) can be executed with all beaters.

Just one stroke from a buzz roll can be used as an effect or for especially short rolls (figure 3.28). One can elongate this buzz effect by controlling the pressure with which the stick is held to the instrument. The stick can be dropped without pressure, like dropping a Ping-Pong ball on a table (figure 3.29), or pressure can be applied to speed up the bounce. A diminuendo will result naturally in all cases.

Figure 3.28
Individual
buzz stroke

Figure 3.29
Elogated bounce

With an *open* or *double-stroke roll*, only two articulations are made with each stroke and all the individual attacks can be heard. An open roll may be specified on drums to evoke a military sound.

Percussionists will decide which type of roll to use depending on the beaters and the resonance of the instrument. With sticks on small tight drums (small to medium tom-toms, tenor drums, timbales, small to medium roto-toms, snare drums, field drums, and bongos), a roll, unless otherwise indicated, will mean a buzz roll. Buzz and open rolls are possible on all instruments when sticks are used. When four beaters are held, buzz rolls (with sticks or any beater) can only be effectively executed for short durations; rolls longer than a few strokes will suffer. The use of buzz rolls should be avoided when four beaters are held.

Single-stroke rolls are more appropriate on larger drums with loose heads (even with sticks), on non-drum instruments with sticks, and on all instruments with mallets. Single-stroke rolls will not work as well on snare drums, bongos, or other small drums because the sound is very short and has little resonance to fill the space between the strokes. These distinctions are rarely notated and are almost always left up to the performer.

Rolls generally start with a slight emphasis. The second of two untied rolled notes will be re-attacked (figure 3.30a). Dotted line or regular ties can be used if a sustained roll is desired (figure 3.30b).

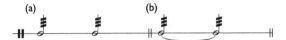

Figure 3.30
Untied and
tied rolls

Rolls on sustaining instruments, like a vibraphone, are not often necessary and can sometimes be a distraction. These notes may be best left to ring naturally.

Rolling on Two Surfaces

A roll on two instruments or two notes is a trill between those two instruments or notes. In notation, a tremolo between two notes with separate stems (figure 3.31a) is less familiar to percussionists than a tremolo on two notes on one stem (figure 3.31b). Notation (b) also makes the rhythm easier to read; however, only notation (a) indicates which note should start the tremolo.

Figure 3.31
Two surface rolls

Rolling on Four Surfaces

There are a variety of roll types with rolls on four surfaces. Roll-type indications are almost exclusively found in marimba transcriptions (written by marimbists) or in scores that have been edited by a percussionist. If the composer feels that controlling these specific roll textures is important, it is probably best to experiment with a performer after the piece has been written and learned, so the different roll types can be heard in context. Percussionists sometimes switch back and forth between roll types throughout the learning process, trying to find the one that is just right for each situation. Roll type is usually not important compositionally and may be a decision best left to the performer.

There are three main types of rolls: the traditional roll, the ripple or Musser roll, and the independent roll. The *traditional roll* is just hand-to-hand, as shown in figure 3.32.

Figure 3.32
Traditional roll

A *ripple or Musser roll* (after marimbist Clair Omar Musser) is similar to the traditional roll, except instead of the two mallets in each hand striking simultaneously, they are staggered to give a less metered texture (figure 3.33). This is sometimes notated with an "S" through the note stem.

Figure 3.33
Ripple roll

With the *independent roll*, the two mallets in each hand alternate independently of the other hand (figure 3.34). The two hands could even alternate at different speeds to create a more meterless texture. This is sometimes notated with an "O" through the note stem. The "S" and "O" notations are not standard and should be explained at the top of the score and part.

Figure 3.34
Independent roll

The above patterns are the most common types of rolls, but any fast pattern can function as such (figure 3.35). (See the second movement of Jacob Druckman's *Reflections on the Nature of Water*.)

Figure 3.35
Other tremolo
figuration

One-Handed Rolls

One hand can execute an independent roll by itself, called a one-handed roll, which leaves the other hand available to do other things. This one-handed roll can be executed on two surfaces or on one surface.

A one-surface roll can be achieved with the independent roll or with a split-bar roll. A *split-bar roll* is executed by placing the two mallets of one hand on either side of a marimba bar—one on top and the other underneath—and then shaking the mallets up and down. This was originally designed for marimba but can be used on all instruments that have both sides accessible. For example:

the "white" notes on marimba, vibraphone, xylophone, and crotales and the
"black" notes if the other side of the instrument is reachable (reaching the
black notes is not practical under normal playing conditions)
cymbals
the edge of gongs
temple bowls
cowbells, almglocken
metal pipes
thundersheet
templeblocks
crystal glasses

When executed on a non-keyboard instrument, this technique is often also called a *mandolin roll*. The choice of an independent or mandolin roll should be made by the performer. The decision is based on sticking and movement issues that will be explored throughout the percussionist's preparation of the piece. An indication of roll type may be included, if at all, only after the piece has been worked out by a performer.

A one-handed roll is limited in speed and dynamic in comparison to its two-handed counterpart. For especially fast or loud rolls, two hands may be required.

One note or instrument can also be sustained with a single-mallet roll. This is a much slower roll and only works well at soft dynamics with soft mallets on resonant instruments (e.g., vibraphone, cymbals, tam-tam, bass drum, and the lower register of the marimba). Rolls on large tam-tams are usually done this way, even at loud dynamics.

Other one-handed rolls include the following:

- A standard triangle roll is executed with one hand. The player moves the beater rapidly back and forth between two sides.
- For a standard tambourine shake roll, the tambourine is held and shaken with one hand.
- With cymbals, a mandolin roll can be executed with one brush by placing the cymbal edge in the middle of the brush's wires and moving the brush up and down. This works only at soft dynamics.
- One-handed rolls on cowbells and almglocken can be executed by moving the beater rapidly up and down inside the mouth of the bell. It requires a small amount of time to take the beater out of the bell and bring it to its next

position (inside another bell or above the next instrument to be struck), so connected passages with one mallet are not always possible.

- One-handed rolls between the rims or shells of drums are executed by moving the beater back and forth between the edges of two closely positioned drums. The same technique can be executed between the edges of two gongs.
- Double-headed beaters can be used to achieve one-handed rolls on a bass drum. The hand rotates back and forth and strikes the drum with alternating ends of the mallet. Rolls with double-headed bass drum beaters cannot be played as loudly as two-handed rolls.

Rolling on Three Surfaces

A rolled three-note (or three-instrument) chord (figure 3.36a) can be executed in a number of ways: (b) two notes against one note; (c and d) two notes against two notes with one common note; (e) three separate notes—two with an independent roll and the other with a single-mallet roll, single-note independent roll, or split-bar roll; and (f) another pattern. The method of execution will be decided by the performer and does not need to be indicated.

Figure 3.36
Three surface rolls

Rolling from the Resonance of a Previous Attack

The start of a roll can be delayed on resonant instruments by tying a struck note to a rolled note of the same pitch. The roll will have an ambiguous beginning, emerging out of the dying resonance of the first struck note. This is especially effective with *forte pianos* where the roll can pick up after the resonance has dwindled to *piano*.

NOTATIONS THAT ARE NOT RECOMMENDED

Symbol Notation

Symbol notation uses small pictures or icons to denote different instruments, mallets, and playing techniques, such as shown in figure 3.37. This system was an unsuccessful attempt to transcend language barriers. Few composers ever used it, and as a result, percussionists have not become familiar with the symbols. When playing music that uses symbol notation, most performers must constantly look back to the instrument key at the beginning of the part to translate. Use of this system is not recommended.

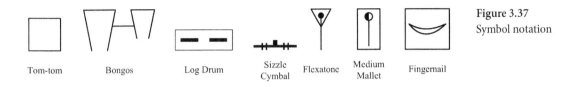

Figure 3.37
Symbol notation

Tom-tom   Bongos   Log Drum   Sizzle Cymbal   Flexatone   Medium Mallet   Fingernail

Altered Keyboard Notation (Timbre-Staff)

Altered keyboard notation (or timbre-staff) is a notational concept that takes the setup/notation relationship idea to its full extent. This system uses a five-line staff with a crossed-out treble clef. Accidentals are used to signify additional instruments with the intention that the instruments will be set up like the white and black notes of a piano keyboard (for one successful example, see Stephen Hartke's *Meanwhile*). This is rarely the best notational option, because percussion instruments come in a variety of shapes and sizes. For example, the timbre-staff notation shown in figure 3.38 would theoretically be set up in keyboard formation (a timbre-rack) as shown in figure 3.39.

Small Tom   --Bongos--   --------4 Cowbells-------   --3 Woodblocks--   ----3 Claves----

Figure 3.38
Altered keyboard notation

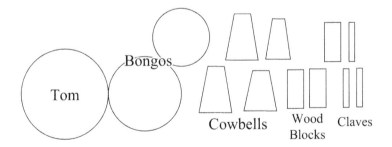

Figure 3.39
Timbre-rack

Tom   Bongos   Cowbells   Wood Blocks   Claves

This timbre-rack is hardly an ideal or intuitive setup for these instruments. Timbre-racks like this often require special rack systems to mount the instruments in the proper positions; designing such mounting systems can be time-consuming. Most percussionists would set up these instruments more as shown in figure 3.40. This setup is easier to construct setup and far more intuitive. The accompanying notation may be as show in figure 3.41.

Figure 3.40
More common
setup

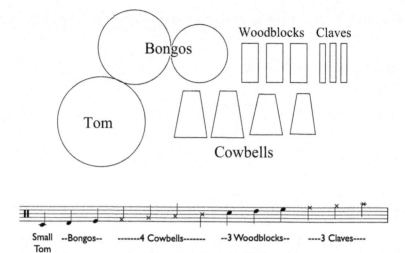

Figure 3.41
More common
notation

With the former arrangement (figures 3.38 and 3.39), the percussionist would likely spend as much time and energy finding a way to mount the instruments to accommodate the notation as he or she would to learn the less familiar notation shown in figure 3.41. Moreover, music with accidentals looks a lot more like a keyboard, wind, or string part than music with no accidentals and "X" noteheads. This can lead to confusion for readers of a score when a timbre-staff is included among determinately pitched instruments. Therefore, use of timbre-staff notation is not generally recommended.

CHAPTER FOUR

Beaters

To Indicate or Not to Indicate?

Unless the composer wishes to have a specific or unusual sound, beater choice is best left to the performer. Far better is a description of the desired sound (e.g., "dark," "heavy," "warm," "sharp," "pointed," "light"), allowing the percussionist to make choices (mallet or otherwise) that produce exactly the sound the composer intends.

There are two situations in which it may be important to consider beaters:

1. When a specific unusual or varied sound is desired—like brushes on snare drum, triangle beater on tam-tam, or the simultaneous use of stick and mallet on a tom-tom—then, of course, this should be indicated.
2. When instruments that require different beaters are used together or in quick succession, the composer should make sure the performer has time to switch beaters or can hold all required beaters at the same time (see appendix G).

If the composer is simply looking for the best and most appropriate sound, then this decision should be left to the performer. Choice of beater is often made based on elements that are out of the composer's control, such as the specific instruments, specific venue, or even the weather. Leaving the decision to the performer encourages him or her to listen and make good choices on the composer's behalf.

Beater Lingo

Often when specifying beaters, the instrument to be used is named. For example, instead of *plastic mallet* for use on xylophone, one might say *xylophone mallet,* or instead of *felt mallet* for use on timpani, one might say *timpani mallet.*

Stick, mallet, and *beater* all mean, more or less, the same thing. The composer should not be too concerned with using the correct terms for the correct types of beaters; percussionists will always understand what is meant. Common uses of these terms are as follows:

A *stick* refers to a regular drum stick. A *mallet* is a stick with a head (e.g., timpani mallet, marimba mallet, bass drum mallet). One would not call a snare stick a *mallet* but might call a mallet a *stick*. For example, one would not say *drum mallet* when referring to a drum stick, but one might say *timpani stick* or *vibe stick*. *Beater* can be used for anything, but it is most commonly used for tam-tam, gong, bass drum, and triangle beaters. For triangle, it would be unusual to say anything but *triangle beater*. Again, this is not an important concern—mallet indications are never unclear because of an unusual use of the terms stick, mallet, or beater.

The different parts of sticks and mallets are as shown in figure 4.1. A typical drum stick has a thick shaft and a bead at the end. The bead (or tip) is usually made of wood, but can sometimes be made of plastic. Mallets designed for use on keyboard instruments have thin shafts with a yarn, cord, rubber, wood, plastic, or brass head. Mallets designed for timpani have a thicker shaft (about the thickness of a drum stick) with a felt or wood head.

Figure 4.1
Beater anatomy

Photos courtesy of
Vic Firth Inc.

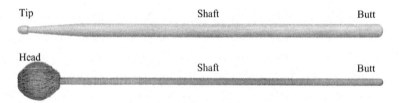

Tip   Shaft   Butt

Head
                             Shaft   Butt

Logistic Beater Issues

◉ Video 4.a—Beater Logistics

The composer must be aware that different instruments often require different beaters. When switching between two instruments, a percussionist may be forced to make a beater change, and proper time must be allotted to do so. Determining the need and time for beater changes can be difficult, so it is always best to consult a percussionist with a specific example.

Difficult beater changes will result in either a compromise of sound quality or a compromise of freedom of movement. Sound quality may be sacrificed if a percussionist does not have time to pick up the beater that will get the best sound out of an instrument (see appendix G). Freedom of movement can be hindered if a percussionist is required to rush to get to the appropriate beater or to hold the beaters in a less than ideal way. In these cases, the percussionist will be slightly handicapped and may not be able to perfectly execute a passage. Difficult beater changes can also create frantic motions or unwanted noise. (See Visuals and Noise in chapter 2.)

When calculating time for a mallet switch, the composer must factor in drop time in addition to pickup time. If the performer needs to drop four mallets and pick up another four mallets, this will take longer than if the performer is using his or her hands with no mallets and then has to pick up four mallets. In addition, it takes longer for a percussionist to pick up four mallets than to pick up two mallets.

Some beaters are not appropriate for some instruments because they may damage the instrument (see appendix G). Instrument damage is an especially important consideration.

Problems with Extreme Register

Larger instruments require larger, softer beaters while smaller instruments require smaller, harder beaters. For example, a mallet one might call "soft" for glockenspiel would be called "extremely hard" if used on vibraphone, and a "medium" bass drum beater would be so large and soft that it would hardly make a sound on a woodblock.

The use of a large bass drum or gong with other instruments in a setup may require some quick switches. The yarn mallets or sticks appropriate for a setup with, for example, marimba, toms, templeblocks, and cowbells, will get a bright thin sound out of a large bass drum or tam-tam, and the mallets that produce a big, full sound from a large bass drum or tam-tam are much too big for the other instruments. Since both the bass drum and tam-tam sound considerably different with a yarn mallet or stick than with their appropriate beaters, it may be wise to allow a short time (maybe only half a second) to switch to a large beater before important bass drum or tam-tam notes.

Instruments like the triangle suffer from the opposite problem when included in a setup. The triangle requires a thin metal beater to sound its best. Sticks and plastic mallets produce a clunky, unappealing sound, and yarn mallets would hardly make the triangle sound at all. Triangle beaters can be used on some other metal instruments, but they are not acceptable for drums or wood instruments.

A similar problem exists with a five-octave marimba. On this instrument, the soft yarn mallets that are ideal for the bass of the instrument do not speak well at the top, and the hard mallets that work best at the top are too bright for the bass and can even break bars at loud dynamics. One remedy for this problem is the use of graduated mallets (e.g., from left to right: a soft mallet, two medium mallets, and a hard mallet, or some other combination). With graduated mallets, one can use the appropriate mallet to bring out the best colors of the entire range of the instrument; on the other hand, this mallet arrangement can create voicing and sticking problems. Most often, composers will just write without regard to these problems and leave it to the performer to figure out a combination of mallets to bring out the best colors from the instruments without disrupting the melodic and harmonic lines. If the composer wrote for a specific graduated mallet arrangement, it would tend to be more idiomatic and better sounding. (See Steven Mackey's *See Ya Thursday*.)

Beater Tricks

A percussionist can hold up to four beaters comfortably and with a lot of control. This technique can be of use when switching quickly back and forth between instruments. For example, the player could hold one vibraphone and one crotale mallet in each hand at the same time (figure 4.2), thus allowing him or her to play two-mallet passages on both instruments.

Figure 4.2
Two pairs of
different beaters

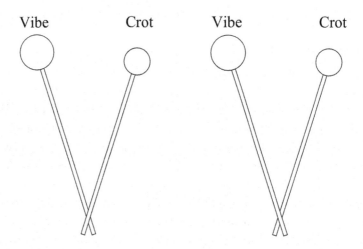

Vibe   Crot   Vibe   Crot

Percussionists can, within reason, hold any combination of four mallets (e.g., a bass drum beater, two drum sticks, and a triangle beater). This opens up possibilities for using many instruments at once, but significantly limits the use of each individual instrument.

Limited use of a triangle beater or other small beater in addition to four other mallets is awkward but possible. With more than four beaters, it is best to speak with the percussionist who is to perform the piece about the specific example. Some marimbists have actually become proficient in a limited six-mallet technique, but this is not widely used. It is best to never request more than four beaters at a time.

A gong beater can often be hung from a large tam-tam stand. This removes the need to pick up or drop the beater, and also always keeps the beater in position to strike the instrument.

If necessary, a drum stick sound can be achieved with the butt end or shaft of a mallet. The butt and shaft of a felt mallet (timpani mallet) is much like that of a drum stick while keyboard mallet shafts are thinner and produce a lighter, brighter sound (see The Shaft and Butt of Beaters, next).

Specialty sticks called *flip sticks, combo sticks,* or *two-headed sticks* are commonly available. Usually a drum stick is paired with a felt or yarn mallet so the player can flip the beaters over to create a totally different sound. Other specialty sticks exist but are not as common. Specialty sticks that are not readily available and that might have to be custom made are best used in solo or chamber pieces. In large ensemble situations where preparation time is not as abundant, it is best to request what is most common. Flip sticks should not be used in sets of four; it is very difficult, awkward, and time consuming to flip mallets over while holding a set of four. In this case, it would be more efficient to drop the mallets and pick up a new set.

At loud dynamics, the color differences between soft and hard beaters are far less noticeable. At soft dynamics, a yarn mallet and a drum stick will produce very different timbres from a tom-tom, but at *forte* these two different beaters have rather similar sounds. As a result, beater changes at loud dynamics may not be necessary.

The Shaft and Butt of Beaters

The shaft or butt of a stick or mallet can be used for effects. The butt can be used everywhere, as can the head, but the shaft, for reasons of angle, can only be used in certain instances. The following is a list of instances where the shaft of the mallet can be used successfully:

on the edge of the bars of all keyboard mallet instruments except the
    glockenspiel
on the rim of all drums
on the edge and bell of cymbals
edge of gongs
nipple of nipple gongs
triangle
temple bowls, mixing bowls, rice bowls
cowbells, almglocken
brake drums (with drum sticks or with mallets held upside down—not with
    mallets held normally)
thundersheet
edge of a tambourine, flat across the head of a tambourine
woodblocks, templeblocks
machine castanets
flat across the head of bongos and congas (These instruments have sunken rims
    so the entire shaft of a stick can be struck flat against the head. On all other
    drums the rim would get in the way. This works with sticks and with mallets
    held upside down, not with mallets held normally.)
flat on the head of a bass drum (with drum sticks, not with mallets)
flat across the face of gongs (with drum sticks or with mallets held upside down,
    not with mallets held normally)

The tip of a drum stick has a pointed and focused sound; the butt end has a much larger, darker, and fuller sound; and the sound of the shaft is larger still. The butt and shaft of a timpani mallet are far different from those of a keyboard mallet: the thick butt and shaft of a timpani mallet sounds like that of a drum stick while the thin butt and shaft of a keyboard mallet has a much smaller, brighter sound. Although mallet shafts come in a variety of materials (rattan, birch, or fiberglass for keyboard mallets; wood [maple, hickory, etc.], bamboo, or graphite for timpani mallets), one can assume that the shaft sound will be with wood.

Again, requesting a switch to the butt ends of the beaters is not reasonable when the player is holding a set of four.

Sticks

◉ Video 4.b—Sticks and Mallets

Sticks (also called *snare drum sticks, snare sticks,* or *drum sticks*) almost always have wooden tips (figure 4.3). Plastic-tip sticks might be used in special instances to get thinner, higher sounds out of cymbals, gongs, and other metal instruments. Drum sticks with a variety of thicknesses, weights, and tip sizes are available for different timbres and functions.

Figure 4.3
Drum stick

Photo courtesy of
Vic Firth Inc.

Drum sticks are not the only wooden sticks used. The rattan shafts of keyboard mallets are often requested for a brighter, lighter wood color. Much smaller wooden sticks like chopsticks and even wooden barbecue skewers can be used for delicate instruments or brighter sounds.

Mallets

◉ Video 4.b—Sticks and Mallets

Yarn, cord, rubber, plastic, and felt mallets come in a variety of hardnesses. Yarn is most commonly used on marimba, cord on vibraphone, rubber on marimba and xylophone, plastic on xylophone, glockenspiel, and crotales, and felt on timpani (figure 4.4; see also appendix G). For soft rolled passages, a softer mallet is best. For faster articulated rhythms, a harder mallet is best. Again, these decisions are often best left up to the performer.

Yarn and felt mallets have a soft outer layer. These mallets will sound softer and less articulate at soft dynamics and harder and more articulate at loud dynamics. This is a very subtle color difference. Cord, rubber, and plastic mallets are more or less the same color throughout the dynamic range. Often percussionists make use of a special

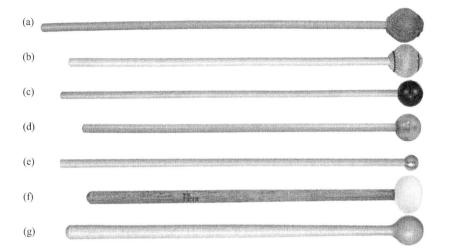

Figure 4.4
Mallets: (a) yarn,
(b) cord,
(c) rubber,
(d) plastic,
(e) brass, (f) felt
timpani, (g) wood
timpani

Photos courtesy of
Vic Firth Inc.

yarn mallet, called a *two-toned mallet*, which is very soft at soft dynamics and very hard at loud dynamics. This can give the performer a great variety of color from just one mallet but the color difference depends on dynamics.

Brass and wood mallets should be assumed to be available in one hardness. It is technically possible to find mallets of metal or wood with slightly different hardness (depending on the material, density, etc.), but it would be very strange to request a soft pair and a hard pair of brass mallets.

Bass drum beaters are essentially overgrown timpani mallets. They are wrapped in felt and come in a variety of hardnesses (figure 4.5a and 4.5b). Most often, just one mallet is used, but a pair can be used for rolls or faster passages that require two hands. Soft double-ended bass drum beaters exist (not pictured in figure 4.5) and can be used to play rolls with one hand by striking the drum with alternating ends of the beater.

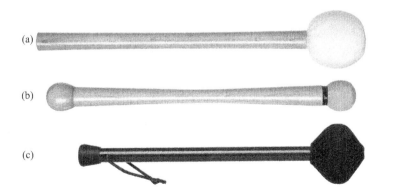

Figure 4.5
(a) Bass drum
beater, (b) double-
ended wood/
chamois bass
drum beater,
(c) gong beater

Photos courtesy of
Vic Firth Inc.

Gong beaters are about the size of bass drum mallets, but are heavier and usually wrapped with yarn instead of felt (figure 4.5c). They come in a variety of sizes for different size gongs.

Slap mallets are used for special effects. These mallets have a relatively large flat surface made of leather which creates a loud contact sound. Operating a set of four slap mallets is especially awkward; they are best used in pairs.

Triangle Beaters and Knitting Needles

◐ Video 4.c—Triangle Beaters, Brushes, Hammers, Rute, Superball Mallet

Triangle beaters are small metal rods. They come in a variety of thicknesses and materials for different dynamics, colors, and articulation (figure 4.6). Besides their obvious use on triangle, triangle beaters are good for getting very high pitches out of cymbals and gongs. Triangle beaters are also perfect for scraping cymbals, gongs, and bell trees.

Figure 4.6
Triangle beaters

Photo courtesy
of Black Swamp
Percussion

When a very light metal beater sound is needed, knitting needles work well. Knitting needles do not sound as good on a triangle, but are great for producing delicate bright sounds from cymbals and gongs.

Brushes

◐ Video 4.c—Triangle Beaters, Brushes, Hammers, Rute, Superball Mallet

Brushes are made with metal wire or plastic (figure 4.7). Light wire brushes are most common. Plastic brushes are usually heavier and louder. Heavy wire brushes called *rakes* are even louder and heavier than plastic.

Figure 4.7
Brushes

Photo courtesy of
Vic Firth Inc.

Brushes can be used for a single stroke or a scrape (see John Cage's *Second Construction*). A scrape with a brush is not like a scrape with a triangle beater; it is more like a brush stroke for a painting. Brush scrapes are best used on drums and at soft dynamics on cymbals and gongs. A brush scrape is a one-handed operation and can be executed while the other hand does something else. By scraping in a circular motion around the instrument, the percussionist can create this effect for as long as needed. A scrape is notated by writing "scrape" or with a special symbol above the note (figure 4.8).

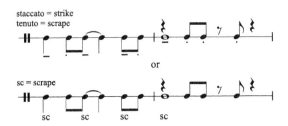

Figure 4.8
Brush scrape
notation

A tremolo with brushes is a normal single-stroke tremolo in which the brushes rapidly strike the drum. If a scrape tremolo is desired (rapidly scraping back and forth), the composer should indicate this by writing "scrape tremolo." A scrape tremolo can be executed with one hand while a normal tremolo requires two hands. A normal tremolo can get much louder than a scrape tremolo.

On keyboard instruments, brushes will strike not one but a few pitches. The composer should expect that a target pitch will be accompanied by the surrounding notes.

Brushes speak at a rather soft dynamic. Scrapes and even regular strokes cannot be nearly as loud as similar attacks played with sticks. When especially loud dynamics are required on drums, percussionists can compensate by playing rimshots (see chapter 6). Volume can also be increased by using thicker plastic brushes or heavy wire rakes. For loud scrapes on cymbals and gongs, a triangle beater or coin is more appropriate.

As a result of their dynamic limitation, brushes can be perfect for involved soft playing. With very fast multi-percussion passages, especially-soft playing can be very difficult with sticks, and brushes may work far better. Rute sticks are another softer alternative to sticks (see Rute Sticks, next).

A one-handed mandolin roll can be executed on cymbals by placing the cymbal edge in the middle of a brush's wires and moving the brush up and down. This works only at soft dynamics.

The butt end of brushes is usually a thick metal wire that can be used for all triangle beater purposes.

Rute Sticks

▶ Video 4.c—Triangle Beaters, Brushes, Hammers, Rute Sticks, Superball Mallet

A rute is a bunch of wooden dowels or twigs tied together (figure 4.9). Traditionally (see Mahler's Symphonies Nos. 2 and 6), the rute is rather large and struck on the shell of the bass drum, producing more of the sound of the rute than of the shell (see Rute in chapter 8). This instrument has now been adapted to the size of a snare stick and can be used as a beater for a special effect on drums, cymbals, and other instruments. These smaller rutes were originally made for softer drumset playing (for low-volume ensembles and practice). Both rute types are common, so "rute stick" should be specified to avoid confusion.

Figure 4.9
Rute sticks
Photo courtesy of
Vic Firth Inc.

Chime Hammers (Tubular Bell Hammers)

▶ Video 4.c—Triangle Beaters, Brushes, Hammers, Rute, Superball Mallet

Chime hammers are made of rawhide or plastic (figure 4.10). Percussionists usually pad one side so a single hammer can be flipped to act as both a hard and a soft beater. Chime hammers are best used in pairs; maneuvering a set of four hammers is very awkward, difficult, and ineffective. Four mallet passages on chimes are more effectively executed with regular plastic or yarn mallets; these beaters will sound considerably different than chime hammers.

Figure 4.10
Chime hammers
Photo courtesy of
Vic Firth Inc.

Superball Mallet

 Video 4.c—Triangle Beaters, Brushes, Hammers, Rute, Superball Mallet

A Superball mallet is a Superball attached to a barbecue skewer or other slightly flexible piece of metal or wood. A Superball mallet, dragged against a surface, creates a groaning sound like that of a finger rub (see Friction Roll in appendix C). The Superball may be slightly easier to use than a finger because the degree of friction tends to be more consistent. The use of either a finger or a Superball can be the choice of the performer. (See George Crumb's *Idyll for the Misbegotten* and Lukas Foss's *Thirteen Ways of Looking at a Blackbird.*)

A Superball mallet rub is a very quiet effect and will easily be lost in ensemble textures. A Superball rub may activate any of a number of harmonics from the rubbed instrument, so the pitches produced will be variable and unpredictable.

Beaters as Instruments

Sticks and mallets can be struck together for a clave-like effect.

Hands

 Video 4.d—Hands

Playing with the hands is most common on drums (see chapter 6 for details on hand drum techniques). On other instruments, hands can be used for special effects or if there is not enough time to pick up sticks. For example, if a percussionist is playing a set of drums with his or her hands and needs to hit a suspended cymbal or a woodblock, using the hands or fingers may be more reasonable than picking up a stick or mallet. Hands cannot usually play as loud as sticks or mallets.

Hand drummers can achieve a wide variety of colors and articulations by using different parts of the hands, different beating spots, and different amounts of dampening. Players can wear rings, thimbles, or special gloves to augment or alter the hands' capabilities. (See the leather and felt gloves in William Kraft's *Concerto for Timpani.*)

Bows

 Video 4.e—Bows

A handful of percussion instruments can be bowed with a bass or cello bow. The most commonly, easily, and successfully bowed percussion instruments are:

vibraphone
crotales
cymbals
small gongs

The following instruments are less commonly but still successfully bowed:

crystal glasses
flexatone

The following instruments can be bowed easily but may not speak well (i.e., they produce weak or inconsistent dynamic, uneven sustain, or unattractive sound):

marimba
xylophone
large gongs

The following instruments can be difficult to bow and may not speak well:

cowbells
almglocken
woodblocks
templeblocks
temple bowls
thundersheet
tubular bells
triangle

Two hands are usually required to bow crotales and all non-keyboard instruments—one to hold the instrument in place and the other to bow. Only one hand is needed with other keyboard instruments, so two bows can be held or the non-bowing hand could do something else like strike the instrument with mallets.

Percussion instruments do not speak nearly as well as the strings of traditionally bowed instruments, so a gradual swelling dynamic is most easily executed. A sharp attack on the start of a bowed note is almost impossible (unless struck with a mallet). Sustaining a loud note for an extended period of time or managing two different dynamic shapes with two different bows is very difficult to execute. The figuration shown in figure 4.11 is most natural. The bowed sound and the resonating sound can be notated separately; this is the most accurate notation. It can be done with note lengths or, on vibraphone, with pedal indications, as shown in figure 4.12.

Figure 4.11
Bow figuration

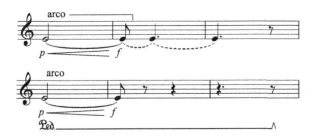

Figure 4.12
Detailed bow
notation

Bowing takes time and is awkward, so fast passages are not possible. The composer should allow time for the performer to pick the bow up, get it into place, make the instrument sound, and put the bow down. On keyboard instruments, more time is required to move the bow from the "white" notes to the "black" notes. To do so, the player must lift the bow up and over the instrument to the other side before getting it into position for the next note. Also, when bowing the accidentals, the music stand can often get in the way, and extra time may be needed to maneuver around it.

When a bow re-attacks an already ringing note, it will tend to dampen the instrument before making it sound again. A smooth re-attack is possible but difficult. As a result, especially long bowed notes may not work because the bow changes may be too apparent. The bow's tendency to dampen can be used as an effect, especially with the vibraphone, where the player can stop the bow short to immediately dampen the sound. This is like a dead stroke (or dead bow; see Dead Stroke in appendix C).

Multiple players with two bows each could be used to execute more complicated bowed passages. (See Steve Reich's *Sextet*.) Two players can also play on either side of one vibraphone—one bowing the naturals and the other bowing the accidentals. (See the four players on one vibraphone in Elliot Cole's *Postludes*.)

Bowed cymbals, indeterminately pitched gongs, and thundersheets will produce a pitch (or several pitches) from the harmonic spectrum of the instrument. The pitch(es) produced vary depending on the speed of the bow, the volume, the spot on the instrument that is bowed, the place the instrument is held by the other hand, and how much of the instrument is muffled by the holding hand or stand. With all the variables, many different pitches can be created on one instrument, but unfortunately they cannot be controlled. The pitch is unpredictable, and it is unreasonable to request specific pitches, specific pitch relations, or even a consistent pitch.

Keyboard instruments, tuned gongs, triangles, cowbells, almglocken, woodblocks, templeblocks, temple bowls, and crystal glasses have a clear and constant pitch when bowed. Flexatones have a clear pitch that will bend as the tension of the metal is manipulated.

The number of bows needed should be specified in the instrument list.

CHAPTER FIVE

Keyboard Percussion

Instruments covered in this chapter are the marimba, vibraphone, xylophone, glockenspiel, crotales, and tubular bells. Keyboard percussion instruments are also commonly called *mallet instruments* or *mallet percussion*.

Ranges and Construction

The ranges indicated here are correct for notation. The marimba, vibraphone, and tubular bells sound as written. The xylophone sounds one octave higher than written. The glockenspiel and crotales sound two octaves higher than written. The ranges in parentheses are not always available. The marimba is notated in treble or bass clef or on a grand staff. The other instruments are almost always exclusively notated in treble clef.

Marimba

◐ Video 5.a—Marimba
Sounds as written (figure 5.1).

(a) 4.3 octave—common
(b) 5 octave—common (shown in figure 5.2)
(c) 4 octave—somewhat common (becoming obsolete)
(d) 4.5 octave—somewhat common
(e) 4.6 octave—rare
(f) 5.5 octave—rare
(g) bass marimba—rare (becoming obsolete)

Vibraphone

◐ Video 5.b—Vibraphone
Sounds as written (figure 5.3). The vibraphone is also called *vibes*.

(a) 3 octave—standard (shown in figure 5.4)
(b) 3.5 octave—rare
(c) 4 octave—rare

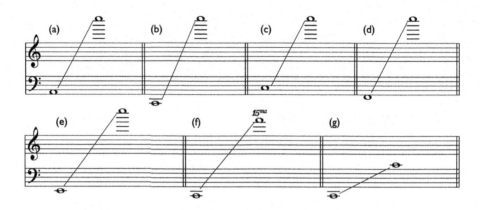

Figure 5.1
Marimba range

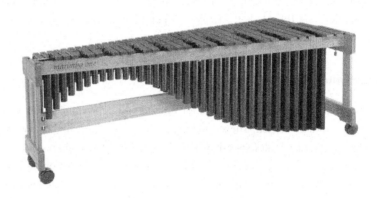

Figure 5.2
Marimba

Photo courtesy
of Marimba One
Marimbas

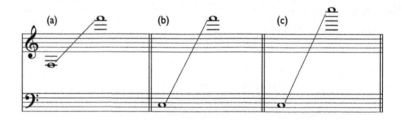

Figure 5.3
Vibraphone range

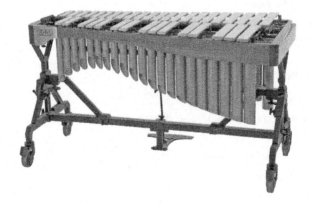

Figure 5.4
Vibraphone

Photo courtesy
of Pearl/Adams
Percussion

Xylophone

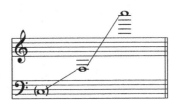 Video 5.c—Xylophone

Sounds one octave higher than written (figures 5.5 and 5.6). Extended range (four-octave) xylophones are common but not standard.

Figure 5.5
Xylophone range

Figure 5.6
Xylophone
Photo courtesy of
Musser Percussion

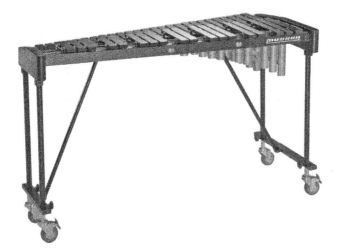

Glockenspiel

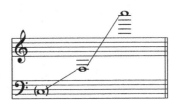 Video 5.d—Glockenspiel, Crotales, Tubular Bells

Sounds two octaves higher than written (figures 5.7 and 5.8). The lower F is the most common range expansion; the upper D is less common. Even larger ranges (up to a fifth below and a third above) are occasionally available. The glockenspiel is commonly called "bells" or "orchestra bells" in the United States; however, "bells" in the UK refers instead to tubular bells. For this reason, it is best to only use *glockenspiel* in writing.

Figure 5.7
Glockenspiel range

Figure 5.8
Glockenspiel

Photo courtesy of
Majestic Percussion

Crotales

🔊 Video 5.d—Glockenspiel, Crotales, Tubular Bells

Sound two octaves higher than written (figures 5.9 and 5.10). The two octaves can be used separately or together. The crotales are also called *antique cymbals*

Figure 5.9
Crotales range

Figure 5.10
Crotales

Photo courtesy of
Zildjian Cymbals

Tubular Bells

🔊 Video 5.d—Glockenspiel, Crotales, Tubular Bells

Sound as written (figures 5.11 and 5.12). Additional individual chimes outside of this range, higher and lower, are sometimes available. The tubular bells are also called *chimes.*

Figure 5.11
Tubular bell range

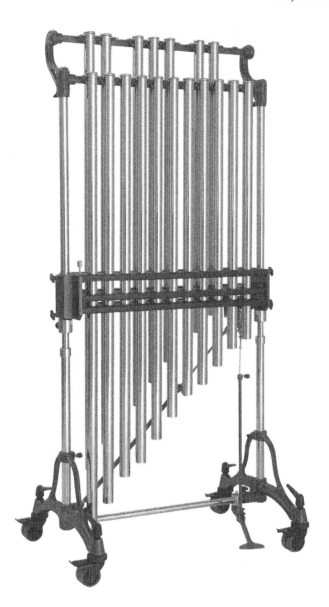

Figure 5.12
Tubular bells

Photo courtesy
of Pearl/Adams
Percussion

Resonators

🔊 Video 5.f—Resonators

Marimbas, vibraphones, xylophones, and some glockenspiels have resonators. The resonators are tubes that are closed at one end and tuned to the pitch of the bar under which they hang. The air inside the tube resonates sympathetically when the bar is struck; this reinforces the fundamental tone and makes the sound louder and fuller.

As a special effect, resonators can be scraped horizontally with a yarn or cord mallet. This sound varies considerably depending on the material of the resonators, which is determined by the make and model of the instrument. A resonator scrape should not be done with hard plastic, wood, or metal beaters, as it can damage the resonators.

Pedals

Vibraphones and chimes have pedals that control the resonance in much the same way as the sustain pedal of a piano does. (See Damper Pedals in chapter 3 for more information.) Pedal glockenspiels exist but are rare.

Vibraphone Motor

The vibraphone has a motor that spins small disks (fans) inside the resonators. The disks, when horizontal, close off the resonator and eliminate its dynamic reinforcement. The motor spins the disks, which rapidly opens and closes the resonators to create a vibrato-like effect. This is not a vibrato with pitch fluctuation but, rather, a pulsing tremolo effect (like flute vibrato). (See Alban Berg's *Lulu*.)

The motor can be turned on and off and the speed can be adjusted during performance. This is notated "motor on" or "motor off," and "fast motor," "slow motor," "medium slow motor," and so on. The composer should be aware that it takes time to turn the motor on and off or to adjust its speed, and these operations can be especially awkward for a percussionist with mallets in hand.

For more specific motor speed, beats per minute may be indicated. Exact b.p.m. cannot be expected of most vibraphone motors; tempo notation should be used only as an approximate guide. Such motor speeds would have to be set before the start of the piece and could not realistically be adjusted with much accuracy during performance.

A simple gear system located on the top end of the instrument controls the opening and closing of the disks. This gear system can be operated manually if a very slow and careful open/close is needed. A continuous opening and closing, like that of the motor, is difficult with this method. Manual operation of the gears requires one hand so only the other hand is free to play.

Vibraphone is most often used with the motor off. This is sometimes referred to as a *metallophone* (by Steve Reich), but percussionists are most accustomed to seeing "vibraphone, motor off." Unless "motor on" is specified, motor off will be assumed. Vibraphone must be plugged into a power outlet when the motor is in use; extension cords are usually required. The composer should indicate the use of the motor in the instrument list at the front of the score and part.

Removing Notes from the Set

Specific tubular bell and crotale notes can be removed from the set if only a few pitches are needed. Crotales can be mounted on cymbal stands or placed on a trap table. Smaller chime racks that hold about four notes are common; a single chime can also be hung from a cymbal stand or held up by hand.

Crotales/Finger Cymbals

Crotales are essentially large tuned finger cymbals mounted and arranged like a keyboard. When determinately pitched finger cymbals are requested, crotales will generally be used. In these situations, two crotales of the same pitch may be held and struck together like finger cymbals.

Writing for Keyboard Percussion

Thumbs and Pinkies—Writing Idiomatically for Keyboards

🔊 Video 5.f—Thumbs and Pinkies

Composers often write using a piano, and are therefore thinking with ten fingers. A percussionist can hold up to four mallets comfortably and has quite a bit of freedom, but certainly not as much as a ten-fingered pianist. The dexterity that composers enjoy on the piano can easily result in compositions of keyboard percussion music that is extremely difficult. By composing on the piano with just thumbs and pinky fingers, the logistic problems that keyboard percussionists face will become immediately apparent.

One will first notice, when playing the piano with only these fingers, that only four notes can be articulated simultaneously. This may seem obvious, but when using ten free fingers, composers can forget and occasionally slip in a five- or six-note chord. Playing a simple scale with one hand is not nearly as easy—C major with alternating thumbs is actually appropriate. If the four-fingered pianist wants to pivot between two adjacent minor thirds in one hand (e.g., C–E♭ and D♭–F♭) the whole arm has to swivel back and forth. In addition to these limitations, imagine that each thumb and pinky is 16 inches long and the piano keys are three times as wide!

As silly as it may sound, this "thumbs and pinkies" technique is rather accurate. One is able to imagine how percussionists move across the keyboard, and this can help the composer write idiomatically for these instruments.

Percussionists can, however, play larger intervals than the thumbs and pinkies will usually allow. The interval stretch in one hand varies with the instrument (the largest interval on a vibraphone is much less than the largest interval on a glockenspiel) and with placement in the range of the instrument (the bars get wider on the low end of the instruments). For these reasons, it is hard to give an exact limit on interval size. The limit in the lowest octave of a five-octave marimba where the notes are largest is about an octave, comfortably. Larger intervals are possible as one moves up in the instrument's range, but it is best to speak with a percussionist about a specific example.

Here is a list of the largest intervals in one hand for each instrument. Slightly larger intervals are possible but should be used carefully:

- marimba and vibraphone—octave
- xylophone and glockenspiel—11th
- crotales—major sixth

Percussionists can play any smaller interval down to a unison. Articulating two adjacent notes with one mallet is not practical.

The composer must keep in mind that mallet instruments are large and awkward. A five-octave marimba is over eight feet long! The size of a fifth on the low end of a marimba is about equivalent to two octaves on a piano, so a composer can take what is known about accuracy problems with large leaps and runs that quickly span large distances on piano and apply that fourfold to keyboard percussion instruments.

There is one important limitation that the thumbs and pinkies technique does not address: mallet instruments are never touched like a piano, so the performer has no way of feeling his or her way around the keyboard. Percussionists rely entirely on being able to see the keyboard to locate the correct notes. Of course, muscle memory is in play and that helps with interval sizes and distances across the keyboard, but this is abstract. Most percussionists are required to play on many different instruments—not only marimba, vibraphone, xylophone, and glockenspiel but also different brands of marimbas, vibraphones, xylophones, and glockenspiels for which bar size can vary slightly. This has a considerable effect on a player's ability to become truly familiar, as a pianist would, with the distances between notes and the sizes of intervals. There are some solo marimbists who play nothing but marimba and always play on the same instrument; for the rest of the percussion community, the ability to see the instrument is important.

As a result, if the two hands are playing far apart from each other, accuracy will be more of a challenge. For example, try the following exercise: sit at a piano with your eyes focused on middle C and notice the span of your peripheral vision. Without moving your head, observe the range you can comfortably move your hands in both directions and still see what notes you are playing. Now, divide that interval by 4. This is the range within which a passage could comfortably fit on a mallet instrument—probably not much more than an octave. The composer can, of course, expand beyond that, but he or she must keep in mind that the player may only be able to look at one hand at a time. For this reason, the composer may want to have difficult large leaps in only one hand at a time while the other plays tighter passages.

Additionally, fast white-note scales or arpeggios are surprisingly difficult. The visual uniformity makes it difficult to stay oriented, so C major is actually our most difficult key.

Here are some more specifics that one can discover with the thumb and pinky technique:

- Fourths, fifths, and sixths are the most comfortable intervals with a single hand, while larger and smaller intervals are more awkward.
- Leaping large intervals with the whole hand is difficult, while alternating the two mallets of one hand is reasonable.
- Keeping one hand on each keyboard—naturals or accidentals—at a time is preferable (as in the piano part of Stravinsky's *Petrouchka*).

The reader may try the passage shown in figure 5.13 on a piano with thumbs and pinkies to get a feel for keyboard percussion playing. This passage has a few tricky bits but is mostly idiomatic. Mallet indications are 1, 2, 3, 4 from left to right (figure 5.14)—that is, 1 is left pinky, 2 is left thumb, 3 is right thumb, and 4 is right pinky. "R" and "L" mean right and left when both mallets (fingers) of the same hand are used together. (Mallet indications are rarely included in scores.)

Figure 5.13
Example of idomatic marimba writing
SOURCE: Courtesy of Matthew Fuerst

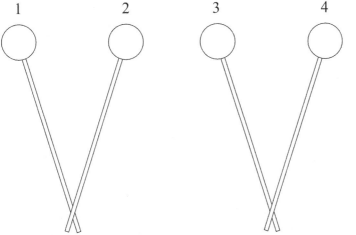

Figure 5.14
Mallet numbering

Tubular bells are far more awkward to play than other keyboard percussion instruments because the beaters used are large and heavy and must be held up high in the air. It is especially difficult to hold more than two chime hammers; four-mallet passages are more easily executed with regular plastic or yarn keyboard mallets, although they sound considerably different from chime hammers. Generally, tubular bells are best for slow passages that require one or two hammers.

Balance Problems

The sounds of the glockenspiel, crotales, and xylophone cut through an ensemble, and tubular bells can usually power their way through. The sounds of the marimba and especially the vibraphone blend well and tend to get covered in an orchestral setting. Harder mallets and stronger dynamics can help, however. The pulsing of the vibraphone's motor can also be used to make the sound of an instrument more conspicuous (in the same way a blinking light is more noticeable than one that stays constant).

Glissando

🔊 Video 5.g—Glissando, Keyboard Rolls, Overtone Interference, Glock/Vibes Extension

Glissando on keyboard instruments is usually executed by running the mallet along the white notes. (See Igor Stravinsky's *Petrouchka*, Olivier Messiaen's *Oiseaux Exotiques*, and Roger Reynolds's *Autumn Island*.) A black note gliss is possible but not as effective because the bars are not all contiguous. If the starting or ending notes of a glissando are not to be struck normally, then they could be notated in parentheses (figure 5.15b and 5.15c), with a grace note (figure 5.15d), or not at all (figure 5.15e). Time can be notated with exact note lengths (figure 5.15a), with a note value in parentheses (figure 5.15b), with note stems (figure 5.15c), or with rests (figure 5.15d and 5.15e).

Figure 5.15
Glissando
notation

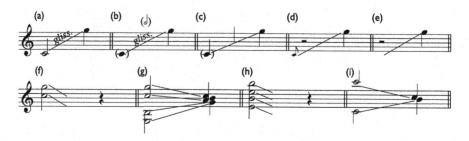

The first note of a glissando can be struck with either the hand performing the glissando or the other hand; the final note is then preferably struck with the "non-glissing" hand; otherwise, there will be a slight break between the glissando and the final note. In figure 5.15a, if the glissando is to be executed by the right hand, the C and G would most likely be struck with the left (non-glissing) hand.

If one hand is performing a glissando, the other hand can be doing something else; however, if the other hand is busy (or if both hands are playing glissandi), then the final note of the glissando may not be able to be struck normally without a slight break beforehand. For example, in figure 5.15g and 5.15i, there would have to be a slight break before the end of the glissandi because both hands must prepare to strike the final notes.

Glissandi are more audible and usually more effective at faster speeds. In older scores, in which too much time is given to execute a glissando, percussionists often start an octave lower. Appropriate glissando speed is an octave per quarter note at ♩=120 or faster. Glissandi that cover smaller distances in longer periods of time can be achieved with a quick chromatic scale. Chromatic scale glissandi should be written out. Glissandi are most effective with hard mallets like rubber or plastic. Hard yarn or cord will also work, but soft yarn will not speak well. An example of glissandi use within figuration is shown in figure 5.16.

Figure 5.16
Passage with integrated glissandi

SOURCE: From Samuel Solomon's *Gliss Ditty.*

Rolls

🔊 Video 5.g—Glissandi, Keyboard Rolls, Overtone Interference, Glock/Vibes Extension

Rolls with hard mallets, like those used for the xylophone, glockenspiel, and crotales, or rolls in the upper register of a marimba will always sound "beat-y"—that is, the individual strokes will be heard. Rolls can be seamless with softer mallets in the mid and lower register of the marimba, and under ideal conditions, rolled four-note chords can sound like an organ. With sustaining instruments such as the vibraphone, glockenspiel, crotales, and tubular bells, the rolls are more of an effect than a necessity. (For detailed information on rolls, see Rolls in chapter 3.)

Overtone Interference

🔊 Video 5.g—Glissandi, Keyboard Rolls, Overtone Interference, Glock/Vibes Extension

The composer should be aware that on a five-octave marimba, the notes in the lowest octave have strong and clear overtones; three octaves and a major third above (a major 24th) is especially apparent (figure 5.17). If a minor tenth (or minor 17th, minor 24th, etc.) is struck, the dissonance between that interval and the overtone is audible. It sounds almost as if all three notes had been struck. This applies to 11ths, 18ths, and so on as well.

Figure 5.17
Marimba overtones

These pitches can also be used as an effect. (See Harmonics later in this chapter.)

Glockenspiel as an Extension of the Vibraphone

🔊 Video 5.g—Glissandi, Keyboard Rolls, Overtone Interference, Glock/Vibes Extension

The glockenspiel is timbrally similar to the vibraphone and is often used to supply notes that are not available in the vibraphone range. Unfortunately, vibraphone mallets do not work well on a glock, and glock mallets are much too bright for the vibraphone. If four-mallet passages are needed on both instruments, then the player will have to switch mallets. If only two-mallet passages are needed on each instrument, then the player can hold two vibraphone mallets and two glockenspiel mallets—one in each hand (see figure 4.2). The composer should specify that the glockenspiel sound and the vibraphone sound match as closely as possible so the player can make the appropriate mallet choices. If two players are used, one for each instrument, then appropriate mallets can be used. It should still be specified that the vibraphone and glock sounds blend as if they were one instrument, so mallet choices can be made accordingly.

Sometimes very hard vibraphone mallets can work in the low to middle register of the glockenspiel. Similarly, soft glockenspiel mallets can work at soft dynamics on a vibraphone, but with an especially bright timbre.

Figurative Writing for Crotales

As a result of their high pitch, lengthy ring, and shimmering overtones, the pitches of crotales are not always clear within fast passages. A fast figure may sound more like many triangles than as a series of notes. This can be a problem when individual pitches of a fast passage are important and need to be heard, or it can be a nice effect as a shimmering gesture. (See John Adams's *Short Ride in a Fast Machine* and his *Harmonielehre*.)

Stacked Instruments

🔊 Video 5.h—Stacked Instruments, Multiple Players

Keyboard instruments can be stacked one in front of the other to be played at the same time or in quick succession. The marimba and vibraphone are commonly stacked, with the vibraphone in front so the pedal is accessible (figure 5.18). Occasionally the marimba can be positioned in front of the vibraphone with the vibraphone pedal extended, but the former configuration is most common. The marimba/vibraphone combination is perfect because the same mallets can be effectively used on both instruments. The xylophone and glockenspiel also stack well for this reason.

With stacked instruments, the instrument farthest from the performer should be notated on top. With the setup shown in figure 5.18, the staves for the marimba would be on top, even though the marimba's range extends far below that of the vibraphone (figure 5.19).

Figure 5.18
Stacked marimba
and vibraphone

Figure 5.19
Stacked
instrument
notation

SOURCE: From John
Aylward's *Songs of
the Wild Iris.*

Using a smaller range of the marimba instead of its full five octaves is far better if fast, difficult passages are written between the instruments. The reach over the
vibraphone can get tricky with the lowest octave, and the mallets necessary for the
vibraphone are not ideal for the lowest register of the marimba. In general, it is best to
avoid writing difficult passages for the instrument farthest from the player.

Many more logistical problems can arise with stacked instruments than with just
a single instrument. To be safe, it is best to request only one instrument per hand at
one time. If a keyboardist plays a piano and a synthesizer at the same time, he or she
cannot be expected to play both instruments at the same time with one hand; the
same is true here. With stacked instruments, it is not certain what will be in reach,
depending on the size of the instruments and how they are set up in relation to each
other. For example, if a chord has three notes on the marimba and one note on the
vibraphone, not all the notes may be reachable. It is acceptable to have four notes on
the marimba, four notes on the vibraphone, or two notes on each (figure 5.20).

Figure 5.20
Stacked
instrument chord
configurations

When stacked, only the "white" notes of the vibraphone are exposed to bowing. If "black" notes need to be bowed, the vibraphone must be pulled away from the marimba. This requires about five seconds and may make a little noise. If the vibraphone is stacked behind the marimba with the pedal extended, it is then entirely unavailable for bowing.

Multiple Players

Video 5.h—Stacked Instruments, Multiple Players

Mallet instruments, especially the marimba, can be played simultaneously by more than one player. This can save space in a big setup or can compensate for the unavailability of multiple mallet instruments. Additional players could even play simple parts from the opposite side of the instrument. (See Steve Reich's *Music for Eighteen Musicians.*) The composer should make sure that the players on the same instrument will not run into each other and should leave at least an interval of a third between the two parts.

Extended Techniques

Striking the Edge of the Bar

Video 5.i—Edge of Bar, Marimshot, Node

The edge of the bar can be played with the shaft of a mallet. One hand can play on only one keyboard ("white" or "black" bars) at a time. Large intervals in one hand are not possible; those larger than a sixth should be avoided unless they are in the uppermost register. There is a considerable distance from the edge of the white keys to the edge of the black keys, so the composer must allow a little time for this jump. Articulations on the edge of the bar are typically notated with "X" noteheads; this notation should be explained. (See Joseph Schwantner's *Velocities.*)

Marimshot

Video 5.i—Edge of Bar, Marimshot, Node

A marimshot is an effect similar to a rimshot whereby the mallet head and shaft strike the bar simultaneously. This can serve a similar function as a Bartók pizzicato.

The note(s) that the shaft strikes may or may not be the same note as the head of the mallet strikes, depending on the angle at which the player strikes the note. The shaft produces primarily a bright percussive sound and the pitch of the extra notes will not sound very loud. When proper time is given, the shaft can be positioned so only the indicated note is struck. Marimshot can also be executed on the xylophone.

With the vibraphone, under normal playing conditions, a marimshot works only on the "white" notes. Because the accidentals are not raised as they are on the marimba and xylophone, the proper angle for a marimshot cannot be achieved on the "black" notes. Also, the additional notes that are sometimes struck by the shaft will be more apparent if the pedal is depressed and they are allowed to ring.

Marimshot should be explained at the beginning of the score and percussion part.

Node

🔊 Video 5.j—Edge of Bar, Marimshot, Node

Different tone colors can be produced from the marimba, vibraphone, xylophone, glockenspiel, and crotales by changing the beating spot on the bar relative to the node. The node is the least resonant and brightest sounding spot, and it sounds considerably different from the normal beating spot (figure 5.21). The node is located where the bar is mounted—that is, halfway between the center and the edge of the bar (where the strings run through) for the marimba, vibraphone, xylophone, and glockenspiel, and directly in the center for crotales.

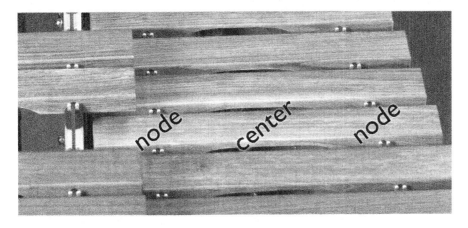

Figure 5.21
Keyboard instrument nodes

These sounds can be notated with "N" or "+" for the node and "C" or "○" for the center, with a dotted line or arrow to indicate motion from one to the other (figure 5.22). These notations should be explained at the beginning of the score and percussion part. The color difference is most apparent with hard mallets at mezzo-dynamics. (See also Roger Reynolds's *Autumn Island*.)

Figure 5.22
Center/node
notation

SOURCE: From
Ryan Streber's
Compassinges.

Mouth Vibrato

🔊 Video 5.j—Vibrato, Pitch Bend, Altered Tuning

The player can create a vibrato effect on the vibraphone by opening and closing his or her mouth over a ringing bar. Owing to the size of the human mouth, this effect only works in the range of the instrument shown in figure 5.23.

Figure 5.23
Mouth
vibrato range

Obviously, the player will have difficulty executing a mouth vibrato in the middle of a quick passage, so it should be isolated, with time allowed to get the mouth into and out of position.

Glockenspiel Vibrato

🔊 Video 5.j—Vibrato, Pitch Bend, Altered Tuning

Vibrato on the glockenspiel can be created by waving a hand up and down over the struck note. This is a very subtle effect.

Pitch Bend

🔊 Video 5.j—Vibrato, Pitch Bend, Altered Tuning

A downward pitch bend is possible on the marimba, vibraphone, xylophone, and glockenspiel by the player's holding a hard rubber or plastic mallet at the bar's node and then, after the bar is struck with another mallet, dragging the plastic mallet toward the center or end of the bar. This gradually adds the mass of the plastic mallet to that of the bar, lowering the pitch and dampening the bar. Pitch bend works best in the middle range of the marimba, the middle and upper ranges of the vibraphone, and the lower ranges of the xylophone and glockenspiel. Pitch bending on mallet instruments takes a little time to prepare and can generally only be done on one note at a time. (See Christopher Deane's *Mourning Dove Sonnet*, George Crumb's *Madrigals*, and Jacob Druckman's *Animus II.*)

A downward pitch bend is also possible with crotales and tubular bells by dipping them into water after they have been struck. (See Water in chapter 7.)

Altered Tuning

🔊 Video 5.j—Vibrato, Pitch Bend, Altered Tuning

The pitch of individual notes can be lowered up to a quarter-tone by attaching putty or clay to the bar. This will also dampen the bar, darken the color, and shorten the sustain. The more putty added, the more degraded the quality of sound; pitch alteration beyond a quarter-tone is therefore not effective. This technique is most successful on the vibraphone.

Prepared Instruments

◐ Video 5.k—Prepared Instruments, Harmonics, Clusters

The vibraphone is the most eligible candidate for preparation. Coins, paper clips, and other such items can be taped to individual bars to sizzle when that note is struck. Aluminum foil can also be placed over the resonators of individual notes for an interesting buzzing effect. (See Jay Alan Yim's *Jam Karet*.)

Harmonics

◐ Video 5.k— Prepared Instruments, Harmonics, Clusters

In the middle to low register of the vibraphone and marimba (below C5), a harmonic two octaves above the pitch of a bar can be produced by slightly dampening the bar (with a finger or mallet), striking toward the node, and then quickly removing the dampening. From C2 to A2 on the marimba, a harmonic three octaves and a major third above the pitch of the bar is also prominent. Harmonics are far more successful on the vibraphone, where the pitch can be left to resonate alone. Vibraphone harmonics can also be bowed. Harmonics are somewhat unpredictable and are difficult to produce with consistency. (See George Crumb's *Madrigal I* and Christopher Deane's *Mourning Dove Sonnet*.)

Clusters

◐ Video 5.k—Prepared Instruments, Harmonics, Clusters

Clusters can be produced by striking a keyboard instrument with a dowel lengthwise. The dowel could be padded for a soft mallet sound (sometimes called a *cluster bar* or *cluster mallet*), or it could be a snare drum stick for a bright clanking sound. One dowel can effectively hit either "white" or "black" notes; two dowels must be used to hit both "white" and "black" notes at the same time. The dowel can be a custom size to hit a certain number of notes and can be angled to hit fewer notes. Clusters are most effective on the vibraphone and tubular bells, where the notes can ring freely and sustain the cluster sound.

Church Bell Effect

A church bell effect can be achieved by playing random pitches and rhythms on tubular bells. This is notated with a wavy line. (See Tchaikovsky's *1812 Overture* and Mahler's Symphonies 6 and 7.) A set of pitches on which to play is often indicated.

The glockenspiel and crotales can be treated the same way for a high, tinkly wind chime effect.

Miscellaneous

Xylophones and even marimbas with synthetic bars are fairly common. They do not have the beautiful tone of rosewood bars and usually ring unnaturally long, but they can withstand more abuse and stay better in tune.

Keyboard glockenspiel parts, such as Dukas's *Sorcerer's Apprentice,* Debussy's *La Mer,* Messiaen's *Chronochromie,* and Resphigi's *Pines of Rome,* are now usually played on a glockenspiel because keyboard glocks are uncommon. *La Mer* is sometimes played on the celeste, another possible substitution. Octave transpositions must sometimes be made to fit keyboard glock parts within the small range of the glockenspiel.

A xylorimba is a xylophone with an extended range called for in scores by composers of the early and mid-twentieth century (e.g., Messiaen). It is now an obsolete instrument and should not be requested. In performances of older music, xylorimbas are simply replaced with xylophones and marimbas.

MIDI mallet instruments (e.g., MalletKat) are currently poor substitutes for acoustic instruments, but are a practical way to include synthesized, sampled, or other electronically produced elements within a percussionist's setup because they can be triggered with sticks or mallets.

CHAPTER SIX

Drums

Instruments covered in this chapter are the timpani, tom-toms, snare drum, field drum, tenor drum, concert bass drum, pedal bass drum, bongos, congas, timbales, roto-toms, frame drums, tambourines, djembe, doumbek, boobams, and drumset. The parts of these instruments are labeled as shown in figure 6.1.

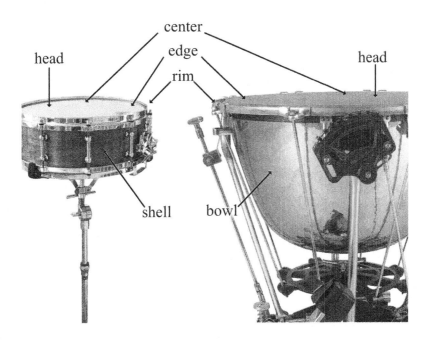

Figure 6.1
Drum anatomy

Photo of timpano courtesy of Pearl/ Adams Percussion

There are three main categories of techniques that can be used to play all drums: techniques unique to snare sticks (derived from snare drum and drumset playing), techniques unique to mallets (derived from timpani playing), and techniques derived from hand drumming.

Sticks on Drums

⬤ Video 6.a—Sticks and Mallets on Drums

Drum sticks can be used on all drums, but they are less appropriate on timpani and certain hand drums (such as frame drum, djembe, and doumbek), as they can damage the drum head.

Unique to drum sticks is the *buzz* or *closed roll*, where the sticks bounce and make numerous articulations per stroke to create a very rapid tremolo. With an *open* or *double-stroke roll*, only two articulations are made with each stroke and all the individual attacks can be heard. An open roll may be specified on drums to evoke a military sound. The composer need not specify the roll type. (See Rolls in chapter 3 for more information.)

A *rimshot* is executed by holding one stick down with the tip touching the center of the head and the shaft touching the rim, and then striking it with the other stick (figure 6.2). This takes half a second to get into position and slightly dampens the head, so only rhythms slow enough to be executed with one hand are possible.

Figure 6.2
Two-handed
rimshot

A rimshot can also be created by striking the drum with one stick at an angle to hit both the head and the rim simultaneously. This produces a slightly different sound, requires no preparation time, allows the drum to resonate, and makes two-handed passages possible. This rimshot, however, is more difficult to execute consistently. Specification of which type of rimshot to be used is rarely notated, and is usually decided by the performer based on the passage.

A common abbreviation for rimshot is "R.S.," but as with all abbreviations, the first appearance in a part should be written out in full. Rimshots are most naturally and almost always executed at a loud dynamic.

Rimshots can damage timpani and should not be requested on that instrument.

A *side-stick* (also called *cross-stick, rim-knock,* or *rim-click*) is a technique often found in drumset playing whereby one end of the stick is held against the center of the head and the shaft strikes the rim (figure 6.3). This takes about half a second to get into position.

Figure 6.3
Side-stick

On drums smaller than 10 inches (26 cm), like bongos, small toms, and small roto-toms, a side-stick is ineffective because the stick is too long.

Rimshot and side-stick rolls are an unreasonable request. Very fast articulations are possible with a one-handed rimshot (the second of the two described above), but the sound produced is so sharp that the articulations will not blend to create a roll effect. Rolls with a two-handed rimshot and side-stick are awkward and will not work.

Here is some basic drum jargon: a note with one grace note is called a *flam,* two grace notes is a *drag* or *ruff,* and three is a *four-stroke ruff* (figure 6.4).

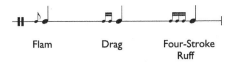

Flam   Drag   Four-Stroke
                                    Ruff

Figure 6.4
Drum ornaments

Execution of these ornaments can vary. If a big, fat, closed ornament is desired whereby many articulations (not just two or three) are crushed out by one hand before the main note, the notation shown in figure 6.5 is appropriate.

Figure 6.5
Buzz ornament

Mallets on Drums

◉ Video 6.a—Sticks and Mallets on Drums

Unique to the use of mallets on drums is the sound of rolls. Single-stroke rolls are used instead of buzz rolls, and at softer dynamics on resonant instruments (like timpani and bass drum), they can create a seamless sustaining sound. Felt mallets (like timpani mallets) are preferable on drums, as the felt contributes very little contact sound; yarn or cord mallets (marimba or vibraphone mallets) sound similar to felt at loud dynamics, but the contact sound of the yarn is present at soft dynamics.

Hands on Drums

◉ Video 6.b—Hands on Drums

The use of the hands is more common on some drums than on others, but it is acceptable on all drums. Since so many different sounds can be produced with the hands, hand drumming notation can become complicated. Hand drumming is traditionally an improvised art, so the best notation may be just the rhythm and dynamics, with instructions to improvise and vary the timbres used; the performer will use these indications to design the best-sounding and most idiomatic articulations. (See The Written/Improv Divide in chapter 1.)

More detailed notation will vary from instrument to instrument, as each hand drum has its own unique techniques; however, these techniques all derive from a few basic sound concepts (see also Manipulations of Timbre in appendix C):

- Using more hand surface will produce a lower pitch and a darker sound, and using less surface will produce a higher, brighter sound.
- Playing toward the center of the drum will produce a lower pitch and a darker sound, and playing toward the rim of the drum will produce a higher, brighter sound.
- Muffling the drum head with the other hand toward the center will shorten the note and cut out some lower pitches, making the sound brighter.
- Pushing on the head with the fingers, hand, or elbow will stretch the head and raise the pitch.

For example, if a player strikes a djembe in the center of its head with an open palm, a low sustained fundamental pitch will result. If the player strikes directly on the edge with just one finger while dampening the drum head with the other hand, a bright sharp sound will result.

At least two pitches can be produced on all drums when hands are used: a low pitch, usually the fundamental; and a high pitch played at the edge of the drum. These two pitches can be referred to as the *bass tone* (or *dum*) and the *rim tone* (or *tak* or *tek*); syllables like *dum* and *tak* are used in South Asian drumming traditions, and have been adapted and applied to many other drums and playing styles. Big, deep drums like the djembe or conga have three main pitches: the bass tone, the rim tone, and a stroke simply called *tone,* which is a harmonic pitched about an octave above the fundamental and an octave beneath the rim tone.

A *slap* can be executed on all drums. It is a high-pitched, accented sound achieved with a dead stroke toward the center of the drum. A slap is sometimes left to ring (called an *open slap*), in which case the attack is not a dead stroke but produces the same accented bright sound. In conga and djembe playing, the bass, tone, and slap sounds are used primarily, and the rim tone is used only occasionally.

Notation of these pitches does not need to be any more complicated than indicating "high and low" or "high, medium, and low." In these cases, the specific techniques used to execute the high, medium, and low pitches will be determined by the performer.

Sound and note length can be controlled with open and muffled strokes. With a muffled stroke, the hand stays on the head after striking to muffle the sound (like a dead stroke). To muffle a rim tone, the percussionist needs to muffle with the other hand; the rim tone is executed at the very edge of the drum, so the striking fingers, if left on the head, would not cover enough of the head to dampen it. Bass, tone, and slap sounds are executed toward the center of the drum, so the player can muffle with the striking hand. Closed and open tones can be notated on additional lines or with +'s and o's.

A rub with the hand or fingernails can be used. This is executed by wiping the hand back and forth across the head in rhythm. The flesh of the hand is used for a softer, darker sound or the fingernails for a louder, brighter sound.

When the head is dampened while playing rim tones, the pitch can be altered by moving the dampening hand across the head toward the striking hand. The pitch of the overtones will become higher as the dampening hand gets closer to the striking hand and lower as the dampening hand moves farther away.

A friction roll can be used as a long tone or rhythmically. (See Friction Roll in appendix C.)

See the section Hands in chapter 4 for more effects. For more information on hand drumming styles and techniques, listen to and consult specialists in Indian, Middle Eastern, African, and Afro-Cuban music.

Playing on the Rim or Shell

🔊 Video 6.c—Rim, Shell, Beating Spot, Mutes, Pitch Bending

The rim of a drum can be struck with the shaft of a stick—the head of the drum will resonate quietly. A change in pitch of the drum head will change the rim sound only slightly. That is, rim pitch is affected primarily by the drum size: smaller = higher, larger = lower.

The rim sound can also be affected by changing the striking point on the stick. For instance, striking with the tip of the stick will have a brighter timbre than striking closer to the hand.

The shell can also be struck for a similar effect. This is common in timbale playing, where bell patterns are played on the metal shell of the drum. Except at loud dynamics, it is best for the composer not to request passages that require two sticks on one surface of the shell of a drum; the playing surface is vertical so it is difficult to achieve consistent playing positions with the two hands. It is more reasonable to have each stick play on opposite sides of the drum shell (or on two different shells); the two sounds will be slightly different and should be treated as such. If soft passages that require two hands are requested on the shell of a drum, then the performer may use an additional drum turned on its side, so that the shell faces upward and both sticks can easily strike the same surface. (See also Striking the Bowl in the Timpani section later in this chapter.)

Beating Spot

⬤ Video 6.c—Rim, Shell, Beating Spot, Mutes, Pitch Bending

As described earlier, different places on a drum head sound considerably different; the center has a thumpy, dark sound and the edge has a pingy, bright sound.

The center of a drum head sounds especially dead if the bottom of the drum is sealed off. On timpani, the bowl has only a small opening at the bottom, so the center of a timpano head sounds especially dead and thumpy. With other drums that have the bottom open or covered with another head, the center sound is more resonant.

To notate the beating spot, the composer can use different lines on the staff or letters—"C" for center and "E" for edge. On timpani, about a third of the way in from the edge is called the *normal* beating spot, which could be notated "N." For other drums, the normal beating spot is the same as the center because the difference in timbre from edge to center is not as apparent as it is on timpani. When a passage travels gradually from one beating spot to another, a dotted line or arrow can be used. These notations should be explained at the beginning of the score and percussion part. (See Elliott Carter's *Eight Pieces for Four Timpani*, the second movement of Béla Bartók's *Sonata for Two Pianos and Percussion*, and John Cage's *Third Construction*.)

After it has been written out the first time, the text "moving gradually to the edge" will be understood and only the dotted line or glissando indication is necessary (figure 6.6).

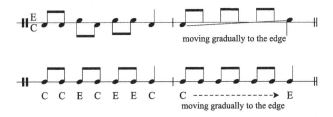

Figure 6.6
Center/edge
notation

Mutes

🔊 Video 6.c—Rim, Shell, Beating Spot, Mutes, Pitch Bending

Light dampening with a piece of cloth or tape is often used to make drums drier, darker, and clearer in pitch and to clean up soft articulate passages on timpani and other large resonant drums. Heavy dampening is commonly used with pedal bass drums where towels, sheets, or something similar is inserted into the drum, giving it a full but punchy sound. This type of muting does not need to be specified by the composer. A composer may occasionally request heavy dampening for effect. (See the mini scores placed on timpani heads in William Kraft's *Concerto for Timpani*.) (See Note Length, Articulation, and Phrasing in chapter 3 for more information.)

Pitch Bending

🔊 Video 6.c—Rim, Shell, Beating Spot, Mutes, Pitch Bending

The pitch of all drums can be manipulated by pressing on the head with an elbow, fist, finger, or stick. Pushing on the head stretches it to raise the pitch. This also dampens the head.

A drum sound will often naturally have a slight pitch bend. When the drum is struck loudly, the force of the stick pushes on the head so that, post-attack, the head quickly relaxes back into position and produces a small downward glissando. This is most apparent on drums with looser heads, played at loud dynamics.

Timpani and roto-toms have mechanisms that bend the pitch.

Drum Size

Indication of drum size is notated as "small," "medium small," "large," and so on; dimensions are unnecessary. The composer's requesting an approximate pitch or pitch range is appropriate for a more specific indication.

Two-Headed Drums

Some drums have both a top and a bottom drum head. In most cases, only one of the heads is struck—the other just resonates sympathetically. Both heads are struck in certain ethnic drumming and on bass drums in marching bands, but in most Western music it is not necessary or practical to strike both heads. On rare occasions, it is more convenient to play on the second head, but this should be the performer's choice.

Concert tom-toms are traditionally single-headed, while drumset toms usually have two heads. Two-headed toms are more easily capable of the boom-y sound popular with rock drummers. Nearly all drums with snares have two heads.

Multiple Drums in Setups

◈ Video 6.d—Multiple Drums

When using multiple drums together in a setup, the composer needs to consider pitch, dynamic, and timbral relationships. It may be best not to specify each drum type—for example, the composer may notate "seven graduated drums" instead of naming each of the seven drums. This allows the performer to find the drum combinations that sound best, given the available instruments.

Drum pitch relationships can be found in appendix F. Timpani are almost always written with specific pitches. Roto-toms are often but not always used with pitch specification. All other listed drums are used primarily without pitch specification. When combining drums of determinate and indeterminate pitch, the composer should be sure that those of indeterminate pitch are capable of the requested relationships—for example, a bongo may be tuned in between but not above two roto-toms pitched C4 and G4.

Drums with deeper shells typically are louder than those with shallower shells. For example, a large tom-tom can get much louder than a large roto-tom (roto-toms have no shell—see figure 6.26).

Plastic-headed drums and calf-headed drums have slightly different timbres. Generally, it can be assumed that bongos and congas have calf heads, and all other drums have plastic heads, although this can vary with the percussionist's preference. Calf heads have a rounder sound with not as bright an attack; plastic heads give the attack more of a pop or crack. When used together in a setup, these different sounds may be apparent, especially at soft dynamics with snare drum sticks. This is a minor issue—bongos, congas, and other drums are frequently and successfully used together—but it should be noted that if the percussionist is using snare sticks and playing soft melodic passages between calf and plastic-headed drums, smooth phrasing may be difficult.

Idiomatic Writing for Drums

It is very easy to visualize exactly what a percussionist must do to play passages on drums, and it is therefore relatively easy to write idiomatically for a set of drums. Once the composer decides how the drums are to be set up, he or she can "air drum" passages to see if they lay well. The composer could even set up objects like pillows or plates to try out passages.

Most percussionists are experienced with improvising on indeterminately pitched instruments. Instead of a completely written out drum part, all they may require is the rhythm, dynamics, and shape of the figures to get the correct feel. (See The Written/ Improv Divide in chapter 1.) This guarantees an idiomatic part.

Many percussionists who do not regularly play drumset are less proficient with complicated foot pedal work, so the composer may want to keep pedal bass drum passages relatively idiomatic. Pedal passages are far easier when the bass drum (or other pedal instrument) is doubled by a hand stroke or written as a steady rhythm. As shown in figure 6.7, (a) is more difficult than (b) or (c).

Figure 6.7
Pedal bass drum within figuration

Also, when using a pedal, control over dynamics is not nearly as strong as when using hand-held beaters, so dynamically sensitive passages should be written with caution.

Timpani

🔊 Video 6.e—Timpani

Timpani is the plural of *timpano*. Timpani are notated in bass clef. A set of four drums is most common: I is 30–32 inches (76–81 cm), II is 28–29 inches (71–74 cm), III is 25–26 inches (63–66 cm), and IV is 23–24 inches (58–61 cm). I is the lowest of the timpani. A fifth, or V, piccolo timpano, is 20–22 inches (51–56 cm) and also common. Sometimes another combination of these drums (e.g., two II drums, a III, two IVs, and a V) or additional drums could be used if they are available. It is always best, however, to write for a standard set of four drums, as shown in figure 6.8.

Figure 6.8
Timpani

Photo courtesy
of Pearl/Adams
Percussion

Ranges

Timpani have pedals that manipulate the tension of the head and thus the pitch of the drum. The overall range of timpani is as shown in figure 6.9. Individually, the drum ranges are as shown in figure 6.10.

Figure 6.9
Full timpani range

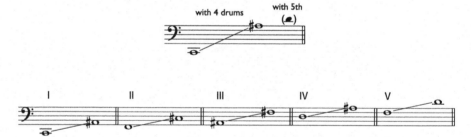

Figure 6.10
Individual
timpani ranges

The top half-step in each case is a stretch. These notes sometimes sound choked, depending on the quality of the instruments. The lowest range of each of the drums sounds tubbier and the pitch is less clear. On the other hand, these pitches are more resonant in soft playing. The choice to put pitches on the lower range of a particular drum should be the performer's, based on the specific instruments available. These low ranges are shown in figure 6.11.

Figure 6.11
Timpani
low ranges

There are three conditions under which the composer should consider the individual ranges:

when writing a part with fixed pitches
when writing for just a few drums
when dealing with glissandi

For fixed pitches, it is best if those pitches fit well into the ranges of the drums (e.g., if G, A, B, and C are requested on a standard set of drums, the top two pitches will not sound best). If only a few drums are used (in a setup with other instruments or if there is a constraint on space), the composer should decide which drums he or she will use and then write only for pitches in those drums' ranges. Glissandi should happen within the range of one drum. For example, a glissando from low G to high f♯ will not work; it must be split up (figure 6.12).

II   III

Figure 6.12
Broken glissando

Instead, the note could be only partially reached with a glissando and then struck (figure 6.13a), or the notes could be rolled to cover the points where drum change is needed (figure 6.13b).

(a)

II   IV

(b)

II   III   IV

Figure 6.13
Glissando
work-arounds

If the pitches are constantly changing, the composer does not need to be concerned with the range of the individual drums. The timpanist will determine which drums to use and on which drums to put pitches. The composer should not provide a tuning plan—a guide to where and when to change pitches on drums; a tuning plan can vary depending on availability of drums and player preference. A provided tuning plan will most often just get in the way of the player's own plan.

In very rare cases, the timpani range is extended far upward. Roto-toms are often used for these high pitches, as timpani small enough are not available, although roto-toms are far from an ideal match to the timpani sound. (See Darius Milhaud's *Creation du Monde* and Maurice Ravel's *L'Enfant et les Sortilèges*.) The use of these extreme ranges should be avoided.

The lowest possible note of a particular drum can be notated with a downward arrow notehead (figure 6.14). At this point, the drum head is very slack and has less recognizable pitch. This notation should be explained in the score and part.

Figure 6.14
Lowest pitch
notation

Two drums can be tuned to the same pitch for added volume. Although two different drums tuned to the same pitch have different sound qualities, this will not be noticed at a loud dynamic. Occasionally, composers wanting especially loud notes call for two mallets to strike one drum simultaneously. Although the two mallets do not produce much more sound than one mallet, it is a nice visual effect. (Remember that one drum hit with one mallet can still be quite loud.)

Changing Pitch

Melodic capabilities on timpani are limited, but not as limited as one may think; complex pedaling is difficult but very possible. Charles Wuorinen's *Bassoon Variations* takes timpani to its melodic limit. The average timpani part of Béla Bartók's—*Sonata for Two Pianos and Percussion,* Piano Concerto No. 2, and Violin Concerto No. 2 (figure 6.15)—or Richard Strauss's—*Der Rosenkavalier Suite* and *Salome's Dance of the Seven Veils,*—are good examples of melodic capabilities within reason.

Figure 6.15
Melodic figuration

SOURCE: From
Bartók's Violin
Concerto No. 2.

When pedaling extensively, the player will have to sit down on a stool to operate two pedals at once. This should be taken into account when composing for a setup that includes timpani with other instruments. If the player is standing to play other instruments in a setup, and then needs to sit for an involved timpani passage, the composer needs to allot some time for the player to get into position on the stool.

Specific pitches do not necessarily need to be notated for quick articulations between the first and last pitches of a glissando. Note stems attached to the glissando line can indicate rhythm (figure 6.16).

Figure 6.16
Glissando with
articulations

When the final note of a glissando is not re-attacked, it should be written as a note in parentheses (figure 6.17). A slur is often used for this purpose, but timpanists will sometimes re-attack the second of two slurred notes; the parentheses indication is less ambiguous.

Figure 6.17
Glissando without
a final articulation

Multiple Timpanists

Multiple timpanists are useful when many pitches are needed. This was especially true in the nineteenth century, when primitive tuning mechanisms made quick pitch changes impossible. With modern timpani, multiple timpanists may be replaced by one player executing quick tuning changes. More than one timpanist can still add volume and play more complicated passages, however. Any more than two sets of timpani is impractical; five timpanists, each with one drum, is reasonable, but five players, each with four drums, is likely to be a problem because of the availability of space and instruments. (See Mahler's symphonies, Hector Berlioz's *Symphony Fantasique* and *Requiem* [twelve timpani!], Carl Nielsen's Symphony No. 4, and Gustav Holst's *The Planets* [figure 6.18].)

Figure 6.18
Multiple
timpanists

SOURCE: From
"Jupiter," from
Gustav Holst's *The Planets.*

Obsolete Notation

The reader may notice that in old scores (most notably early ones of Mozart), the timpani notes are notated as C and G, for example, but "Timpani D & A" is written at the top of the part. It was common practice at the time to treat timpani like a transposing instrument. Later, timpani parts were notated on their correct lines but without accidentals. For example, it would be notated as F and B with "Timpani E♭ & B♭" indicated at the top of the part. These notational practices should no longer be observed.

In some works by Schumann, Verdi, and other composers, there are timpani notes that are out of harmony with the rest of the orchestra. Players of the day did not have time to retune the drum with the old hand-screw drums, and because the drums of the time did not produce a clear pitch anyway, it did not matter much if the pitch was a step off. The instruments of today are much clearer pitched, and pedal mechanisms allow for very quick and efficient tuning. Many timpanists and conductors fix these "wrong" notes in those scores.

Striking the Rim and Bowl

It is not advisable to notate on-the-rim playing for timpani. Timpani rims are often sunken below the edge of the bowl, so the bowl itself could be struck if a player aims for a rim sound. The edge of the copper bowl is soft metal and can easily be banged out of shape, effectively ruining the drum.

Striking the side of the bowl is less damaging, as long as the bowl is not struck too loud. Loud playing can easily dent the bowl, effectively ruining the instrument. Timpanists will go to great lengths to ensure the safety of their instruments, and may choose to use poor-quality drums when bowl playing is requested. The indication to strike the copper bowl of the timpani is often notated with an "X" notehead.

When the bowl or rim is struck, the head does not ring much; when the pedal is adjusted, it adjusts the pitch of the head and not the pitch of the bowl. For these reasons, it is not effective to move the pedal while striking the bowl or rim.

Prepared Timpani

Crotales, temple bowls, or an upside-down cymbal can be placed on a timpano head and struck, rolled on, or bowed while the percussionist pedals up and down. A thumb-piano can also be played while resting on a timpano. These produce haunting effects. In each case, the overtones of the timpano head resonate sympathetically with the pitches produced by the instrument resting on it; the moving pedal gives the impression that these pitches are glissando-ing. The effects are soft and will not be noticed if the pedal moves up and down too slowly. The pitch of the drum head will not be heard. (See Per Nørgård's *I Ching* and George Crumb's *Music for a Summer Evening*.)

Playing too many crotales on a timpano is unwieldy and passages will be difficult for the player to execute; it is best to use no more than six notes in these situations. If quick passages or passages with many notes are needed, it is more appropriate to use a regular set of crotales on a stand.

Small items, like a coin or the ring from a soda can lid, can be placed on timpani heads to rattle. This works best at soft dynamics, because at loud dynamics the item will bounce off and fall onto the floor. Objects can be placed on the head and secured with tape to rattle at loud dynamics without falling off, but this will muffle the head.

Harmonics

By pressing a finger or mallet against the drumhead about halfway between the center and edge, and then striking toward the edge, the player produces the harmonic an octave above the fundamental (figure 6.19). This is a subtle effect, and a moment of preparation is necessary to get the finger or mallet into position.

Figure 6.19
Timpani harmonics

SOURCE: From Elliott Carter's Adagio, from *Eight Pieces for Four Timpani.*

Sympathetic Resonance

Two timpani tuned in unison will ring sympathetically with one another. If the player strikes one drum loudly and then muffles it, the sympathetic resonance of the other drum can be heard (figure 6.20). This effect is extremely subtle, but a glissando (on the drum not struck) can be used to make the sympathetic resonance more noticeable.

Figure 6.20
Timpani sympathetic resonance

Timpani can also be used as resonators for other non-percussion instruments that are played into the heads of the drums while the pedal is adjusted (with trumpets in Jefferson Friedman's *Sacred Heart: Explosion* and trombones in Christopher Rouse's *Seeing*).

Tom-Toms

🔊 Video 6.f—Tom-toms, Snare Drums, Bass Drums

A tom-tom (or just *tom*) can have one or two heads (just the top *batter* head, or both top and bottom heads) and comes in a variety of sizes and pitches from very high to very low (figure 6.21). "Tom-tom" refers to a drum with no special features.

Snare drums, field drums, tenor drums, timbales, roto-toms, bongos, and congas have special characteristics that make them more than just tom-toms, but they could all technically be described and even used as tom-toms.

Figure 6.21
Tom-toms

Photo courtesy
of Pearl/Adams
Percussion

Concert tom-toms are traditionally single-headed, while drumset toms usually have two heads. Two-headed toms are more easily capable of the boom-y sound popular with rock drummers.

These drums are almost always used as indeterminately pitched instruments. They can be tuned if necessary, but the pitches are not especially clear. Roto-toms are often used when tuned tom-toms are requested because the pitch is easily adjusted. It is not advisable to specify pitches for drums with snares because the snare sound can obscure the pitch. With the exception of roto-toms, the pitch of a drum cannot be changed within a piece; changing the pitch of roto-toms is possible but awkward.

Chinese tom-toms have a unique shape, with two calfskin heads. They come in a variety of sizes and have a dry and dark sound. They are not as widely available as Western tom-toms or the other drums described in this chapter.

Snare Drum, Field Drum, and Tenor Drum

🜄 Video 6.f—Tom-toms, Snare Drums, Bass Drums

The snare drum (also *side drum* or *military drum*) can come in a variety of sizes, from piccolo to field drum. A piccolo snare drum is just a few inches deep and is very bright and responsive. A standard snare drum (figure 6.22a) is 4 to 6 inches (10–15 cm) deep, and a field drum (figure 6.22b) can be 12 to 16 inches (30–40 cm) deep. A tenor drum is simply a field drum without snares. Snare drum shells are made of wood, brass, fiberglass, steel, or other materials.

Snare drums have both a top and a bottom head and have snares. Snares are wires that run across the bottom head of the drum and vibrate when the top head is struck; this gives the snare drum its unique sound. The snares can be lowered away from the head by use of a snare *throw off* or *clutch,* indicated as "snares off." The snares can be turned on or off easily during performance, but there must be some time (about a

(b)

(a)

Figure 6.22
(a) snare drum,
(b) field drum

Photos courtesy
of Pearl/Adams
Percussion

second or two) allotted to do so; without proper time for this switch, extra noise may be produced. A snare drum with the snares off is just a tom-tom. If there is no indication for snares on or off, "snares on" is assumed.

Snares add a bright timbre to the drum. The snare drum, even at soft dynamics, has a lot of cutting power, and thus has difficulty blending well with darker sounding instruments. Because of the very tight articulation that the snares create, rolls on snare drums, especially those at soft dynamics, should always be executed as buzz rolls with drum sticks. Single-stroke rolls with mallets or hands tend to sound choppy and unappealing.

The sound that the snares produce depends on the material or combination of materials used and the tightness of the snares against the head, neither of which is commonly specified by the composer. Any indication with respect to the timbre of the snares is rare, but a "wet" or "dry" sound may be specified. Drumset players sometimes use a wet snare; a dry snare is more of a marching band sound. Both are used in concert music for a variety of effects, but generally a concert snare sound is dry.

Snares are sensitive and often vibrate sympathetically with just about everything else. The wetter the snare, the more sensitive it is. Timpani, tom-toms, a marimba, or a vibraphone located close to a snare drum—or French horns, whose players are often positioned right in front of the percussion section in an orchestra—are common causes of snare noise. If a snare drum is used with other toms, those toms might vibrate the snares and sound as if they have snares themselves. The size and volume of an orchestra can usually cover the buzzing snares, but that buzzing can be a real problem in chamber and solo settings. To cut down on the noise, percussionists try to turn on the snares only when absolutely necessary. It may be wise for a composer to leave a bit of time before and after each snare drum entrance so that the snares can be turned on and off.

Although it is usually a drawback, a composer could use the sympathetic buzzing as an effect to enhance the sound of a wind, brass, or other percussion instrument.

Concert Bass Drum and Pedal Bass Drum

🔊 Video 6.f—Tom-toms, Snare Drums, Bass Drums

There are two main types of bass drums: the concert bass drum and the pedal bass drum. A typical concert bass drum is very large and resonant and is played either upright (Figure 6.23a) or on its side. A typical pedal bass drum (sometimes called a *kick drum*) is smaller and much drier (usually muffled by towels or blankets inserted inside the drum); it is played with a mallet made of wood, plastic, or hard felt that is attached to a pedal (Figure 6.23b). Concert bass drums come in a variety of sizes from 25 to 40 inches (63–102 cm) in diameter; pedal bass drums range from 16 to 22 inches (41–56 cm). Large concert bass drums can also be played with a pedal, and pedal bass drums can be played with sticks or mallets.

Figure 6.23
(a) concert bass drum, (b) pedal bass drum

Photo of concert bass drum courtesy of Pearl/Adams Percussion

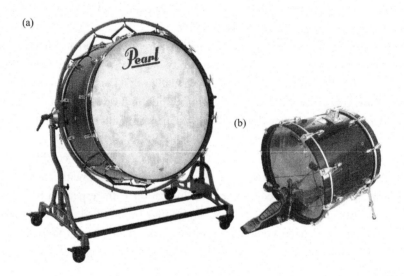

(a)

(b)

A pedal bass drum is usually played with the foot facing the drum, but the drum can be placed behind the player so the pedal is operated by the heel of the foot. This is advantageous if there is no room for the bass drum under a mallet instrument or within a setup.

Double bass drum pedals are becoming more frequently used. This is a device that allows for both feet to play one bass drum. The feet cannot play quite as fast as the hands, but can play faster than one might think. Some percussionists can do this better than others. When both feet are involved, the percussionist needs to sit down; standing is possible but difficult.

Tambourines, sleighbells, shakers, or other such instruments can be placed on a concert bass drum head to rattle when the head is struck.

Bass Drum/Cymbal Attachment

Bass drum and crash cymbals can be played by a single player with a bass drum/ cymbal attachment. A bass drum/cymbal attachment mounts one cymbal to the bass drum so it can be crashed by another cymbal. The player operates the cymbal with one hand and the bass drum mallet with the other. The bass drum must be upright, not flat on its side. Playing the cymbals in this manner is awkward, and fine control over dynamics and muffling is sacrificed. (See Stravinsky's *Petrouchka*, Mahler's Symphonies Nos. 1 and 3, and Rossini's overtures.)

Bongos and Congas

◉ Video 6.g—Bongos, Congas, Timbales, Roto-toms

Bongos and congas are traditionally played with the hands, but sticks and mallets also work well (although some players might object to the use of sticks and mallets on these instruments, especially congas, as they can damage the drum head). Both instruments almost always have calfskin heads. Bongos (figure 6.24a) are high pitched and come in pairs, with one 8-inch and one 10-inch drum (20 and 25 cm) attached to each another. These drums are always attached together, so if only one drum is requested, the other drum is usually still present in the setup. If more than two bongos are used, they are tuned to graduated pitches because only the two drum sizes are available. Other sizes of bongos exist but are rare.

(b)

Figure 6.24
(a) bongos,
(b) congas

Photos courtesy of Latin Percussion

(a)

More than two bongos may be difficult to arrange in a setup. The player may need to unscrew and re-screw the drums together to set them up in an odd configuration.

If it is inconsequential to the piece, it may be best to use a pair of bongos with other drums instead of three or four bongos. Since only the two sizes of bongos is common, any more than four bongos (with four different pitches) in one setup is unreasonable.

Congas are deeper than bongos and are generally used in pairs, but any number (reasonably, up to four) is acceptable (figure 6.24b). These drums come in three basic sizes, from low to high: the *tumba*, the *conga,* and the *quinto*. For nontraditional music notation, these terms is unnecessary; "low," "medium," and "high" are more appropriate.

Bongos and congas complement each other—two bongos and two congas cover a nice range and have similar timbral qualities. Although congas are large, they are not especially low in pitch. An overtone about an octave above the fundamental is the most prominent pitch. The fundamental is heard most with a bass stroke of the hand; this pitch is very low. The pitch produced with sticks, mallets, or the tone stroke of the hands is relatively high—just under the pitch of bongos. If necessary, the heads of the congas can be tuned loosely so even sticks and mallets will produce low pitches.

Figure 6.25
Timbales

Photo courtesy of
Latin Percussion

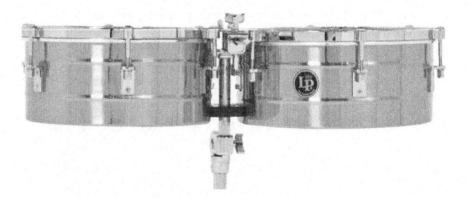

Timbales

◐ Video 6.g—Bongos, Congas, Timbales, Roto-toms

Timbales are a traditional Afro-Cuban instrument, derived from (but only very loosely resembling) timpani. They are similar to a regular snare drum without snares, but always have metal shells and only one head (figure 6.25). They are almost always used in pairs. In traditional music, bell patterns are often played on the metal shells of timbales.

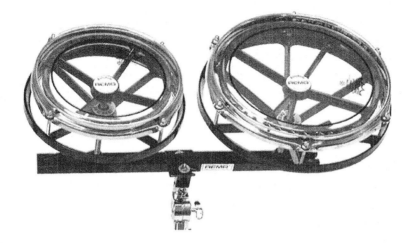

Figure 6.26
Roto-toms

Photo courtesy of
Remo Percussion

Roto-Toms

◉ Video 6.g—Bongos, Congas, Timbales, Roto-toms

Roto-toms are tunable single-headed toms with a thin frame instead of a shell (figure 6.26). They come in the following sizes: 6, 8, 10, 12, 14, 16, and 18 inches (15, 20, 25.5, 30.5, 35.5, 41, and 46 cm).

The pitch of a roto-tom can be raised or lowered by spinning the entire drum. Unlike timpani, it is not easy to change the pitch while playing. The design of these drums is best for fixed pitches; if the pitch is to be changed during a piece, there should be enough time (8 to 10 seconds) to do so accurately. Glissandi are possible, but difficult—upward glissandi are more reasonable than downward—and the player must have one hand free to spin the drum. Pitch specification is not necessary for roto-toms.

When used with pitch specification, roto-toms are notated at pitch in treble and bass clef. Although there are some important pieces in which roto-toms are notated in alto clef (see Michael Colgrass's *Variations for Four Drums and Viola*), percussionists prefer treble and bass. The best-sounding pitches are in the middle of a drum's range; the highest pitches will sound choked and the lower pitches will be flabby and unclear. The ranges are shown in figure 6.27.

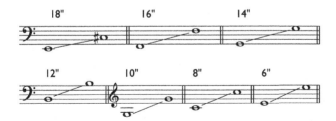

Figure 6.27
Roto-tom ranges

Since they have no shell, roto-toms project the least well of all drums. This is not to say they are not loud, but the sound—and especially the pitch—can get lost in a heavily orchestrated passage or one that features other drums.

Although commonly used as an upward extension of timpani, the sound of roto-toms is quite different and the match is far from perfect.

Frame Drums

🔊 Video 6.h—Frame Drums, Tambourines

Frame drums are very shallow single-headed drums (figure 6.28). They can be found in many different sizes, from 6 to 20 inches (20–51 cm). Frame drums are traditionally held and played with the hands and fingers. The guidelines for hand drum notation described in the Hands on Drums section apply here as well. To design a more detailed notation, the composer should take a close look at the instrument with a percussionist.

Figure 6.28
Frame drum

Photo courtesy of
HUBB Percussion

Steve Reich requests "tambourines without jingles" that are tuned to specific pitches and played with sticks in his *Tehillim*. Tunable frame drums with heads designed to withstand a drumstick are occasionally available, but these instruments sound not unlike roto-toms; roto-toms are far more common and are often substituted when tunable frame drums are not available.

An *ocean drum* is a two-headed frame drum; the space between the two heads is filled with small metal ball bearings that can rattle along with drum articulations or be swirled around for a sustained sound. This instrument is an effective substitute for a *geophone*, an instrument requested by Olivier Messiaen in his *Des Canyons aux étoile. . .*

Tambourines

🎵 Video 6.h—Frame Drums, Tambourines

A tambourine is a type of frame drum to which many tiny cymbals, called "jingles," are affixed (figure 6.29). The tambourine has been used for centuries by many cultures around the world. As a result, there are many different types of tambourines and many different playing styles.

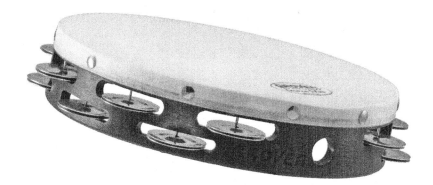

Figure 6.29
Tambourine

Photo courtesy of Grover Pro Percussion.

The traditional orchestral tambourine is 10 inches (25.5 cm) in diameter and has a single head. The sound of the drumhead is secondary; rather, it is the sound of the jingles that is most important. The jingles are made from a variety of materials that produce different sounds; the composer may specify "bright" or "dark" sounding jingles, but this is not common or necessary. The tambourine is usually held, but can be mounted or rested on a table. It is traditionally played with a hand, but sticks and mallets can be used.

The tambourine is usually held in one hand, so fast rhythms that require two hands can present problems. Percussionists employ a variety of techniques to make faster rhythms possible: for fast soft passages, they often rest the tambourine on a leg and play it with both hands; for loud passages, the player uses his or her knee like an extra fist to strike the tambourine. The techniques chosen will vary depending on the passage, the particular instrument used, and the player's preference. The specific means of execution should not be a concern of the composer. (See Georges Bizet's *Carmen*, Pyotr Tchaikovsky's *Nutcracker*, and Edgard Varèse's *Amérique*.)

Rolls can be executed by shaking the tambourine or rubbing a thumb or finger along the edge of the head. (See Friction Roll in appendix C.) To specify, the composer can write "shake" or "thumb roll"; however, specifying the roll type is not necessary. (See Igor Stravinsky's Tableau 4 of *Petrouchka* [1947 version] and Benjamin Britten's "Storm" from the *Peter Grimes Four Sea Interludes*.)

If the tambourine is mounted to be played loudly with a stick, percussionists will often substitute a drumset tambourine in place of a regular orchestral tambourine. Drumset tambourines are made of plastic, have no head, are brighter and drier than orchestral tambourines, and are built to withstand the abuse of snare drum sticks (figure 6.30). Use of this type of instrument does not need to be specified by the composer. The drumset tambourine is simply a mountable version of an average rock-style tambourine.

Figure 6.30
Mountable drumset tambourine

Photo courtesy of Latin Percussion

There are many ethnic tambourines from all over the world. The *pandeiro* and the *riq*[1] are probably the most notable in this context, although there are many others of equal musical and cultural importance. A pandeiro is a Brazilian instrument that is usually larger than a normal orchestral tambourine and has thicker jingles (see figure 6.31a). With this instrument, the head sound is more important than the jingle sound. The riq is a Persian instrument, slightly smaller than a normal orchestral tambourine, and also has thicker jingles (see figure 6.31b). It is held vertically, like a frame drum, and played mostly with individual fingers. Unique to the riq is the striking of the jingles—not just the head. One hand primarily plays the jingles while the other hand moves between the jingles and the head. (See Adam Silverman's *Naked and on Fire*.)

Pandeiro and riq playing is typically improvised. In a concert setting, the composer may find it more appropriate to supply a guide for improvisation, rather than a completely written-out part (see The Written/Improv Divide in chapter 1). For more detailed pandeiro and riq information, consult a percussionist.

All pandeiro, riq, and frame drum techniques can be applied to all tambourines.

---

1. *Pandeiro* and *riq* are among a few acceptable spellings of the names of these instruments.

Figure 6.31
(a) pandeiro,
(b) riq

Photos courtesy of
Remo Percussion

(a)

(b)

Djembe and Doumbek

🔊 Video 6.i—Djembe, Doumbek

The djembe and doumbek are just two of an enormous number of similar ethnic hand drums. They are played almost exclusively with the hands and are generally held either between the legs (djembe; figure 6.32a) or under the arm (doumbek; figure 6.32b). Each instrument has its own characteristic playing styles and techniques. The guidelines for hand drum notation described earlier in Hands on Drums apply here as well. To design a more detailed notation, the composer should take a close look at the instrument with a percussionist.

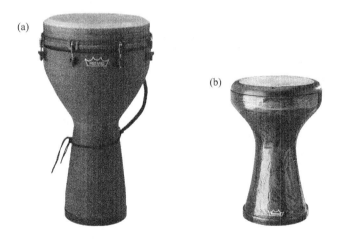

(a)

(b)

Figure 6.32
(a) djembe,
(b) doumbek

Photos courtesy of
Remo Percussion

Djembes are large wooden hourglass-shaped drums with a booming bass and wide range of timbres. (See Iannis Xenakis's *Okho.*) A doumbek (also *darabuka* or *goblet drum,* with many other variant spellings and names depending on country of origin and transliteration) is smaller than a djembe and made of ceramic or metal. (See Adam Silverman's *Naked and on Fire.*)

Boobams

Boobams are tube-shaped drums 4 to 6 inches (10–15 cm) in diameter and between 10 and 25 inches (25–63 cm) deep. They were originally made of large pieces of bamboo (hence the name), but are now more commonly made from wood, plastic, and fiberglass. They are often also known as *Octobans*, a product of the Tama drum company, although there are several other manufacturers with similar products. Boobams are sometimes tuned to specific pitches. (See six pitches of boobams in Christopher Rouse's *Ku-Ka-Ilimoku*.) They are only better suited for this than other drums because they are of uniform size and can more easily be positioned like the pitches of a keyboard. They are, however, far less widely available than similar drums (bongos, for instance) and are no clearer in pitch.

Drumset

🕑 Video 6.j—Drumset

The drumset (also *drum kit, trap set, trap kit*, or just *traps*) is the most successful, versatile, and ubiquitous multi-percussion setup (figure 6.33). It has evolved over a century to become a fixture in countless styles of music from all over the world and has attracted many thousands of performers who identify themselves as "drummers." It is capable of polyphonic music with a rich variety of articulations and is better than any other instrument at clarifying time, meter, and rhythm.

Figure 6.33
Drumset

Photo courtesy
of Pearl/Adams
Percussion

The drumset characteristically has a core setup of three instruments: pedal bass drum, snare drum, and hi-hat. Common add-ons include one or more tom-toms and two or more suspended cymbals, often a ride and crash cymbal (not to be confused with a pair of crash cymbals). The low tom of a drumset often stands on the floor (see figure 6.33) and is called a *floor tom*. Drumsets are commonly rearranged or augmented with other percussion instruments. The composer should not feel restricted to these instruments just because he or she feels the need to use a "drumset." Another setup of drums, with or without cymbals or pedal instruments, may be what the composer is imagining.

The drumset is traditionally used to evoke the sounds of specific styles of music (jazz, rock, etc.). For example, Leonard Bernstein's *Symphonic Dances from West Side Story* uses a drumset in a jazz and Latin style. On the other hand, John Adams's *Chamber Symphony* uses a drumset-like setup for an exclusively Adams sound. (See also Milton Babbitt's *All-Set*.) Steven Mackey's *It Is Time* and James Dillon's *Ti.re-Ti.ki-Dha* find a middle ground, referencing the instrument's roles in popular music while advancing it into new contexts.

In its traditional role in popular music, the drumset player is often expected to keep time—that is, to play an ostinato figure characteristic of the indicated style (e.g., swing, hard rock, shuffle). This defines the *feel* of a piece of music. If the drummer changes to a different feel—a shift in metric feel (e.g., from 4/4 to 2/2) or a shift in rhythmic inflection (e.g., from straight time to swing)—that can change the song entirely. For this reason, drummers have a lot of power and can often make or break the success of the musical product.

In popular music styles, if the drummer reads from music, it is rarely a completely written-out part. Usually the drummer plays off a song chart (see figure 6.34) and responds to tempo, meter, feel, structure, orchestration, dynamics, phrase lengths, and rhythms in the rest of the ensemble. Charts may also offer spots in which to put a drum fill; a drum fill is a short embellishment about a bar or half a bar long, usually at the end of a phrase. The composer may further control a drumset part by notating specific rhythms for fills, places to put important cymbal crashes, or specific ostinati to play, but it is often most effective for drummers to interpret a vague notation so they can be free to react to the specific ensemble and venue.

Since the drummer often functions like a conductor, driving the whole ensemble, it is essential that he or she know exactly what to expect. A drum chart well marked with useful information is welcome, especially when there are many different charts in one concert or recording session. Note the following in figure 6.34:

- *Indication of feel* (e.g., "moderate swing" or "jazz waltz"): This is essential information, as it determines the material the drummer will play.
- *Metronome mark*: The drums are a strong communicator of tempo, and a precise tempo indication ensures accuracy.

Figure 6.34
Example
drum chart

- *Dynamics*: The dynamic also influences the material the drummer will play and gives clues to the orchestration.
- *Rhythms present in the rest of the ensemble*: This can be notated on or above the staff. The *tutti* passages are notated on the staff while the more ornamental hits appear above. Indications of orchestration (e.g., "w.w." or "brass") and additional dynamics and articulations are very much welcome in the cues.
- *Phrase lengths*: The number above the measures outlines the specific phrase lengths (e.g., 4, 8, 12). Music notation software often places these courtesy numbers in musically inappropriate places (for example, a "4" would appear in bar 6 because it is the fourth bar of the repeat symbols). Phrase beginnings and ends will often be shaped and ornamented by the drummer, so it is important that they are clearly and accurately notated.
- *Beaters*: Sticks are assumed unless a specific sound is desired (e.g., brushes), but beater indications are not necessary.

The slash marks are a common indication for the drummer to "play time."

For traditional popular music styles, these notations are often far more effective than a completely written-out part. A competent drummer already knows what music to play, so the notation need only show how the composition is structured. It is recommend the composer study rock, jazz, and musical theater recordings to understand how the drumset may be used in these contexts.

Composers using a drumset for nontraditional purposes may prefer to notate the part completely, in which case the notational guidelines presented in chapter 3 apply. Figure 6.35 shows a common notational system for a drumset.

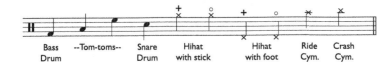

Figure 6.35
Drumset notation

When a drumset is used in acoustic ensembles, balance can be a significant challenge. The composer must be careful to write for this instrument and orchestrate the ensemble around it in a way that makes balance possible. Rock music is amplified, and the drumset sound characteristic of this style is that of the drummer playing loud. This sound has become what most listeners and composers expect, even in non-rock settings. At soft dynamics, the drumset music will change color, change character, and sometimes become unplayable; more commonly, drummers are forced to play too loud. However, drummers can make instrumentation substitutions for softer dynamics, such as using a tight hi-hat instead of a ride cymbal, or using side-stick on snare drum instead of hitting the drumhead. Rute sticks (see chapter 4) are often used for soft playing, but these beaters are not always an effective substitute for sticks, as they produce a much duller sound on cymbals. Brushes are another effective soft-dynamic alternative, but the playing style and resulting material tend then to be different.

CHAPTER SEVEN

Metal

Instruments covered in this chapter are the cymbals, gongs, triangle, finger cymbals, cowbells, almglocken, temple bowls, mixing bowls, brake drums, metal pipes, anvil, bell plates, thundersheet, junk metal, tin cans, pots and pans, ribbon crasher, spring coil, church bells, hand bells, steel drums, sleighbells, tambourine, metal wind chimes, mark tree, bell tree, and flexatone.

Cymbals

There are two main types of cymbals: suspended cymbals and crash or hand cymbals. *Suspended cymbals* are suspended on a stand and struck with beaters. *Crash cymbals* are two cymbals struck together. In a drumset context, certain suspended cymbals are also called crash cymbals, but composers should reserve this term for the pair of hand crash cymbals.

When a cymbal is struck and then muffled immediately, it is called a *choke*. This term is applied to both suspended and crash cymbals, as well as to gongs. This can be notated by writing "choke" or by any other indication to muffle or play a short note.

Myriad factors influence a cymbal's color and response—size, shape, thickness, cup size, bow, pattern of hammering and lathing, and so on. Percussionists often use different cymbals for different functions, even within a single part written for one cymbal. Specification in this regard by the composer is unnecessary.

Multiple Cymbals

Cymbals do not sound at a pitch but, rather, a pitch spectrum. The perceived pitch of a cymbal can change depending on volume, beater, and even with its placement in relation to the listener. As a result, cymbals have to be far away from each other in pitch to be easily distinguishable; little is gained from using more than four regular suspended cymbals. If different types of cymbals are used (e.g., sizzle, china), then the listener can easily hear the differences.

Multiple crash cymbals to be played simultaneously requires multiple players.

Suspended Cymbals

🔊 Video 7.a—Suspended Cymbals

A regular orchestral suspended cymbal (figure 7.1) is designed for the widest pitch spectrum and longest ring time. It can be any size from about 14 to 22 inches (34–56 cm) in diameter. The ring time will vary with the size—the larger the cymbal, the longer the ring. A *fortissimo* crash on an average 18-inch (46 cm) suspended cymbal will reach *piano* after about four seconds, and a *piano* stroke will be inaudible after about two seconds.[1]

Figure 7.1
Suspended cymbal

Photo courtesy of
Zildjian Cymbals

Rolls on cymbals are usually single-stroke rolls. Yarn, cord, felt, or soft rubber mallets can produce seamless swooshing rolls; fast passages on cymbals with these beaters always result in a roll because the individual strokes will not be heard clearly. With sticks, hard rubber mallets, or plastic mallets, each individual attack is audible. With snare sticks at soft dynamics, the articulation is so clear that a buzz roll may be preferable. (See Rolls in chapter 3.)

Suspended cymbals can also be bowed. The pitch should not be specified. (See Bows in chapter 4.)

Different spots on a cymbal sound differently (figure 7.2). The edge of the cymbal has a large pitch spectrum and a washing sound. The *bell* (also called the *dome* or *cup*) of the cymbal is brighter, has a more articulate attack, and gives a more centered sound. (See Manipulations of Timbre in appendix C.) A normal beating spot is on or near the edge. A specification of "bell" can be negated by writing "edge."

---

1. Ring times are approximate and vary with the individual instruments.

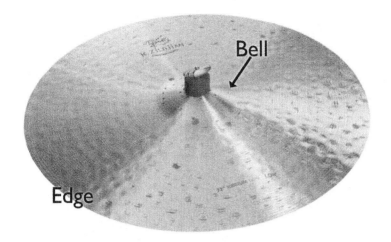

Figure 7.2
Anatomy of
the cymbal

Photo courtesy of
Zildjian Cymbals

SPECIAL SUSPENDED CYMBALS

There are many different types of suspended cymbals, most of which developed from drumset traditions. The most common are ride, crash, splash, sizzle, and china cymbals.

A *ride cymbal* (see figure 7.2) is large (17 to 24 inches, 43–61 cm) with a very bright and dry sound. A suspended crash cymbal (not to be confused with a pair of crash cymbals) is usually a bit smaller (12 to 18 inches, 30–46 cm) and has a full spectrum of sound with a relatively short ring time. In a non-drumset context, the notation "crash cymbals" will always indicate a pair of crash cymbals; drumset crash cymbals may also be called "small suspended cymbals."

The *splash cymbal* is the smallest cymbal (6 to 12 inches, 15–30 cm), is very bright, and has a very short ring time. A *sizzle cymbal* is usually about the size of a ride cymbal. It is perforated with holes into which small metal rivets are placed; when the cymbal is struck, the rivets sizzle. (See Henri Dutilleux's *Cello Concerto*, George Crumb's *Quest,* and Ryan Streber's *Cold Pastoral.*) The same effect can be achieved by taping a coin or placing a thin metal chain on a normal cymbal. (See the Preparations section at the end of this chapter.)

China cymbals (figure 7.3) come in a wide range of sizes (8 to 24 inches, 20–61 cm). They have a unique shape and a "trashy" sound with a short ring time. (See Olivier Messiaen's *Turangalîla-Symphonie*, John Cage's *Third Construction,* and Judd Greenstein's *We Shall Be Turned.*) In traditional Chinese music, these cymbals are often used in pairs and struck together, like crash cymbals.

Hi-Hat

🔊 Video 7.a—Cymbals

The hi-hat (figure 7.4) is a pedal mechanism with two cymbals—one suspended upside down and another above it suspended right side up. When the foot pedal is

Figure 7.3
China cymbal

Figure 7.4
Hi-hat

Photo courtesy of
Zildjian Cymbals

depressed, the cymbals are brought together. (See John Adams's *Chamber Symphony,*
Luciano Berio's *Laborintus II,* and The Police's *Driven To Tears.*) Hi-hat cymbals are
rather thick and about 14 inches (35.5 cm) in diameter; however, any type of cymbal
can be put onto a hi-hat stand.

When the pedal is depressed and released, the hi-hat cymbals crash together like
crash cymbals. When the pedal is depressed and not released, the cymbals produce
a very short "chick" (or "sock") sound, and then muffle each other. Similarly, a sustained or short sound can be produced when the cymbals are struck with a beater
while the pedal is either up or down (open or closed, respectively).

The beauty of this instrument lies in the infinite variety of articulation possible
by means of pedal manipulation from very tightly closed to very open. The hi-hat
is unique among percussion instruments in this regard, making it one of the more
expressive of all indeterminately pitched instruments. Generally, an "open" hi-hat

(pedal up) is not completely open but, rather, slightly open so that the cymbals still touch and sizzle against each other. When completely open, the top hi-hat cymbal functions as a suspended cymbal.

A hi-hat's normal resting position is open. To keep it closed, the player must hold the pedal down with a foot. The pedal can be disengaged so the hi-hat remains closed; this facilitates use of the closed hi-hat in a setup where the player's feet may be otherwise occupied. It takes a second or two, with a free hand, for the player to reengage the pedal.

One staff line with open (○) and closed (+) symbols can be used for hi-hat notation (figure 7.5). A slightly open symbol (ø) can be used as a separate sound from the completely open sound; otherwise, the open symbol (○) indicates a slightly open sound. A dotted line between the open and closed symbols indicates a gradual change from one to the other.

A two-line staff can be used to notate complicated hi-hat parts—one line for the hand and one for the foot. Both lines use the open (○) and closed (+) symbols.

Hand Crash Cymbals

🌀 Video 7.b—Crash Cymbals

Hand crash cymbals (or just *crash cymbals*; (figure 7.6) come in many different sizes and thicknesses. (See Mahler's and Shostakovich's symphonies and Tchaikovsky's *Romeo and Juliet* overture.) An undampened *fortissimo* crash will reach *piano* in up to four seconds. A *piano* crash will be inaudible after about a second and a half. The ring of the cymbals is controlled with muffling, which is executed by bringing the edges of the cymbals into the player's torso.

Figure 7.6 Hand crash cymbals

Photo courtesy of Zildjian Cymbals

Crash cymbals are heavy and awkward instruments that require a lot of energy to play. The composer should avoid especially fast articulations, rapid muffling, and very quick changes from loud to soft dynamics.

Crash cymbals will make noise if they are not put down carefully, so enough time (about two or three seconds) must be allotted for the performer to pick up or put down these instruments. The cymbals must be held to allow them to ring; therefore, with long notes, the composer must take into account the ring time of the cymbals before giving the performer time to put them down.

Just as the length of the cymbal resonance can be controlled, so too can the length of the attack. By letting the cymbals sizzle against each other for a split second after the crash, the player can elongate the attack. By pulling the cymbals apart immediately after the crash, he or she can make the attack more articulate. These articulations are not usually notated.

A scrape with the edge of one cymbal against the inside face of the other might be appropriate for soft long notes. This creates a long swish that is not very loud. Composers need to allow a second or two for the player to silently get the cymbals into position for a crash cymbal scrape.

Crash cymbal rolls are rarely used. Where they are notated in works by Bartók, Mahler, and Copland, some percussionists argue that the composer in each case was actually indicating a suspended cymbal roll. Regardless, this type of roll is now part of percussion playing. A loud crash cymbal roll can be achieved by rapidly striking the cymbals together, but this is difficult to execute consistently and can quickly tire the player. For softer crash cymbal rolls, the player holds the cymbals together and moves them against each other in a circular motion. Again, consistency is difficult. A far more effective crash cymbal roll requires two people: one player holds the cymbals together parallel to the floor while the other rolls on them with mallets, as for a suspended cymbal. For this technique, some time is needed to get the cymbals into position. A two-person crash cymbal roll should be clearly described in the score.

Crash cymbals can be mounted on a hi-hat stand. This allows soft crashes to be executed with just one hand or foot, without any pickup/put-down time needed. Also, a hi-hat stand can make the aforementioned crash cymbal roll possible to execute with just one person. Loud crashes are not possible on a hi-hat stand.

Bass Drum/Cymbal Attachment

Bass drum and crash cymbals can be played by one player with a bass drum/cymbal attachment. The attachment mounts one cymbal to the bass drum so it can be crashed by another cymbal. The player operates the cymbal with one hand and the bass drum mallet with the other. The bass drum must be upright, not flat on its side. Playing the cymbals in this manner is awkward, and fine control over dynamics and muffling is sacrificed. (See Stravinsky's *Petrouchka*, Mahler's Symphony Nos. 1 and 3, and Rossini's overtures.)

A cymbal can also be mounted face up on a cymbal stand to be used in the same manner.

Gongs

 Video 7.c—Gongs

Gong is a general term (like *drum*) that refers to a group of instruments. It is not wise to use this term in writing without some additional qualification (e.g., nipple gong or Chinese opera gong). Although the tam-tam is colloquially referred to simply as "gong," it should not be so in a score.

Tam-Tam

 Video 7.c—Gongs

Like cymbals, tam-tams (also called *chau gongs*; figure 7.7) produce a blossoming pitch spectrum rather than a specific pitch. They are usually rather large but come in many sizes, from 8 to 50 inches (20–127 cm). As for ring time, a *fortissimo* tam-tam note reaches *piano* after about nine seconds, and a *piano* note reaches *pppp* after five seconds. Only one hand with one mallet is needed to roll on a large tam-tam because of its extended ring time. (See Mahler's and Shostakovich's symphonies.)

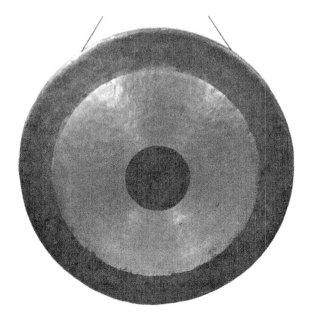

Figure 7.7
Tam-tam

A *wind gong* is a very thin tam-tam with a dark sound, quick response, and short decay.

Nipple Gong

🔊 Video 7.c—Gongs

Nipple gongs (also called *Thai gongs* or *Javanese gongs*) are tuned to specific pitches (figure 7.8). They may be used with (see Per Nørgård's *I Ching*) or without (see Messiaen's *Et Expecto Resurrectionem Mortuorum*) pitch specification. A full chromatic set of gongs is rare—three octaves requires 37 gongs, the largest of which is over 30 inches (76 cm) in diameter—so the composer should check with the group for whom he or she is writing to see what pitches are available. It may be possible to rent pitches that are not immediately available. Upper-range gongs are more commonly available than the largest gongs because these large instruments are expensive; a single pitch in the lowest octave costs thousands of dollars.

Figure 7.8
Nipple gong

Pitches within the range shown in figure 7.9 may be available. Nipple gongs are large, and many of these instruments are awkward to set up and difficult to play. Logistically, use of up to five gongs is reasonable.

Figure 7.9
Nipple gong range

The most clear fundamental pitch of a large nipple gong is achieved with a gong or bass drum beater striking directly on the nipple. With a smaller beater, such as a marimba mallet, harmonics above the fundamental may be more prominent; smaller beaters do, however, work well for smaller gongs. The area around the nipple has a higher and less clear pitch.

Gongs work best for slow passages because they swing back and forth after they are struck. Fast passages can become nearly impossible to execute effectively because of all the moving targets.

Chinese Opera Gong

◗ Video 7.c—Gongs

Chinese opera gongs (also called *Peking opera gongs, Chinese fight gongs,* or *gliss gongs*; figure 7.10) are fairly small (8 to 12 inches, 20–31cm) and have a short ring time and a pitch bend. Smaller gongs have an upward pitch bend while larger gongs gliss downward. Pitch bend direction may be specified. (See Jean Piché's *Steal the Thunder*, Bright Sheng's *H'un [Lacerations]*, and Chen Yi's *Qi*.)

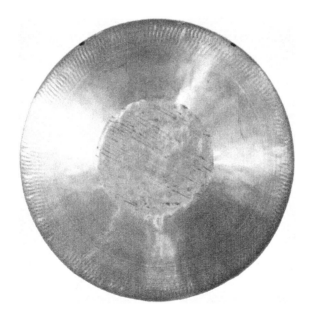

Figure 7.10
Chinese
Opera gong

Other Gongs

There are many other types of gongs from Asian traditions; those just described are the types that have become standard in Western composition. If the composer would like to use other gong sounds, he or she may give the performer a free choice of gong type. This way, the percussionist can use unusual gongs that are available to him or her, without hindering future performances of the work for which those gong types might not be available.

Gong Stands and Racks

There are a variety of ways to suspend gongs. Most stands hold a single gong a few inches off the floor; large tam-tams are almost always mounted on these stands. Other stands with height adjustments can hold a gong three to six feet off the ground; these are usually best for smaller instruments. Large racks can hold several gongs at one time. Small gongs can even be placed on a boom cymbal stand (a cymbal stand with a boom arm).

Gongs can also be laid down on a trap table. The table slightly mutes the gong, which can help clarify fast rhythmic passages. Placing a Chinese opera gong on a table can be effective; the gong rings just long enough for its glissando to sound, which creates an almost comical effect. Laying nipple gongs on a table is the best option when they are used without pitch specification. (See Henry Cowell's *Set of Five* and John Cage's *Credo in US*.)

Triangle

🔊 Video 7.d—Triangle, Finger Cymbals

The triangle (figure 7.11) is usually held in one hand and played with the other; any necessary dampening is executed by the fingers of the hand holding the instrument. The triangle can also be hung from a music stand; this allows both hands to be free but makes dampening slightly more difficult. (See Liszt's *First Piano Concerto*, Bartók's *Miraculous Mandarin*, and Bizet's *Carmen*.)

Figure 7.11
Triangle

A triangle roll is executed by moving the triangle beater back and forth between two sides in one of the three corners. Fast rhythms can be executed in this manner or with two beaters. If two beaters are used, the triangle must be hung from a stand.

A triangle can be muted to varying degrees to control note length and articulation. Fast notes tend to wash together, so slight muting is often required for clarity.

The use of muting is usually decided by the performer but can be prescribed by the composer. (See Note Length, Articulation, and Phrasing in chapter 3.)

Triangles come in a variety of sizes. Larger triangles sound fuller, louder, and produce a wider spectrum of pitches, while smaller triangles sound lighter, softer, and produce predominantly the uppermost partials. Like cymbals, triangles produce a pitch spectrum rather than a specific pitch; therefore, using more than four triangles graduated in pitch is a bit unreasonable. When multiple triangles are to be played by one player, they are always hung from a stand. (See Joseph Schwantner's *Percussion Concerto.*)

A large triangle can be bowed with a bass or cello bow. This technique cannot be executed quickly, and so a generous amount of time should be given for the player to get the bow into position and make the instrument sound.

Triangle vibrato can be achieved by shaking the instrument back and forth after it has been struck. This can only be done when the triangle is held—not when it is mounted. This effect is very subtle.

A *ranch triangle* is much larger and thicker than normal triangles and rings only a short time. These instruments originated as a means to call the family in for dinner. (See Lou Harrison's *Symphony No. 2 "Elegiac."*)

Finger Cymbals

🔊 Video 7.d—Triangle, Finger Cymbals

Finger cymbals (figure 7.12) are usually used for single notes, but quicker rhythms are possible. These instruments are played by striking the edges of the two cymbals together—not like crash cymbals by which the cymbals are struck together on their flat surfaces. Finger cymbals are not very loud but they have a lot of cutting power owing to their high pitch. They can also be hung from a stand and struck with a plastic mallet, brass mallet, or a triangle beater. (See Leonard Bernstein's *West Side Story,* Jacob Druckman's *Animus II,* and Luciano Berio's *Circles.*)

Figure 7.12
Finger cymbals

The two cymbals in a pair are often matched to be the same pitch, but this is not always the case. Crotales are a not too distant relative of finger cymbals, so if pitches are specified for finger cymbals, crotales will likely be used.

Two pairs of finger cymbals are sometimes used as metal castanets. (See Castanets in chapter 8.)

Cowbells and Almglocken

🔊 Video 7.e—Cowbells, Almglocken, Temple Bowls, Mixing Bowls

Cowbells (figure 7.13a) come in many sizes. They can be mounted by clamping them to a stand or placing them on a towel; the latter method will dampen the instruments. (See John Adams's *Chamber Symphony,* Leonard Bernstein's *West Side Story,* and John Cage's *Third Construction.*)

Figure 7.13
(a) cowbell and
(b) almglocken

Photo of cowbell
courtesy of Latin
Percussion

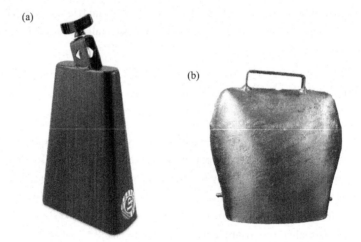

(a)

(b)

Two different beating spots on the cowbell can be used: the edge closer to the opening (the lip) and further back toward the closed end (the crown). The crown beating spot is slightly brighter and drier. These beating spots can be notated with a "o" for the lip and "+" for the crown. This notation should be explained at the top of the score and percussion part.

If necessary, rolls can be executed with one hand by moving the stick or mallet rapidly up and down inside the cowbell. This technique is a bit awkward, and very loud dynamics are not possible.

Almglocken (figure 7.13b) means "cow bells" in German. This term (also *Swiss cowbells*) is used to denote European-style cowbells that are tuned in chromatic sets (see Messiaen's *Et Expecto Resurrectionem Mortuorum*). As with tuned gongs, specific pitches are not always readily available, and almglocken may need to be rented. Almglocken in the upper range are more commonly available than the largest almglocken. American cowbells have pitch but are less resonant than almglocken, so the pitch dies away quickly. If specific pitches are requested for cowbells, almglocken will likely be used.

Almglocken within the range shown in figure 7.14 may be available.

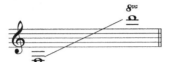

Figure 7.14
Almglocken range

"Cowbells" (*Herdenglocken*), as used in Gustav Mahler's Symphony No. 6 and Richard Strauss's *Alpine Symphony*, are not hit rhythmically but, rather, knocked back and forth randomly to evoke the sounds of cows grazing in a field. These cowbells have a metal clapper hanging inside, so when they are suspended and set into motion, the clapper swings back and forth and knocks into the sides of the bell; this is how a cowbell would operate around the neck of a cow. These cowbells are usually used in sets of about a dozen randomly pitched bells. Only starting and stopping points need be notated, not specific rhythms. These instruments are not especially common, but percussionists can effectively simulate this ambient cowbell texture with mallets on any set of cowbells.

Agogo bells are generally smaller than cowbells. They come in pairs, with the bells attached to each other by a curved metal rod; usually only one pair is used at a time. They can be held, clamped to a stand, or placed on a towel. Agogo bells can be used as the top pitches of a set of regular cowbells. (See Tan Dun's *Concerto for Water Percussion* and Tania Leon's *A La Par.*)

Temple Bowls and Mixing Bowls

🕉 Video 7.e—Cowbells, Almglocken, Temple Bowls, Mixing Bowls

Temple bowls (also called *prayer bowls, temple bells, bowl gongs, singing bowls, meditation bowls, cup gongs,* or *rin;* figure 7.15) are resonant pitched metal bowls. Although the pitch is quite clear, temple bowls are most often used without pitch specification. These instruments are usually sold by size rather than by pitch, so finding a specifically pitched bowl may require much trial and error. For this reason, it may be best for the composer to not specify the pitch. Temple bowls are usually used in groups of up to five; using more is possible but may be unreasonable—one, two, or three is the most common arrangement. (See George Crumb's *Ancient Voices of Children* and *Music for a Summer Evening,* and John Cage's *First Construction.*)

Temple bowls are most often struck on the edge or side, but they can also be rubbed along the edge with a wooden stick or hard rubber mallet. By striking the bowl to start it vibrating and then rubbing the wooden stick around the bowl's lip, a sustained tone can be achieved.

Figure 7.15
Temple bowls

A metal mixing bowl (standard kitchen variety) can be struck on its edge or side to produce a ringing pure tone like that of a temple bowl, but with lower pitch and shorter ring time. Mixing bowls can also be filled with beads (or ball bearings, marbles, etc.) and stirred in a circular motion to slide the beads around the walls of the bowl. This produces a sustained swishing sound with variable dynamics. Stirred beads can get only so loud before they start flying out of the bowl. Mixing bowls can be flipped over and struck on the bottom. This produces a sound similar to an opera gong. Some bowls with thinner metal may produce an upward pitch bend.

Brake Drums, Metal Pipes, Anvils, and Bell Plates

◑ Video 7.f—Brake Drums, Metal Pipes, Anvils, Bell Plates

Junk yards usually carry a large selection of brake drums and metal pipes (figure 7.16). Brake drums are very loud. Metal pipes are far less loud.

Figure 7.16
Brake drum
and metal pipes

These instruments are almost always used without specified pitches, even though brake drums and especially metal pipes will tend to have a single identifiable pitch (see The Problem of Pitch in chapter 1). (See Elliott Carter's *What Next?,* Christopher Rouse's *Ogoun Badagris,* and Lou Harrison's *Song of Queztecoatl* and *Canticle No. 1.*)

Some recent works make use of a two-octave set of tuned metal pipes, from about A4 to B6. Construction of such a set of pipes is very time-consuming. (See Paul Lansky's *Threads* and Adam Silverman's *Naked and on Fire.*)

Real anvils (like those used by blacksmiths and cartoon characters) are very rare in instrument collections and are commonly and successfully replaced with instruments like square metal pipes (figure 7.17a), bell plates (figure 7.17b), railroad tracks, barbell weight plates, or even brake drums.

(b)

(a)

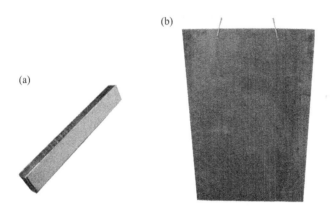

Figure 7.17
(a) anvil
(b) bell plate

Bell plates are thick sheets of metal that can come in any number of sizes, from small hand-sized plates to large planks four feet (123 cm) tall. These instruments are sometimes requested with pitch specification. As for nipple gongs and almglocken, only a small number of bell plate pitches may be available—chromatic sets do exist but are very rare.

Thundersheet

🔊 Video 7.g—Thundersheet, Junk Metal, Tin Cans, Pots and Pans, Ribbon Crasher

A thundersheet is a large, thin sheet of metal. It is most often shaken for long notes with sweeping or sporadic dynamics. It is unusual but possible to articulate rhythms on a thundersheet by striking it with sticks or mallets. (See John Cage's *First Construction* and George Crumb's *Music for a Summer Evening.*)

Junk Metal, Tin Cans, and Pots and Pans

◐ Video 7.g—Thundersheet, Junk Metal, Tin Cans, Pots and Pans, Ribbon Crasher

Just about any piece of metal—garbage cans, garbage can lids, hub caps, baking sheets, metal shelving, bicycle parts, shopping carts, and so on—can potentially be used in a percussion piece. When "junk metal" is requested, percussionists tend to choose instruments that have an unfocused pitch and a short ring time. Metal that is thin and not very dense (like that used for a metal garbage can) sounds "splatty." Denser, higher quality metals resonate longer and with a clearer pitch. Specification of pitch clarity and length of resonance may be appropriate when requesting found metal objects.

Tin cans are a staple of early percussion ensemble works, especially those of John Cage. These instruments are easy to acquire, as most restaurants and cafeterias discard several each day. Cans come in a wide variety of sizes, from tiny tuna cans to large trash cans. These instruments are struck on their bottoms and have a "splatty" quality to their sound. (See John Cage's *Third Construction*.)

Pots and pans are also easy to acquire—percussionists often have options both in their instrument collections and in their kitchens. A standard cooking pot or sauté pan struck on the bottom has a more focused clear tone than tin cans. Some pans made of thin metal have a slight pitch bend. Most baking pans sound similar to tin cans.

Ribbon Crasher

◐ Video 7.g—Thundersheet, Junk Metal, Tin Cans, Pots and Pans, Ribbon Crasher

A ribbon crasher (figure 7.18) is pile of four or five metal strips mounted loosely to a pair of metal posts. When struck, the metal strips briefly bounce and rattle against one another. The sound, as the name suggests, is like a dull "crash." This instrument frequently is used in music that calls for "junk" percussion.

Figure 7.18
Ribbon crasher

Photo courtesy
of RhythmTech
Percussion

Spring Coil

🔊 Video 7.h—Spring Coil, Ship Bells, Handbells

A spring coil (figure 7.19) is a large metal spring—the kind used for shock absorption on trucks and off-road vehicles. It can be suspended and struck or scraped with a large triangle beater, plastic mallet, or brass mallet. The sound is "twangy," like a low-pitched triangle. (See Jacob Druckman's *Animus II* and Luciano Berio's *Folks Songs*.)

Figure 7.19
Spring coil

Church Bells

🔊 Video 7.h—Spring Coil, Ship Bells, Handbells

Church bells are also called *ship bells* or *Berlioz bells*. Since Berlioz's *Symphonie Fantastique* is so frequently performed, some orchestras and conservatories own a pair of large church bells that are tuned C4 (middle C) and G3 or C3 and G2 for the last movement. These bells are played with chime hammers. Other pitches are available on rare occasion (a low E♭ for *Pictures at An Exhibition*, low E for *Also Sprach Zarathustra*, or a low F and B♭ for *Tosca* and *La Bohème*, for example). Chimes and/or bell plates commonly substitute if real bells are not available.

Hand Bells

🔊 Video 7.h—Spring Coil, Ship Bells, Handbells

Tuned hand bells (or *church hand bells*) are tuned to specific pitches and most commonly found in churches that have a hand bell choir. These instruments are rarely found in percussion instrument collections, however. Hand bells are played by bouncing a clapper, mounted inside the bell, against the inside of the bell. One player can operate up to four small bells (two in each hand) or two larger bells (one in each hand), but can quickly drop and pickup different pitches. The clapper often has two striking surfaces—one soft and one hard. The bell can be struck against a padded surface for a short articulation. Bells may also be suspended and played with mallets.

Smaller hand bells without pitch specification (like tea bells or dinner bells) are common. They are used for tremolos rather than specific rhythms. There are many different kinds: the regular tea or dinner bell (see David Lang's *Table of Contents* and Joan Tower's *Percussion Quartet*) or other exotic bells like elephant bells (see Lou Harrison's *Canticle No. 3*).

Steel Drums

🔊 Video 7.i—Steel Drums

Steel drums (or *steel pans*) are made out of large oil barrels. Lead pans (that is, "lead" as in leader—not the metal) (figure 7.20a) and double second pans (figure 7.20b) are most common. Lead pans are also called *tenor pans*.

The ranges are as shown in figure 7.21: (a) for lead pan and (b) for double second pans. These ranges are augmented by a whole step either up or down (but not both).

Figure 7.20
Steel drums:
(a) lead pan and
(b) double seconds
Photos courtesy of
Panyard

(a)   (b)

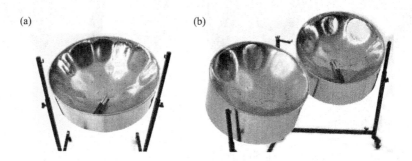

Slight variations in range, configuration, and sound quality can be expected from drum to drum, as a standard system is not yet widely used. These ranges, however, can be safely assumed.

Other types of pans exist, such as double tenor pans, double guitar pans, triple cello pans, and bass pans, with ranges that reach as far down as A1 (the A three ledger

Figure 7.21
Steel drum ranges

lines below the bass clef staff). Bass pans are very large (each made from an entire oil barrel) and have only two to four pitches each. The composer should work with the group for whom the piece is written to learn the ranges, configurations, and sound qualities of the specific instruments they may have available.

Steel drums are instruments that most percussionists do not practice on a regular or even occasional basis. Unlike all other determinately pitched mallet instruments, pitches are not laid out like a keyboard (see figure 7.22), and involved passagework can be a considerable challenge for a performer unfamiliar with the instrument.

Expert players are becoming more numerous, however, as steel drum bands become increasingly common at universities across the United States. Slow passages, isolated notes, or ostinati are easily learned and executed by any percussionist (see Pierre Boulez's *Sur Incises*), but the composer can ask much more of an experienced player (see Steven Mackey's *It Is Time*). The composer is encouraged to work with the performers involved to take advantage of their particular skills.

Steel drums should always be played with special steel drum mallets, which are very lightweight soft rubber mallets. If regular marimba or vibraphone mallets are used, they will tend to bang the instrument out of tune. For this reason, the composer should use caution when writing for steel drums in setups and allow time for the performer to switch to steel drum mallets. Brushes or chopsticks may be used for special effects.

Steel drums may be played with a set of four steel drum mallets, but with less dexterity than four-mallet keyboard playing. For example, two mallets in one hand cannot reach across a pair of drums, so a four-note chord must require four mallets on one drum, or two on one and two on the other (see figure 7.22).

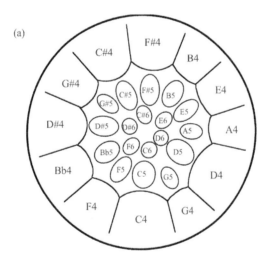

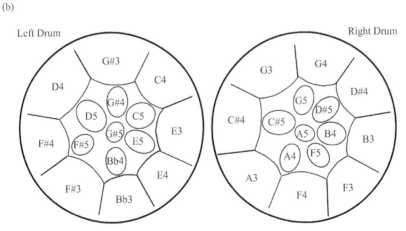

Figure 7.22
Layout of
(a) lead pan
and (b) double
second pans

Tambourines

🔊 Video 6.h—Tambourines, from the previous chapter

The tambourine (figure 7.23) is a type of frame drum to which many tiny cymbals, called "jingles," are affixed. Tambourines have been used for centuries by many cultures around the world. As a result, there are many different types of tambourines and many different playing styles.

Figure 7.23
(a) orchestral tambourine and (b) headless rock tambourine

Photos courtesy of Grover Pro Percussion and Latin Percussion

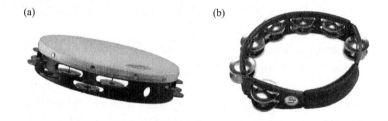

(a)   (b)

With traditional orchestral tambourines (figure 7.23a), the sound of the drumhead is secondary; rather, it is the sound of the jingles that is most important. Rock-style tambourines are completely without heads (figure 7.23b). Only with ethnic tambourines such as the Brazilian pandeiro, the Persian riq, and the Indian kanjira is the drum sound a prominent element of the playing style.

See the complete entry for tambourines in chapter 6.

Sleighbells

🔊 Video 7.j—Sleighbells, Metal Wind Chimes, Mark Tree, Bell Tree, Flexatone

The player can articulate rhythms on the sleighbells (figure 7.24) by holding them down (with the handle facing up) and striking the top of the handle with a fist. The sleighbells can also be shaken back and forth in a steady rhythm, like a shaker. Rhythms faster than eighth notes at ♩=144 are indistinguishable, however. Sleighbells can also be sustained by shaking them, notated with a tremolo. The composer should allot enough time for the percussionist to pick up the sleighbells without creating any unwanted jingling, although players can hang or mount sleighbells, if necessary. (See Leroy Anderson's *Sleigh Ride*, Gustav Mahler's Symphony No. 4, Aaron Copland's *Billy the Kid*, and Edgard Varèse's *Ionisation*.)

Metal Wind Chimes, Mark Tree, and Bell Tree

🔊 Video 7.j—Sleighbells, Metal Wind Chimes, Mark Tree, Bell Tree, Flexatone

Metal wind chimes (figure 7.25) are sets of four to twelve metal tubes that hang from a wooden board. When disturbed by the wind or by a performer's hand, the

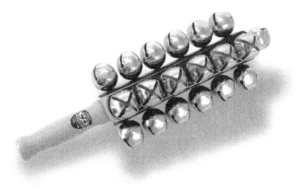

Figure 7.24
Sleighbells
Photo courtesy of
Latin Percussion

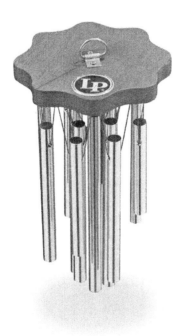

Figure 7.25
Metal wind chimes
Photo courtesy of
Latin Percussion

tubes collide with one another or with a central hanging wooden beater to create an ambient tinkling. The reader may be most familiar with the versions of this instrument that hang from porches, backyard trees, and store front doors.

Wind chimes are usually made of metal, but are also made of bamboo, glass, or shells. A notation of "wind chimes" usually is interpreted as metal wind chimes, but a "metal" specification is recommended. (The composer should be careful not to write "chimes" if wind chimes are desired; "chimes" indicates tubular bells.)

Metal wind chimes are usually rather high pitched (C5 and above), but deeper chimes are sometimes available. (See Wind Chimes in chapter 9 for complete details.)

The mark tree (also called *bar* chimes; figure 7.26) is commonly mistaken for wind chimes. It is a row of small metal chimes organized in pitch from high to low. A glissando up or down is produced by running a finger or beater through the chimes.

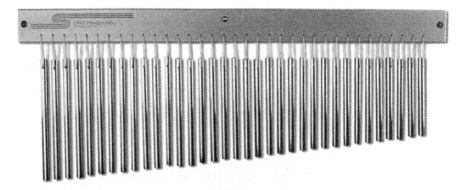

Figure 7.26
Mark tree

Photo courtesy
of Grover Pro
Percussion

Mark trees continue swinging back and forth after they are struck and are usually left to exhaust themselves naturally (which takes about six seconds). Dampening a mark tree requires a couple seconds to execute effectively; some mark trees have a muffle bar with which the performer can muffle more quickly. Glissando direction and duration (no longer than three seconds) should be indicated (figure 7.27). (See Per Nørgård's *I Ching,* John Zorn's *For Your Eyes Only,* and Frank Zappa's *Dog Breath Variations/Uncle Meat.*)

Figure 7.27
Mark tree notation

An isolated register of a mark tree can be played like a set of wind chimes and used in place of that instrument. Random individual notes of a mark tree may be struck with a triangle beater or plastic mallet.

Mark trees and wind chimes are sensitive and can be set into motion with just a light brush of a hand, body, or stick. For this reason, accidental mark tree/wind chime solos can occur during rehearsals and performances. This is, of course, the performer's problem, but the composer should be aware of its possibility, especially in setups involving these instruments.

The bell tree (figure 7.28) is a series of cup bells mounted on a stand and organized (inexactly) from high to low. It is similar to the mark tree, but only sounds when struck (with a glock mallet, xylo mallet, or triangle beater)—there are no swinging parts.

Figure 7.28
Bell tree

Photo courtesy of
Latin Percussion

Glissandi, as well as random or relatively pitched single notes, can be played on a bell tree. Glissando direction and duration should be notated. If just a quick glissando is needed, the composer should indicate whether it goes to or starts on the beat (figure 7.29). (See Per Nørgård's *I Ching* and Steely Dan's *Babylon Sisters* and *Gaucho*.)

Bell Tree

sfz   *mp*   *p*

Figure 7.29
Bell tree notation

The bells of a bell tree are not exactly arranged in order of pitch—they are slightly mixed up. The microtonal scale stumbles upward and falls back down every couple of notes. In the context of a glissando, this mixed-up arrangement is not noticeable; it simply makes the glissando sound fuller.

Flexatone

🔊 Video 7.j—Sleighbells, Metal Wind Chimes, Mark Tree, Bell Tree, Flexatone

The flexatone (figure 7.30) is inspired by, but only loosely resembles, the musical saw. It is a small, thin piece of metal on which two mallets are mounted. It is held so the piece of metal can be bent to alter its pitch. When shaken, the mounted mallets bounce back and forth to create a tremolo. Specific pitches are difficult but possible; glissandi without specific pitch are easily executed. Flexatones can also be bowed for a sound more similar to that of a musical saw. Flexatone is played with one hand; bowing requires two. (See Steven Hartke's *Meanwhile*, Steve Mackey's *It Is Time,* and Schoenberg's *Variations*.) Flexatones are available in two sizes (large and small) with the ranges shown in figure 7.31.

Figure 7.30
Flexatone
Photo courtesy of
Latin Percussion

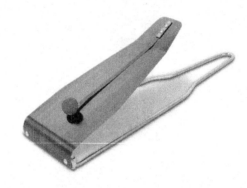

Figure 7.31
Flexatone ranges

Extended Techniques

🔊 Video 7.k—Extended Techniques

Scrape

Cymbals and gongs can be scraped with a coin or triangle beater. The back of a keyboard mallet can work on cymbals, but not very well; a fingernail works only at extremely soft dynamics. To notate a scrape, the composer simply writes "scrape" over the note. The length of the note indicates the length of the scrape, not the length of the sustain. A quick scrape with a crescendo is easiest and most effective, but longer scrapes are possible. It is assumed that the scrape is left to ring unless otherwise indicated. (See the second movement of Joseph Schwantner's *Percussion Concerto* and Ryan Streber's *Cold Pastoral.*)

A scrape is sometimes called a cymbal or tam-tam glissando because there is a glissando of overtones. A quick stroke with a crescendo results in a glissando upward. (See Sacrificial Dance in Stravinsky's *Rite of Spring.*)

Cymbals and gongs are also capable of a "scream" (or *screech*). A scream is a technique whereby a stick is held perpendicular to the cymbal or gong and the tip or butt is dragged across the instrument's face. This produces a sound similar to that achieved by bowing the instrument, but it is even more shrill and abrasive.

Water

All resonant metal instruments, like gongs, crotales, and triangles, can be lowered into a tub of water to bend the pitch downward. This also dampens the instrument. The quiet sound of splashing water will surely accompany the dipping and retrieving of the instrument into and from the water. (See John Cage's *First Construction,* Tan Dun's *Concerto for Water Percussion,* Christopher Rouse's *Cello Concerto,* and the second movement of Joseph Schwantner's *Percussion Concerto.*)

The composer should understand that, logistically, the use of water is often a problem. Most concert halls prefer to not have water on stage. Tarps or towels can be laid down under and around the large tub of water that might be required for these effects. Also, the composer needs to allow ample time for the player to pick up and put down the instrument with minimal drippage and splashing sound.

Preparations

A sizzle effect can be created by the player's attaching a coin, paper clip, or thin metal chain to a resonant metal instrument. This is similar to the traditional sizzle cymbal. (See Cymbals earlier in this chapter.) A manual sizzle can be achieved by holding a triangle beater or coin against the instrument; in this case, the sizzle can be added and taken away as needed while the instrument is resonating.

CHAPTER EIGHT

Wood

Instruments covered in this chapter are woodblocks, templeblocks, log drums, wood planks, wood drums, wooden boxes, cajón, Mahler hammer, claves, castanets, rute, guiro, slapstick, ratchet, and bamboo wind chimes.

Woodblocks, Templeblocks, and Log Drum

🔊 Video 8.a—Woodblocks, Templeblocks, Log Drum

Woodblocks (figure 8.1) are bright and high-pitched. They come in a variety of sizes and can be used one at a time or in groups (reasonably, up to six). Very small woodblocks are called *piccolo woodblocks.* (See Aaron Copland's Symphony No. 3, Sergei Prokofiev's Symphony No. 5, and Christopher Rouse's *Ku-Ka Ilimoku.*)

Figure 8.1
Woodblock

Photo courtesy
of Ron Vaughn
Percussion

Templeblocks (also called *Chinese blocks* or *dragon's mouths*; figure 8.2) are slightly darker in timbre than woodblocks. They most often come in sets of five (sets of six are sometimes available) and are suspended from a stand. (See Michael Torke's *Green,* William Kraft's *Concerto for Timpani,* Christopher Rouse's *Violoncello Concerto,* and Jacob Druckman's *Windows.*)

The lowest templeblocks in a set are generally lower pitched than most woodblocks, but the highest of a set are often in a comparable register. When combining woodblocks and templeblocks, or for a set of wood sounds larger than five, the composer may specify a mix of templeblocks and woodblocks, at the performer's

Figure 8.2
Templeblocks

Photo courtesy
of Black Swamp
Percussion

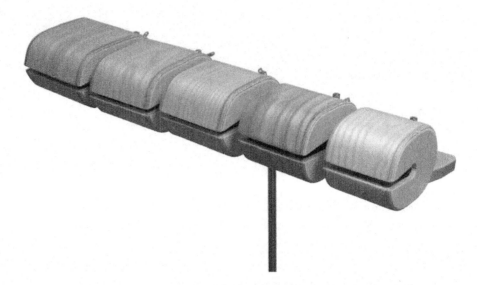

discretion. For example, the notation could be "templeblocks and woodblocks, seven graduated pitches." These instruments are more or less interchangeable.

Many templeblock sets are tuned to a pentatonic scale. Of course, more pitch variety is possible with individually chosen woodblocks or combinations of templeblocks and woodblocks. Plastic versions of woodblocks and templeblocks are also common. They are not as beautiful sounding, but can be struck with harder mallets at louder dynamics without breaking.

Woodblocks and *templeblocks* as names for the instruments may be written as one or two words (e.g., *woodblocks* or *wood blocks, templeblocks* or *temple blocks*). Either is clearly understood and acceptable.

Log drums (also called *slit drums*; figure 8.3) are pitched much lower than woodblocks or templeblocks and have a warm, mellow sound. A log drum usually has two pitches (high and low); multiple log drums can be used together for more pitches. Log drums are especially fragile instruments and should not be played too loud or with too hard a beater. (See Rouse's *Ku-Ka Ilimoku,* Crumb's *Idyll for the Misbegotten,* and Cage's *Third Construction.*)

Log drums with multiple pitches are sometimes available. These are often called *tong drums.* Such instruments are more fragile and cannot be played as loud or with as hard a beater as their two-pitch counterparts, so care must be taken when using these drums in a setup with other instruments.

Wooden Planks

🕬 Video 8.b—Wooden Planks, Wooden Boxes, Cajón, Mahler Hammer

Any piece of wood can be used in place of the more refined sounds of woodblocks or log drums. For instance, a composer may specify type of wood (see "walnut planks" in David Lang's *The So-Called Laws of Nature*), or simply describe the

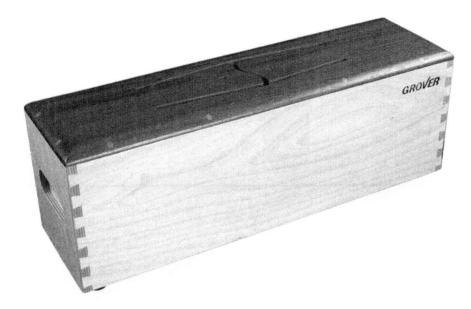

Figure 8.3
Log drum
Photo courtesy
of Grover Pro
Percussion

desired color, register, or degree of resonance. A *simantra*, a large semi-resonant wooden plank, was a traditional instrument used in Byzantine church music that was adapted to concert music by Iannis Xenakis in *Persephassa*. A simantra can also be made of metal, but this instrument would more commonly then be called a "metal pipe" or "anvil." (See Iannis Xenakis's *Persephassa*, Michael Gordon's *Timber*, and James Wood's *Rogosanti*.)

Wood Drums, Wooden Boxes, Cajón, and Mahler Hammer

◗ Video 8.b—Wooden Planks, Wooden Boxes, Cajón, Mahler Hammer

A "wood drum" can be one of a few different similar instruments: a plywood box with one side open, a tom-tom with a circular piece of wood in place of the normal drum head, or a log drum. In cases of the plywood box or wood-headed drum, the sound is dry and bright, but amplified by the body of the box or drum shell. (See Roger Reynolds's *Watershed* and Edgard Varèse's *Déserts*.) Log drums are more resonant and clearer in pitch.

A cajón (pronounced *ka-HONE*; figure 8.4) is a Peruvian and Cuban instrument that is being more commonly used in the United States in popular music. It is a resonant wooden box that is sat upon or held between the legs and played like a hand drum. All hand drum techniques apply (see chapters 4 and 6). Some cajóns have wire snares that run along the back of the instrument's striking surface, adding a unique snap to the sound.

The two, arguably three, "hammer" strokes in Gustav Mahler's Symphony No. 6 have quite a powerful aural and visual effect. This instrument has been used in modern scores by various composers, most notably Christopher Rouse. It is, as Mahler

Figure 8.4 Cajón
Photo courtesy of
Latin Percussion

describes, "a short, powerful, but dull-sounding stroke of nonmetallic character." It is marked at *fortississimo*. Orchestras often use a large plywood box that is struck with a large wooden hammer. Owing to the size of the hammer, quick rhythms cannot be executed—loud isolated notes are most common. This instrument is referred to as a "Mahler hammer," as the "hammer, as used in Mahler Symphony No. 6," or simply as "hammer." (See Mahler's Symphony No. 6, Christopher Rouse's *Gorgon*, Wolfgang Rihm's *Tutuguri VI*, and Elliott Carter's *Tintinnabulation*.)

Claves

🔊 Video 8.c—Claves, Castanets, Rute

Claves (figure 8.5) are a traditional Cuban instrument and serve, in that music, as the rhythmic backbone and time keeper. They are held in the hands—one clave is used to strike while the other simply receives the blow and resonates. Since only one hand is used to produce the rhythm, claves can be played only so quickly.

Figure 8.5 Claves
Photo courtesy of
Latin Percussion

If necessary, a single clave can be mounted on a towel or foam rubber and played with xylophone mallets; this allows for passages that require two hands, but sound quality is sacrificed. (See Aaron Copland's *El Salon Mexico,* Christopher Rouse's *Violoncello Concerto,* John Zorn's *For Your Eyes Only,* Steve Reich's *Music for Pieces of Wood,* and John Cage's *Third Construction.*)

Castanets

🔊 Video 8.c—Claves, Castanets, Rute

The castanet sound is produced with the clapping of two cup-shaped pieces of wood against each other. Traditional castanets (held in the hand and played while dancing) are not generally used in concert music; the castanets used by percussionists are mounted to handles (figure 8.6) or to a stand.

Figure 8.6
Castanets

Photo courtesy
of Frank Epstein
Percussion

Castanets with handles are held and played by striking the player's knee. Mounted castanets (called *machine castanets*) are struck with the hands or mallets and some-times with other hand-held castanets for especially loud passages. Choice of castanet type should be decided by the performer. (See Prokofiev's Piano Concerto No. 3 and Violin Concerto No. 2, and Ravel's *Alborada del gracioso.*)

Rolls can be executed with both types of castanets. At loud dynamics, a double-stroke roll is possible with hand-held castanets whereby the clappers rebound back into each other after striking the knee. This is a fuller sounding roll and is not possible on machine castanets.

Hand-held castanets can technically be used as beaters on drums, but this will damage the castanets and is not recommended.

Two pairs of finger cymbals are sometimes used as *metal castanets.* One pair rests on a table while the other pair is held and used to strike the resting cymbals.

Rute

🔊 Video 8.c—Claves, Castanets, Rute

Rute (or *switch*; figure 8.7) is a bunch of wooden dowels or twigs tied together. Traditionally, the rute is rather large and struck on the shell of the bass drum to produce more of the sound of the rute than of the shell. (See Mahler's Symphonies Nos. 2 and 6.)

Figure 8.7 Rute

This instrument has now been adapted to about the size of a snare stick (figure 4.10) and can be used as an effect on drums, cymbals, and other instruments. The newer rute sticks were originally made for softer drumset playing (for low-volume ensembles and practice). Both rute types are common.

Guiro

🔊 Video 8.d—Guiro, Slapstick, Ratchet, Bamboo Wind Chimes

Guiro (or *gourd*; figure 8.8) is a tube-shaped instrument with a series of grooves along the body. Guiros come in many different sizes and are made of wood, bamboo, plastic, metal, or traditionally, a hollowed-out gourd.

Figure 8.8 Guiro

Photo courtesy of
Latin Percussion

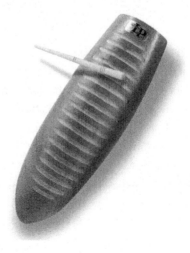

Guiros can be scraped with small wooden or plastic dowels, the shafts of keyboard mallets, triangle beaters, wire rakes, or hair picks. Guiros are usually held in one hand and scraped by the other, but can be mounted if necessary. The length of the note can be controlled to a certain degree and fairly quick rhythms can be articulated by using up and down scrapes (comfortably, 16th notes at ♩=110). Very long sustained notes are not easy but are possible at soft dynamics.

The pitch produced by a guiro depends on the size of the instrument, the speed of the scrape (a faster scrape will produce a higher pitch and louder dynamic), and the placement on the beater (scraping near the tip will be brighter than near the hand). Music for the guiro may be notated with dynamic shapes and/or with glissandi, indicating pitch shape. (See Aaron Copland's *Billy the Kid,* David Lang's *Scraping Song,* and Christopher Rouse's *Violoncello Concerto* and *Percussion Concerto.*)

Longer guiros are sometimes available. These instruments are capable of longer durations.

Washboards are large grooved boards made of wood or metal. They can be much louder than guiros and are often used in place of guiros if especially loud dynamics are required (like Stravinsky's *Rite of Spring*). The grooves are much larger, so larger scrapers, like snare sticks, can be used. In traditional jug band music, the washboard is worn around the player's neck and scraped and struck with thimbles worn on the fingers.

Slapstick

🔊 Video 8.d—Guiro, Slapstick, Ratchet, Bamboo Wind Chimes

A slapstick (figure 8.9) is two pieces of wood slapped together to make a sound similar to that of a whip crack. Often, if "whip" is notated, a slapstick will be used. Using an actual bull whip is rare, for a number of reasons: the desired whip sound is difficult to get consistently, placing a whip crack accurately in time is extremely difficult, and a lot of space is needed to crack a whip without injuring someone. The only

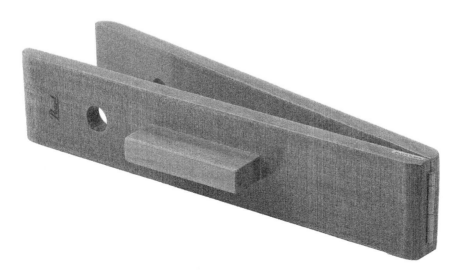

Figure 8.9
Slapstick

Photo courtesy of Pearl/Adams Percussion

advantage to the real whip is the visual effect, which is powerful but usually does not outweigh the whip's musical and logistical drawbacks.

The slapstick cannot be played too quickly (not much faster than eighth notes at ♩=120). Two hands are used to operate a slapstick, but it can be placed on a trap table and operated with one hand, if necessary. Spring-loaded slapsticks also exist that require only one hand. Two of these slapsticks could be wielded by one player for faster rhythms, although spring-loaded slapsticks are difficult to play accurately in time. (See Leroy Anderson's *Sleigh Ride*, Gustav Mahler's Symphony No. 5, Aaron Copland's Symphony No. 3, and Olivier Messiaen's *Turangalîla-Symphonie*.)

Ratchet

🔴 Video 8.d—Guiro, Slapstick, Ratchet, Bamboo Wind Chimes

The ratchet (figure 8.10) is a fairly limited instrument. Very little dynamic control is possible; cranking it faster will give the impression of louder volume, but the volume does not actually increase much. For real dynamic variety, multiple ratchets with different loudnesses can be used.

Figure 8.10
Ratchet

Photo courtesy of
Latin Percussion

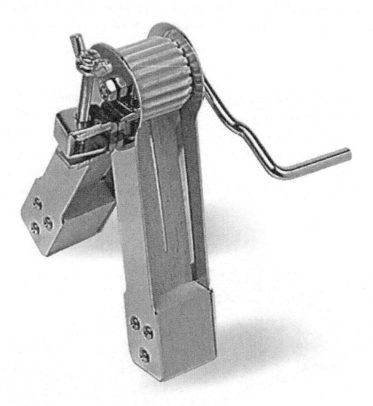

A rhythm executed on a ratchet will not be articulated with single clicks but, rather, with short bursts of many clicks. Note length should be notated accurately.

(See Richard Strauss's *Till Eulenspiegel* and *Der Rosenkavalier Suite,* Christopher Rouse's *Gorgon,* and Moussorgsky/Ravel's *Pictures at an Exhibition.*)

Very large ratchets do exist, but are not common. These are louder and have slower clicks so specific rhythms can be articulated. (See Ottorino Respighi's *Pines of Rome.*)

Bamboo Wind Chimes

🔊 Video 8.d—Guiro, Slapstick, Ratchet, Bamboo Wind Chimes

Bamboo wind chimes (figure 8.11) are sets of six to twenty pieces of bamboo that hang from a wooden board. When disturbed by the wind or by a performer's hand, the hanging bamboo pieces collide with one another or with a central hanging wooden beater to create an ambient tinkling. The reader may be most familiar with the versions of this instrument that hang from porches, backyard trees, and store front doors.

Figure 8.11
Bamboo
wind chimes

Wind chimes are usually made of metal but are also made of bamboo, glass, or shells. Bamboo wind chimes are usually rather high pitched, but deeper chimes are sometimes available. (See Wind Chimes in chapter 9 for complete details.)

CHAPTER NINE

Miscellaneous Instruments

Almost anything can be used as a percussion instrument. The composer should not neglect his or her kitchen, living room, bathroom, garage, or local hardware or toy stores as places to discover usable sounds. Percussionists often use everyday items like glass bottles, plates, silverware, jars, books, children's toys, pet toys, tables, chairs, car parts, floors, walls, and even the performer's body and voice. John Zorn's *For Your Eyes Only* calls for the sounds of hammering nails, breaking glass, and a slamming door! Other parts of regular percussion instruments (like the frame of a keyboard instrument or the stand on which a cymbal or drum is mounted) are often employed as instruments themselves.

All of these everyday items can be added to the list of percussion instruments covered in this chapter: bottles, cabasa, conch shell, crystal glasses, maracas, shakers, rainstick, rice bowls, flower pots, sandpaper blocks, sirens, string drum, cuica, stones, thumb piano, vibraslap, whistles, wind chimes, and wind machine.

Bottles

🎵 Video 9.a—Bottles, Cabasa

Glass bottles can be struck with sticks or mallets (see Paul Lansky's *Threads* and Michael Jackson's *Don't Stop 'Til You Get Enough*). The mouth of a glass or plastic bottle can also be blown over in the same manner as one would play a flute. Specific pitches can be tuned by adjusting the amount of liquid in the bottle. A slight pitch bend can be achieved by changing the amount of lip placed over the hole.

Cabasa

🎵 Video 9.a—Bottles, Cabasa, Conch Shell, Crystal Glasses

The cabasa (or *afuche cabasa*; figure 9.1) is usually held by both hands, but can be mounted for one-handed operation. Different note lengths can be achieved up to one second long.

The cabasa is not a particularly loud instrument, and when louder dynamics are requested, only shorter note values are possible. Rolls can be executed by rapidly

Figure 9.1 Cabasa

Photo courtesy of
Latin Percussion

twisting back and forth or even shaking the cabasa (this only requires one hand); however, rolls on this instrument are not particularly successful. (See The Jacksons, *Your Ways.*)

Conch Shell

🔊 Video 9.a—Bottles, Cabasa, Conch Shell, Crystal Glasses

A conch shell is blown through like a brass instrument. Percussionists should be expected to play no more than one pitch with a steady *fortissimo* dynamic, not very lengthy sustain, and not very fast articulations. (See John Cage's *Third Construction.*) In the hands of a brass player, however, much more is possible, such as more complex dynamics and articulations, longer durations, and limited pitch control (through placement of a hand inside the "bell" of the shell and manipulation of the embouchure).

Crystal Glasses

🔊 Video 9.a—Bottles, Cabasa, Conch Shell, Crystal Glasses

Crystal glasses can be struck (not too loudly or else they will break), rubbed, and bowed. When a glass is rubbed around its top edge with a moistened finger, the glass will quietly hum a pitch. A glass rim generally require about a second of rubbing before it will speak, so fast passages on rubbed glasses are not recommended. Glasses can also be bowed with a bass or cello bow; this is a perfect alternative to rubbing when loud dynamics are needed. Glasses can be tuned to specific pitches by adjusting the amount of water they hold. (See George Crumb's *Black Angels* and Joseph Schwantner's *. . . and the mountains rising nowhere.*)

Maracas and Shakers

◐ Video 9.b—Maracas, Shakers, Rainstick

Maracas (figure 9.2) are gourds (or gourd-like containers made of wood, plastic, metal, or rawhide) filled with beads and attached to a handle. They are generally used in pairs.

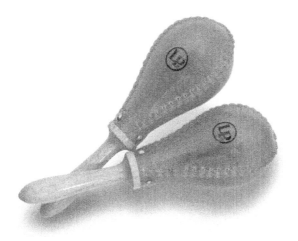

Figure 9.2
Maracas

Photo courtesy of
Latin Percussion

Rhythms are executed with a regular downward stroke or with downward and upward strokes whereby the beads strike the bottom and top of the inside of the gourd. Advanced maraca playing can actually be quite sophisticated. (See Javier Alvarez's *Tezmacal* and Adam Silverman's *Naked and on Fire.*)

Maracas are available in a variety of sizes and materials for many different timbres. A pair of maracas with the same timbre is most often used, but two differently sounding maracas can be requested by the composer (e.g., one high and one low maraca).

Rolls are executed by spinning or rapidly shaking the maracas. A spun roll is produced by holding the maraca upside down and moving it in a stirring motion as if mixing the contents of a bowl. (See George Crumb's *Music for a Summer Evening* and Christopher Rouse's *Violoncello Concerto.*) This type of roll is smooth and seamless but not always loud enough—the shake roll is much louder. The composer's specification of roll type is not necessary.

Maracas can be mounted on a towel or piece of foam and struck with a hand or a beater. This facilitates the playing of maracas included in setups, but the volume and sound quality of the instrument are greatly sacrificed. It is also difficult to get a mounted maraca to speak on time; the beads move inside the maraca in such a way that it will speak slightly after it is struck.

Maracas can be used on drums (as in Leonard Bernstein's *West Side Story* and *Jeremiah*), but this can damage nicer maracas; quality maracas will usually be substituted with more durable maracas. For this purpose, some manufacturers have created specialty maraca mallets that have beads inside the mallet head.

There are an infinite number of other shakers—traditional African or South American sounds, contemporary plastic egg shakers, or even beads in a soda can (figure 9.3). Percussionists often make their own shakers.

Figure 9.3
(a) Shaker,
(b) caxixi, and
(c) egg shakers
Photos courtesy of
Latin Percussion

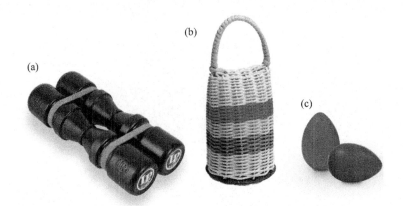

Maracas are typically used in pairs while shakers are used one at a time (although the use of one maraca or two shakers is acceptable). More involved rhythms are often notated for maracas; with shakers, it is more common to simply play steady time.

A shaker will produce two different strokes: a forward stroke and a back stroke; the subtle difference between these two sounds is like that of the up-bow and down-bow of a violin. (See Frank Zappa's *Outrage at Valdez*; Steve Reich's *Tehillim* and *Music for Eighteen Musicians* have parts for maracas that would be very appropriate for shakers; John Cage's *Third Construction* uses maracas and a variety of shakers and rattles.)

When a shaker is shaken quietly, the attacks become less articulate. If articulate soft shaker strokes are desired, then a shaker made specifically for soft dynamics can be used. Percussionists will usually have many types of shakers for various timbres and dynamics.

The tone color of the shaker can be adjusted by covering the surface of the instrument. Covering more of the shaker with one's hand will muffle high overtones. This makes the instrument softer and darker.

The *caxixi* (pronounced *cah-SHEE-shee*; figure 9.3b) is a special type of shaker. It has a harder surface at its bottom for a louder, brighter color. It can be shaken side to side, like a normal shaker, or top to bottom to make use of the different colors.

Various shakers or bells can be attached to a player's ankles, wrists, or beaters to accompany the motion of stomping or playing of other instruments. (See the ankle rattles in James Wood's *Village Burial with Fire*; and the wrist bells in Sofia Gubaidulina's *In the Beginning There Was Rhythm,* and in Adam Silverman's *Naked and on Fire*.)

Rainstick

🔊 Video 9.b—Maracas, Shakers, Rainstick

The rainstick is a long tube filled with beads. When the tube is tipped, the beads fall and filter slowly down the body of the tube, sounding like rain. Its dynamics can be controlled with the speed of the falling beads, which depends on the angle the tube is tipped, but even at its loudest, the rainstick is still rather quiet. The composer should not expect very precise stopping and starting of the rain sound. The rainstick can also be used as a giant shaker.

Rice Bowls and Flower Pots

🔊 Video 9.c—Rice Bowls, Flower Pots, Sandpaper Blocks, Sirens

Ceramic rice bowls are usually struck with chopsticks or thin rattan sticks. Terracotta flower pots are more durable and can be struck with sticks or mallets. These items are often used in sets with or without pitch specification. Bowls and pots are inexpensive and widely available, so finding specific pitches is relatively easy. (See the rice bowls in Henry Cowell's *Ostinato Pianissimo* and the flower pots with pitch specification in Frederic Rzewski's *To the Earth*.)

Sandpaper Blocks

🔊 Video 9.c—Rice Bowls, Flower Pots, Sandpaper Blocks, Sirens

Sandpaper blocks are two pieces of sandpaper attached to blocks of wood (or another material) so that the sandpaper pieces can be scraped together. Rhythms are easily executed and sustained notes can be achieved by scraping in a circular motion. Sandpaper blocks are not very loud. Also, the coarseness of the sandpaper affects the sound and volume. This instrument is usually held in both hands, but one of the blocks (or just a piece of sandpaper) can be secured to a table for one-handed operation, if necessary. (See John Adams's *Chairman Dances* and George Gershwin's *Porgy and Bess*.)

Sirens

🔊 Video 9.c—Rice Bowls, Flower Pots, Sandpaper Blocks, Sirens

Toy siren whistles are inexpensive, easy to find, and ideal for a quick comical effect; they are not loud and have a short sustain. Professional siren whistles are louder, have a longer sustain, and are more suited to musical purposes. Hand-crank sirens (like those used for the music of Edgard Varèse) have a much more serious and alarming sound.

With all types of sirens, the louder they are played, the higher the pitch. Stopping a siren short may not be possible with certain hand-crank sirens, so the sound must instead be muffled while it dies out on its own, taking up to 15 seconds. Notation is usually rather vague; a wavy line can indicate relative pitch and volume. (See the siren whistles in Iannis Xenakis's *Persephassa* and David Rakowski's *Ten of a Kind*; and the crank sirens in John Luther Adams's *Inuksuit* and Edgard Varèse's *Amérique* and *Ionisation*.)

String Drum and Cuica

🔊 Video 9.d—String Drum, Cuica, Stones, Thumb Piano

The string drum (or *lion's roar* or *friction drum*) is a drum with a string attached to the center of the drum head. Rosin is applied to the string; the player holds the string taut and rubs it with a small piece of moistened cloth, thus vibrating the drum head to create a roaring sound. It takes a small amount of time for the player to pick up the piece of cloth and get into position to play the string drum. Sustained notes no longer than two seconds are most common—short rhythmic passages or especially long notes are impractical. (See John Cage's *Third Construction* and Edgard Varèse's *Amérique* and *Ionisation*.) A friction roll on a large drum (see Friction Roll in appendix C) can replace a string drum, although it may not be as loud.

In its original use as a sound effect for vaudeville and silent films, string drums came in a variety of sizes to imitate different animals, such as dog barks, pig grunts, bear growls, and lion roars. The lion's roar was the largest, and is the instrument that has survived into the modern repertoire.

The cuica (or *quica*; figure 9.4) is a traditional Brazilian instrument. It is a small metal drum with a thin wood dowel attached to the inner side of the head. With a wet cloth, the wood dowel is rubbed to create a moaning sound. The pitch can be altered slightly by pressing on the head, and high/low figuration is possible by manipulating different harmonics.

Figure 9.4 Cuica
Photo courtesy of
IZZO Percussion

Requesting specific pitches for the cuica is not recommended. Specific note lengths up to a second long, and rhythms no faster than 16th notes at ♩=100, are possible. The composer must allow some time (about two or three seconds) for the percussionist to pick the cuica up and get it into playing position. (See Christopher Rouse's *Infernal Machine* and John Zorn's *For Your Eyes Only*.)

Stones and Prayer Stones

🔊 Video 9.d—String Drum, Cuica, Stones, Thumb Piano

Two regular stones can be struck together. This is not very loud. (See Iannis Xenakis's *Persephassa* and Alberto Ginestera's *Cantata Para America Magica*.)

Prayer stones are not necessarily special stones but, rather, stones played with a special technique. One stone is held in a cupped hand and is struck by the other stone. The shape of the cupped hand is altered to emphasize different overtones. This is a soft, subtle effect. The player can amplify this effect by resting one stone against his or her cheek and altering the size of the mouth. The mouth, as a larger resonating chamber than a cupped hand, yields a much louder sound and wider variety of timbre. (See George Crumb's *Ancient Voices of Children*.)

Thumb Piano

🔊 Video 9.d—String Drum, Cuica, Stones, Thumb Piano

The thumb piano (or *kalimba* or *mbira*; figure 9.5) is a set of small metal tongs attached to a resonating chamber (such as a wooden box or a hollowed gourd) and tuned to specific pitches. The number of metal tongs varies but there will be at least seven.

Figure 9.5
Thumb piano

The tongs can be tuned by adjusting their length, but this cannot be done during performance—they must be preset. The thumb piano is not especially loud and is often amplified electronically or by the use of a sympathetically resonating acoustic instrument (as with piano in George Crumb's *Music for a Summer Evening* and with a timpano in Per Nørgård's *I Ching*).

Vibraslap

🔊 Video 9.e—Vibraslap, Wind Chimes, Whistles, Wind Machine

The vibraslap (figure 9.6) is a modern invention that replaced the *jawbone of an ass* or *quijada,* in which the teeth rattled inside the jawbone when struck. It has about a one to four second decay but can be muted with a hand for shorter notes. It is usually held, but can be mounted if necessary; mounted vibraslaps will typically have a shorter ring time. It is best struck with a hand, but a stick or mallet could be used. (See John Cage's *Third Construction* and Jacob Druckman's *Aureole.*)

Figure 9.6
Vibraslap

Photo courtesy of
Latin Percussion

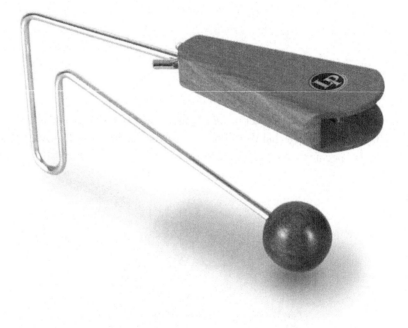

Wind Chimes

🔊 Video 9.e—Vibraslap, Wind Chimes, Whistles, Wind Machine

Wind chimes (figure 9.7) are sets of four to ten metal tubes, pieces of bamboo, pieces of glass, or shells that hang from a wooden board. When disturbed by the wind or by a performer's hand, the hanging items collide with one another or with a central hanging wooden beater to create an ambient tinkling. The most familiar versions of this instrument can be seen hanging from porches, backyard trees, and store front doors.

Figure 9.7
Wind chimes

Photo of metal wind chimes courtesy of Latin Percussion

Wind chimes are usually made of metal but are also made of bamboo, glass, or shell. Wind chimes are usually rather high pitched (C5 and above), but deeper metal or bamboo chimes are sometimes available; glass and shell chimes are usually high pitched.

Some wind chimes have pitches that are random with unusual tunings; others resemble a major or minor chord or pentatonic scale. An isolated register of a mark tree can also be played like a set of metal wind chimes; these pitches are rather close together and include microtones.

Wind chimes can be sustained by the player's noodling his or her fingers through them; they can also be struck with a sharp attack and left to decay, or they can be clapped together and then held to stop the sound dead (often called a *wind chime choke)*. After the chimes have been choked, the player must eventually let go; this can be notated as a separate sound. If a silent release is desired, it must be done very slowly and carefully, and under the cover of loud sounds. A wind chime choke is most effective with bamboo wind chimes. (See the metal and bamboo chimes in Jacob Druckman's *Animus II,* the bamboo and glass chimes in Luciano Berio's *Circles,* and the bamboo chimes in Michael Finnissy's *Hinomi.*)

Notation for wind chimes is vague, usually a single hit with its natural decay or a trill or tremolo to indicate a sustained tone; see figure 9.8. (The composer should be careful not to write "chimes" if wind chimes are desired; "chimes" indicates tubular bells.)

Figure 9.8 Wind chime notation

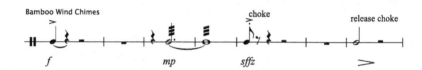

Wind chimes are sensitive and can be set into motion with just a light brush of a hand, body, or stick. For this reason, accidental wind chime solos can occur during rehearsals and performances. This is, of course, the performer's problem, but the composer should be aware of it, especially in setups involving these instruments.

Whistles

🔊 Video 9.e—Vibraslap, Wind Chimes, Whistles, Wind Machine

There are many types of whistles, like bird calls and those used in various African and Latin American music traditions. Bird calls come in many varieties, depending on the bird being mimicked—crow, cuckoo, dove, duck, jay, nightingale, and so on. Non-bird whistles include police, samba, train, siren (see Sirens earlier in this chapter), and slide.

Most whistles can be hung around the neck for quick pickup. Some can be held in the mouth without the help of a hand, so the hands may do other things. Samba whistles have two pitches, but one hand is needed to open and close the hole that controls the pitch. Simple melodies can be executed on a slide whistle; these instruments require two hands—one to hold the whistle and the other to operate the slide. (See the slide whistle in George Crumb's *Music for a Summer Evening* and Gyorgy Ligeti's *Concerto for Violin*; the police whistle in Leonard Bernstein's *West Side Story*; the police and samba whistle in Steven Mackey's *Tuck and Roll* and *Pedal Tones*; and the cuckoo whistle in Engelbert Humperdinck's *Hansel und Gretel.*)

Tin whistles and *penny whistles* are probably better suited for wind players to play (at the risk of orchestra doubling fees). *Ocarinas* are simple enough for percussionists, but instruments with specific pitches may not be easy to find. (See Gyorgy Ligeti's *Concerto for Violin.*)

Wind Machine

🔊 Video 9.e—Vibraslap, Wind Chimes, Whistles, Wind Machine

The wind machine (figure 9.9) has a canvas that is pulled tightly down over what looks like a small water wheel. The wheel is hand-cranked and spun so it rubs against the canvas. Only long notes with big swooping dynamics are possible. Just as with a crank siren, an increase in dynamic always results in an increase of pitch, and vice versa. (See Richard Strauss's *Alpine Symphony* or *Don Quixote*, and Giacinto Scelsi's *I Presagi*.)

Figure 9.9
Wind machine

Repertoire Analysis

This appendix examines the percussion writing in specific percussion ensemble, orchestral, mixed chamber, solo, and concerto contexts. The reader is directed to the online video companion of *How to Write for Percussion* for further analysis, score excerpts, audio and video performances, and interviews with performers and composers of these works.

PERCUSSION ENSEMBLE

Edgard Varèse, *Ionisation* (1929–1931)

 Video A.a

Although percussion ensembles have existed for thousands of years in musical and religious traditions across the world, *Ionisation* is credited as the first notated work for percussion alone. Here, Varèse demonstrates how thirteen percussionists playing nearly forty instruments can be utilized maturely and creatively, keeping each player and each sound essential to the work.

Instrumentation (13 percussionists)

player 1: china cymbal, large bass drum, small tam-tam
player 2: 2 tam-tams, gong*
player 3: 2 bongos, tenor drum, 2 bass drums
player 4: field drum, tenor drum
player 5: high siren, string drum
player 6: low siren, slapstick, guiro
player 7: 3 Chinese blocks,** claves, triangle
player 8: snare drum without snares, 2 maracas
player 9: piccolo snare drum, snare drum, suspended cymbal
player 10: crash cymbals, sleighbells, tubular bells***
player 11: guiro, castanets, glockenspiel
player 12: tambourine, 2 anvils, very large tam-tam
player 13: slapstick, triangle, sleighbells, piano

*A nipple gong is often used for this "gong."

**Chinese blocks can mean templeblocks or woodblocks.

***Varèse requests two pitches that are out of the range of a standard set of tubular bells: B3 and C3. B3 is just below the standard range and is sometimes available. The C3 tube is rare, as it is nearly ten feet tall! These pitches are transposed up the octave for most performances.

John Cage, *Constructions* (1939–1942)

 Video A.b

John Cage's three *Constructions* for percussion were written before he began experimenting in earnest with aleatoric procedures (*4'33"*, as a point of reference, was conceived in 1952). The *First Construction* creates a grand palette of sounds using only metal instruments. The *Second* is humbler, with a contained but more varied instrumentation, including a prepared piano. The *Third* is quintessential percussion ensemble, groovy and drummy with an expertly crafted palette of assorted instruments.

FIRST CONSTRUCTION (IN METAL)

6 percussionists plus assistant

player 1: glockenspiel, thundersheet

player 2: string piano*

assistant: string piano*

player 3: 12 oxen bells,** small sleighbells, thundersheet

player 4: 4 muted brake drums, 8 cowbells, 3 Japanese temple gongs,*** thundersheet

player 5: 8 muted anvils, 4 suspended Turkish cymbals,**** 4 china cymbals, thundersheet

Player 6: 4 muted gongs, tam-tam, water gong, thundersheet

*"String piano" is "Henry Cowell's term for an ordinary piano, the strings of which are performed upon." In addition to pressing the piano keys, player 2 and the assistant both play inside the piano and manipulate the sound with muting and by moving a metal rod over the strings to elicit a glissando of harmonics.

**Almglocken.

***Temple bowls.

****Turkish cymbals are normal suspended cymbals.

SECOND CONSTRUCTION

4 percussionists

player 1: sleighbells, glass wind chimes, Indian rattle,* maracas

player 2: snare drum, 5 tom-toms, 2 pairs of maracas

player 3: 5 muted gongs, tam-tam, water gong, thundersheet
player 4: prepared piano

*"Indian Rattle" in this case refers to a Native American instrument; functionally, any wooden rattle will do.

THIRD CONSTRUCTION

4 percussionists

player 1: 5 tin cans, 3 tom-toms, claves, china cymbal, log drum (2 pitches), North West Indian rattle*
player 2: 5 tin cans, 3 tom-toms, claves, 2 cowbells, Indo-Chinese rattle,* lion's roar**
player 3: 5 tin cans, 3 tom-toms, claves, tambourine, vibraslap, cricket callers,*** conch shell
player 4: 5 tin cans, 3 tom-toms, claves, tin can rattle, maracas, ratchet, bass drum roar**

*Cage seems to be very specific about exactly what type of rattle he requests; however, the names he gives these rattles are less useful than would be a description of the sound or construction of the instrument. Generally, a wood rattle is used for the N.W. Indian instrument, and a bean pod rattle is used for the Indo-Chinese instrument.
**Cage requests two string drums—one large (lion's roar) and one very large (bass drum roar).
***Cricket callers are pieces of bamboo that have been split, so they rattle when shaken.

Iannis Xenakis, *Persephassa* (1969)

 Video A.c

Persephassa is an epic half-hour work for percussion sextet that was written to be played outdoors. Indoors or out, the players are to be positioned around the audience, adding an architectural element to this musical experience. During some sections of the work, the players proceed in tempos independent from one another, and metronomes must be employed to maintain synchronization. The final section features musical material literally spinning around the audience at faster and faster rates.

Instrumentation (6 percussionists positioned around the audience)

A: piccolo timpano, 3 snare drums without snares, snare drum with snares, large bass drum, woodblock, wood simantra,* maracas, metal simantra,* cymbal, tam-tam, Thai gong (F2),** small thundersheet, 2 sea stones, siren whistle
B: pair of bongos, 3 tom-toms, pedal bass drum, woodblock, wood simantra, maracas, metal simantra, cymbal, tam-tam, Thai gong (F♯2), small thundersheet, 2 sea stones, siren whistle

C: pair of bongos, 3 tom-toms, low timpano, woodblock, wood simantra, maracas, metal simantra, cymbal, tam-tam, Thai gong (E2), small thundersheet, 2 sea stones, siren whistle

D: pair of bongos, high tom-tom, conga, medium timpano, bass drum, woodblock, wood simantra, maracas, metal simantra, cymbal, tam-tam, Thai gong (E♭3), small thundersheet, 2 sea stones, siren whistle

E: pair of bongos, 3 tom-toms, pedal bass drum, woodblock, wood simantra, maracas, metal simantra, cymbal, tam-tam, 2 Thai gongs (B♭2, C3), small thundersheet, 2 sea stones, siren whistle

F: pair of bongos, piccolo snare drum, conga, low tom-tom, timpano, woodblock, wood simantra, maracas, metal simantra, cymbal, tam-tam, Thai gong (G2), small thundersheet, 2 sea stones, siren whistle

*A wood simantra is a plank of wood. A metal simantra is a metal pipe.

**Thai gongs are nipple gongs.

Steve Reich, *Drumming* (1970–1971)

◉ Video A.d

Drumming is a 1- to 1½-hour-long work built on a single repeated figure six beats long. This was the first live large-scale work in which Reich used the technique of *phasing*, where one of two players playing the same pattern speeds up slightly to become out of sync with the other. The accelerating pattern grinds against the first and eventually lands one eighth note ahead. The patterns, now combined in canon, yield new melodies. This technique is used as a means of development throughout *Drumming*, as well as providing a type of rhythmic dissonance that resolves when the patterns finally come back together into unison.

Instrumentation: *(9 percussionists)*

4 pairs of tuned bongos (G♯3, A♯3, B3, C♯4)
3 marimbas
3 glockenspiels
2 or 3 female voices
piccolo

Steve Mackey, *It Is Time* (2010)

◉ Video A.e

It Is Time is a forty-minute tour de force for percussion quartet. It was written in close collaboration with So Percussion, a New York City-based percussion quartet;

the parts were specifically tailored to each player's individual skills, taste, and personality, and each of the piece's four sections functions as a mini-concerto for one of the players. As the title suggests, this work is about the perception and manipulation of time. Time is an essential element in most percussion music, as percussion is uniquely excellent at clarifying time, meter, and rhythm. Mackey examines this from all angles—*It Is Time* is a compendium of ways in which time can be lost and found. Moreover, each section of this work contains brilliant uses of the instruments, the sophistication of which is only possible when a veteran percussion composer like Mackey collaborates with a group of thoughtful performers like So Percussion.

Instrumentation (4 percussionists)

metronome
metronome sounds
digital delay
organ
small bells
noah bells* (A, E)
2 wine bottles
tuned frame drum
mounted china cymbal on hi-hat stand
small water gong
vibraphone with variable motor
chimes
4 cowbells
solo baritone voice
marimba
flexatone
steel drums: double seconds, lead pan, microtonal lead pan (all pitches tuned up between 1/6th and 1/4 tone—pitches actually used in the "sharp" microtonal pan are: C♯4, D♯4, A4, A♯4, B4, C5, C♯5, D5, D♯5, E5, F♯5, G5, G♯5)
drumset with toys: wine bottle, 2 woodblocks, tambourine, triangle, 4 crotales (B, C♯, D, E), foot pedal mounted cowbell, 2 bongos

*Noah bells are like small cowbells with the clappers still attached inside the bell.

John Luther Adams, *Inuksuit* (2009)

 Video A.f

Inuksuit is an hour-long "site-determined" work built to be performed outdoors with the performers spread out over a large area. Although the work is particularly impractical, requiring an enormous number of players and an enormous number of instruments in unusual and sometimes awkward locations, the experience of *Inuksuit* is so engaging that it was recreated over two dozen times in the first four years after it was composed. The "concert halls" that have held this work include deserts, forests, city parks, and the Alaskan tundra. The information on instrumentation is quoted from the score.

Instrumentation (9 to 99 percussionists)

Inuksuit employs three Groups of instruments and five types of musical materials: Breathing/Wind, Calls/Clangs, Inuksuit, Waves, and Birdsongs.

Each musician in Group 1 breathes audibly through a megaphone (a bullhorn, a microphone and portable speaker, horn, or trumpet), plays a conch shell trumpet (Tibetan trumpet, air horn, other horn, or trumpet), an air raid siren (timpano, wind machine, or water gong), a hand bell (medium suspended bell, chime, temple bell, or Tibetan cymbals), and a triangle (or small bells).

Each musician in Group 2 plays a snare drum, rubbed with brushes or rolled with light sticks (stones rubbed together, maracas, rattle, shaker, sandblocks, rice swirled inside a single-headed drum, or other friction sounds), a sizzle cymbal, and an array of seven tom-toms and bass drum. (If fewer drums are available, the musicians should produce eight distinctively different sounds from their drums.)

Each musician in the Group 3 plays a whirled plastic tube (blown corrugated metal tubing, bullroarer, or other Aeolian instrument), seven suspended cymbals, a tam-tam, and orchestra bells (or crotales). (If fewer cymbals are available, the musicians should produce eight distinctively different sounds from their cymbals.)

The musicians are encouraged to select instruments carefully, to create varied and imaginative soundings of *Inuksuit*. A larger performance space will likely require lower-pitched instruments and louder dynamic levels. A smaller space may encourage higher-pitched instruments and softer dynamics.

Ryan Streber, *Cold Pastoral* (2004)

 Video A.g

Cold Pastoral was conceived as a visual complement to Part 1 of Steve Reich's *Drumming*, in which four pairs of bongos are set up in a line perpendicular to the edge of the stage and played from both sides. The vibraphone and crotales are set in a similar line with players approaching from both sides. Two of the four players have the task of learning to play the keyboards from the "wrong" side. Streber does an excellent job of choosing indeterminately pitched instruments that effectively color the pitch material from the keyboards without contributing distracting indeterminate pitch material.

Instrumentation (4 percussionists)

vibraphone
crotales
suspended cymbal
sizzle cymbal
hi-hat
tam-tam
snare drum
low templeblock

Nico Muhly, *Ta & Clap* (2004)

 Video A.g

Ta & Clap is a play of rhythm, meter, and tempo, and how each can be obscured by changing instrument colors or clarified by harmony. The work was intended as a complement to John Cage's *Third Construction,* as it can be played from the Cage setup with the addition of two marimbas. Muhly did not, however, request the same instruments as Cage; rather, he left the instrumentation open to the performers' choosing. The idea of open instrumentation is further encouraged by Muhly's request that each repeat of a figure be played on a different set of instruments. This break from any sense of timbral control or consistency illuminates the importance of the rhythmic material and the auxiliary nature of the colors used to communicate them.

Instrumentation (4 percussionists)

2 marimbas
a large variety of instruments of different materials

Adam Silverman, *Naked and on Fire* (2011)

 Video A.h

This work is exemplary of many of the concepts described in chapter 1. Specific pitches are requested for all the instruments that sound clear pitches, including the bowls, gongs, and metal pipes. The remaining instruments are used in sophisticated ways, taking advantage of techniques found in improvised styles.

Instrumentation (6 percussionists)

percussion 1: high triangle, 3 gongs (G2, C♯3, F♯3)
percussion 2: middle triangle, vibraphone
percussion 3: low triangle, 3 singing bowls (B3, C♯4, F♯4)
percussion 4: riq, doumbek with jingles on wrists

percussion 5: 2 octaves of metal pipes (B4–A6)
percussion 6: maracas

Paul Lansky, *Travel Diary* (2007)

⬤ Video A.h

Travel Diary is an example of percussion music in which individual parts function like mini ensembles. The work is a duo, but it could easily be split to be played by four players. The two-person execution, therefore, is impressive. The third movement, featured here, is particularly effective—only a small set of pitches are played on the keyboard instruments at any given time, so the keyboard material functions similarly to the non-keyboard instruments.

Travel Diary has four movements: I. Leaving Home, II. Cruising Speed, III. Lost in Philly, IV. Arrived, Phone Home.

Instrumentation (2 percussionists)

player 1: 5 unpitched noise-like instruments (bottles, flower pots, etc.), claves, 2 congas, 2 bongos, glockenspiel, vibraphone

player 2: small cowbell, 3 unpitched woodblock-like instruments (templeblock, etc., low to high, and different in timbre—i.e., not 3 different pitched woodblocks), triangle, 2 cymbals, pedal bass drum, 4 tom-toms, crotales (low octave), marimba (4.3 octave)

ORCHESTRAL

Béla Bartók

⬤ Video A.i1

Concerto for Orchestra (1943)
Violin Concerto No. 2 (1938)
The Miraculous Mandarin (1919)

These excerpts feature some tasteful uses of percussion in solo and accompanimental roles, including Bartok's exceptional timpani writing.

Sergei Prokofiev

⬤ Video A.i2

Scherzo from *Love for Three Oranges* (1921)
Lieutenant Kijé Suite (1934)

Violin Concerto No. 2 (1935)
Symphony No. 6 (1947)

These excerpts feature Prokofiev's writing for the percussion section, as well as some highlights from his elegant use of the bass drum.

Maurice Ravel

◑ Video A.i3

Daphnis et Chloe (1912)
Alborada del gracioso (1918)
Modest Mussorgsky, *Pictures at an Exhibition* (Ravel orchestration) (1922)

These excerpts feature Ravel's section writing. The orchestration is outstanding but unwieldy, as it often requires two, three, or four more percussionists than are usually found in an orchestra section.

Gustav Mahler

◑ Video A.i4

Symphony No. 6 (1904)
Symphony No. 5 (1902)

Much of Mahler's percussion usage serves to illicit a military sound, with excellent uses of timpani, bass drum, and cymbals. These excerpts also feature clever combinations of triangle and keyboard percussion.

Dmitri Shostakovich

◑ Video A.i5

Symphony No. 11 (1957)
Symphony No. 5 (1937)
Symphony No. 15 (1971)

Like Mahler, Shostakovich's percussion is often militaristic, making expert but traditional use of timpani, bass drum, cymbals, snare drum, and xylophone. The excerpt from his Fifteenth Symphony is exceptional, featuring particularly delicate and artful uses of snare drum, woodblock, castanet, glockenspiel, triangle, xylophone, and timpani.

Leonard Bernstein

◐ Video A.i6

Symphonic Dances from West Side Story (1960)

Bernstein's percussion writing is often excessive, requiring more instruments and more players than are probably needed. The function of the sounds, however, is spot on, from orchestral coloristic additions to the traditional sounds of jazz and Latin dance music.

Carl Nielsen

◐ Video A.i7

Clarinet Concerto (1928)

This excerpt features the snare drum as a sort of anti-soloist, interjecting its unique color and character against that of the clarinet solo. Nielsen used percussion in unique ways in many of his orchestral works, as in the two antiphonal timpanists in his Fourth Symphony and the snare drum cadenza in his Fifth Symphony.

Jean Sibelius

◐ Video A.i7

Symphony No. 1 (1899)

This excerpt features Sibelius's unique timpani writing. Tremolos, both metered and unmetered, can be heard throughout his orchestral music, like a rolling sea on which the rest of the orchestra floats.

Wind Ensemble

◐ Video A.i8

John Phillip Sousa, *The Washington Post March*
Percy Grainger, Arrival on Platform Humlet, from the *In a Nutshell* Suite
Michael Gandolfi, *Flourishes and Meditations on a Renaissance Theme*

Although wind ensemble percussion writing requires much the same considerations as orchestral writing, these three works are a small window onto the world of wind ensemble percussion and provide an opportunity to discuss some of the small differences between percussion in this ensemble and percussion in the orchestra.

SMALLER MIXED ENSEMBLE

John Adams, *Chamber Symphony* (1992)

 Video A.j

Chamber Symphony has three movements: I. Mongrel Airs, II. Aria with Walking Bass, and III. Roadrunner.

Chamber Symphony calls for a single percussionist playing a trap set. "Trap set" was a common nick name for the drumsets of the early twentieth century (*trap* is short for "contraption"), which were collections of many instruments and sound effects—not just drums and cymbals. Adams describes this work as a meeting of Schoenberg's *Chamber Symphony* with the music from Looney Tunes cartoons; the percussion here is certainly a representative of the latter.

Percussion instrumentation

4 roto-toms (E4, C4, F3, and B♭2)
2 bongos
2 timbales
3 tom-toms
conga
snare drum
hi-hat
cowbell
woodblock
tambourine (mounted)
claves

Stephan Hartke, *Meanwhile* (2007)

 Video A.k

Meanwhile has six movements: I. Procession, II. Fanfares, III. Narration, IV. Spikefiddlers, V. Cradle-songs, and VI. Celebration.

The percussion setup for *Meanwhile* is unique, as it is a successful example of a timbre-rack (see chapter 3). The decision to use this method of setup and notation was arrived upon through the close collaboration of Hartke and percussionist Matthew Duvall.

In addition to the percussionist's setup, Hartke requests extensive flexatone playing from the piano, flute, and clarinet players. In the first movement, the pianist plays an instrument Hartke dubs a "Flexatone Gamelan," consisting of three flexatones mounted to a board and played with mallets. Detailed instructions for constructing this instrument are found in the score, including a picture of the final product. The flute and clarinet players each play one flexatone in the final movement.

Instrumentation

viola
cello
flute, doubling flexatone
clarinet, doubling flexatone
piano, doubling "Flexatone Gamelan"
percussion:
    vibraphone
    water gong
    maraca
    timbre-rack consisting of:
        2 accent cymbals (splash cymbals)
        7 piccolo woodblocks
        3 medium woodblocks
        4 templeblocks
        4 muted cowbells
        2 bongos
        slit drum (4 pitches)

Jacob Druckman, *Come Round* (1992)

 Video A.1

Come Round, in three movements, features both the keyboard and non-keyboard percussion instruments expertly blended into the ensemble sound.

Instrumentation

violin
cello
flute
clarinet
piano

percussion:
    marimba
    vibraphone
    4 tom-toms
    bass drum
    bongo
    2 suspended cymbals
    tam-tam

Charles Wuorinen, *New York Notes* (1982)

 Video A.l

New York Notes, in three movements, uses only percussion instruments of determinate pitch, including significant use of timpani in addition to the keyboard percussion instruments. The percussion part was originally conceived for one percussionist, but is so challenging that it is commonly divided for two players.

Instrumentation

violin
cello
flute
clarinet
piano
1 or 2 percussionists:
    marimba
    vibraphone
    timpani
    glockenspiel

Pierre Boulez, *Sur Incises* (1996/1998)

 Video A.l

Sur Incises, in two movements, demonstrates skillful use of a variety of determinately pitched percussion instruments.

Instrumentation

3 pianos
3 harps
3 percussionists:
    player 1: vibraphone, steel pans, crotales
    player 2: vibraphone, glockenspiel, timpani
    player 3: marimba, tubular bells, crotales

PERCUSSION SOLO—DRUMS

Michio Kitazume, *Side by Side* (1991)

◐ Video A.m

Side by Side is an example of effective use of a simple setup. The work opens with the simplest music, a straight pulse, and gradually builds an elegant vocabulary of rhythmic manipulations.

Instrumentation

2 bongos
2 congas
2 tom-toms
pedal bass drum

Elliott Carter, *Eight Pieces for Four Timpani* (1950/1966)

Saëta
Canaries

◐ Video A.m

Carter's *Eight Pieces* makes extensive and functional use of extended techniques to distinguish melody from accompaniment, delineate phrases and sections, and enhance dynamic shapes. The work seems to function as Carter's testing ground for the metric modulation techniques that he would use exhaustively in the First String Quartet (1951).

Casey Cangelosi, *Meditation No. 1* (2011)

◐ Video A.m

Meditation No. 1 for snare drum uses simple techniques beyond standard stick-on-head playing—striking the rim, using side stick and rimshots, and playing with fingers—to expand the functionality of the snare drum. The head sound is not introduced until well into the start of the piece. This is a work with simple instrumentation that achieves variety of timbre and texture enough to sustain an interesting composition without requiring especially unusual or awkward playing styles. *Meditation No. 1* is not easy, however, as it is designed to showcase Cangelosi's exceptionally fast hands and fluid technique.

PERCUSSION SOLO—KEYBOARDS

Jacob Druckman, *Reflections on the Nature of Water* (1986)

◐ Video A.n

Reflections on the Nature of Water is in six movements: 1. Crystalline, 2. Fleet, 3. Tranquil, 4. Gently Swelling, 5. Profound, and 6. Relentless.

With this piece, Druckman has done an exceptionally good job of writing truly marimbistic music—that is, music that lays well on the instrument and sounds native to it. Unlike many works in the marimba repertoire, *Reflections* would not sound better on any other instrument. This work requires an instrument with a low F2, although much of it fits on a 4.3 octave (low A2) marimba. Five-octave (low C2) instruments were not common in 1986. Part of the work's success may be in its limited range, as the use of the lowest register can create problems of mallet choice, balance, and playability.

Paul Simon, *Amulet* (2008)

 Video A.o

This piece, written by the legendary singer-songwriter, was worked out first on guitar and then adapted to marimba in collaboration with marimbist Nancy Zeltsman. Acoustic guitar and marimba have similar qualities, and marimbists commonly adapt guitar works for their instrument. *Amulet* is simple and beautiful, like many of Simon's folk songs. The marimba would likely be a popular instrument in the folk world if it weren't so hard to carry around!

Steve Mackey, *See Ya Thursday* (1992)

 Video A.p

See Ya Thursday is a charismatic single-movement work for marimba that takes advantage of the full five-octave range. Mackey was careful to write with the instrument's particular strengths in mind, and although the execution required is often virtuosic, the sound and character of the work are at home on the marimba.

Steve Swallow/Gary Burton, "I'm Your Pal" and "Hullo Bolinas"

 Video A.q

Gary Burton is considered, by many, one of the greatest vibraphonist in history. His approach to the instrument revolutionized its use in jazz and in written concert music. This excerpt is an improvisation, displaying his exceptional control over this instrument. Note how Burton seems completely unencumbered by the vibraphone's small range (F3–F6).

Donald Martino, *Soliloquy* (2003)

 Video A.q

Soliloquy is a charming work for vibraphone solo that displays many strengths of the instrument but also exposes some of its weaknesses. The opening section intends to be very slow and connected, but it is a considerable challenge to create these lines on an instrument that cannot control sustain. This section would probably be realized better if played by a string or wind instrument. The larger middle section is much more effective; it shifts back and forth between strict *presto* and more rhythmically abstract *a piacare*, showcasing the vibraphone's variety of articulation. The coda is a short return to the sustained music of the opening, although here the music is less linear and more suggestive of clouds of pitches, a texture of which vibraphone is quite capable.

PERCUSSION SOLO — MULTI-PERCUSSION

Iannis Xenakis, *Psappha* (1975)

 Video A.r

Psappha, a warhorse of the percussion solo literature, is a showcase of the power of percussion and the athleticism of the performer. It uses an unusual grid notation without meter or phrase markings. Xenakis gives guidelines for instrumentation, but much of it is left to the performer. *Psappha* is a purely rhythmic work, where the instrument colors are subservient to the bold structures they clarify.

Instrumentation

group A: 3 high drums or woods
group B: 3 medium drums or woods
group C: 3 low drums or woods
group D: 3 medium metals
group E: 1 low metal
group F: 3 very high metals

Xenakis suggests a variety of instruments for each, but the final decision is left to the performer. He adds that accents may be interpreted as:

1. louder
2. a change in timbre
3. a change in weight
4. play another instrument in unison
5. a combination of the above

David Lang, *Anvil Chorus* (1991)

 Video A.r

Anvil Chorus is inspired by the songs blacksmiths would sing to help coordinate multiple smiths working on a single piece of metal. Lang purposely avoided traditional instruments, looking instead for the raw sounds of real-life percussioning that are part of this industrial profession.

Instrumentation

3 resonant junk metals
4 non-resonant junk metals
4 junk metals played by foot pedal
2 woodblocks
bass drum

Roger Reynolds, *Watershed* (1995)

 Video A.s

The instrumentation for *Watershed* was designed as sculpture, considering the look of the setup and the dance of the performer within it. The version of this piece with electronics (called *Watershed IV*) intends to augment these characteristics with multi-channel spatialization, projecting the sound from inside the setup around the whole concert space.

Instrumentation

6 drums: bongos, congas, pedal bass drum, large concert bass drum
11 oddities*
5 metals: 2 tam-tams, 2 cymbals, crotale
4 wooden boxes with snares

*Oddities are "small distinctive noise sources, two of which are metallic, two wooden." Reynolds adds, "unexpected rattles, clunks, buzzes, thuds, and so on are desirable."

Four Pieces for the Author's "Setup #1"

 Video A.t1

The following four pieces were all written for a setup designed by Samuel Solomon. Each piece also uses the same notational system. The project was conceived to overcome a number of musical and logistical obstacles in the life and repertoire of a multi-percussionist. A unique feature of this project is that the composers are given the pitch material of the non-keyboard instruments, so they have the opportunity to use the non-keyboard instruments as a complement to the keyboard instruments in specific and predictable ways.

Nico Muhly, *It's About Time* (2004)

 Video A.t2

It's About Time begins with the vibraphone harmonizing the non-keyboard instruments, thus establishing the pitch material for the rest of the piece in which the non-keyboard instruments may fully participate.

Michael Early, *Raingutter* (2007)

 Video A.t3

Raingutter uses the vibraphone as a central vehicle throughout, while the accompanying sounds shift to different areas of the setup—first, brake drums and cowbell, and then drums, and finally crotales and triangle. The pitches of the non-keyboard instruments are not vital to the success of this work, but they did influence the choice of pitch material used for the vibraphone.

Marcos Balter, *Descarga* (2006)

 Video A.t4

Descarga features a characteristic in much of Balter's work that he calls "false stasis," in which something that is seemingly sustained or static is actually made up of many active parts. Percussion is well suited to this, as its primary means of sustain is tremolo. The pitches of the non-keyboard instruments are not important to the success of this work—in fact, even the specified pitches in the vibraphone and crotales serve more of a timbral than a harmonic function.

Judd Greenstein, *We Shall Be Turned* (2006)

 Video A.t5

In preparation for composing *We Shall Be Turned*, Greenstein spent hours improvising on the setup to experiment and work out material for the piece. As a result, this work makes extensive use of the pitch material in the non-keyboard instruments and successfully blends many of these otherwise disparate-sounding instruments. The sound of this work is beautiful, but the execution is extremely difficult. This is an example of a solo work that functions more like an ensemble piece, and a version of *We Shall Be Turned* for percussion quartet (arranged in 2013 as an experiment for this analysis) is far easier to play and perhaps as successful.

PERCUSSION CONCERTO

James MacMillan, *Veni, Veni Emmanuel* (1992)

 Video A.u

A classic of the percussion concerto repertoire, *Veni, Veni Emmanuel* is a grandiose work with religious undertones. The percussion soloist is featured on a variety of instruments and at four different stations on stage, each with its unique role in the character of the composition.

Percussion instrumentation

2 woodblocks
2 cowbells
sizzle cymbal
large cymbal
2 bongos
2 congas
2 timbales
6 tom-toms
pedal bass drum
6 cencerros or Javanese gongs (no specified pitch)*
6 templeblocks
log drum
marimba (5-octave)
mark tree
vibraphone
2 tam-tams
tubular bells

Additionally, there is timpani in the orchestra, and at the end of the work every member of orchestra plays a small handbell.

*Cencerros is another name for cowbells, in this case, indicating almglocken. Javanese gongs are nipple gongs.

Einojuhani Rautavaara, *Incantations* (2008)

 Video A.v

Percussion soloist Colin Currie pursued this commission from Rautavaara in hope of receiving a percussion concerto more stylistically akin to the great concertos of the nineteenth and early twentieth centuries. *Incantations* is indeed emotionally expressive in the traditional sense and fills what Currie felt was a void in his repertoire. Marimba and vibraphone are the central vehicles for the soloist.

Percussion instrumentation

marimba
vibraphone
crotales
tubular bells
4 roto-toms
2 bongos

2 congas
pedal bass drum
3 tam-tams
3 gongs
thunderstick (a small thundersheet)

Additionally, there is timpani and tubular bells in the orchestra (two players).

Steven Mackey, *Micro-Concerto* (1999)

 Video A.w

Micro-Concerto is Mackey's exploration into the life of percussionists who, by nature of the profession, agonize over the smallest details of playing techniques and instrument construction and setup. His work earns its title as the details of sound and execution are micro-managed, many of the soloist's instruments are small and hand-held, and the accompanying orchestra is as reduced as can be.

Instrumentation

flute
clarinet
violin
cello
piano
percussion solo:
    marimba
    vibraphone
    concert bass drum
    pedal bass drum
    2 tom-toms
    2 congas
    2 timbales
    2 bongos
    almglocke (E♭4)
    claves
    triangle
    2 suspended cymbals
    sizzle cymbal
    china cymbal
    small Chinese gong
    vibraslap (mounted)
    tambourine (mounted)

samba whistle
clicker
2 woodblocks
small cowbell
log drum (E♭)
castanet
small guiro
egg shaker
2 cans
bean pod rattle
2 bottles

See also the analysis of the setup for *Micro-Concerto* in appendix B.

ORCHESTRATING NATIVE SOUNDS

Percussion often plays an important role in the sounds characteristic of the music of different cultures. For this reason, composers commonly use percussion to elicit these styles. For example:

- Beethoven—battling armies in *Wellington's Victory*
- Rimsky-Korsakov—Persian music in *Scheherazade*
- Ravel—Spanish music in *Alborada del gracioso*
- Bernstein—jazz in *West Side Story*
- Gershwin—Afro-Cuban music in *Cuban Overture*
- Lou Harrison—gamelan in *Concerto for Violin and Percussion Orchestra*

Some examples of instruments that conjure the sounds of different cultures or styles follow. These are instruments native to these cultures or Western instruments that imitate native sounds:

- Jazz—drumset (with sticks or brushes), vibraphone
- Rock—drumset
- Ragtime—xylophone, marimba, drumset, woodblocks, whistles
- Marching or military band—snare drum, bass drum, crash cymbals, triangle[1]

---

1. This is originally the sound of the Turkish Janissary bands, to which eighteenth-century composers were making a reference when they used these instruments.

- Afro-Cuban—claves, bongos, congas, timbales, cowbell, suspended cymbals, maracas, guiro, shakers
- Caribbean—steel drums
- Central American—marimba
- Brazilian—shakers, pandeiro, cuica, large drums, small frame drums, whistles, triangle, agogo bells, snare drum
- African—djembe and other hand drums, shakers, cowbells, agogo bells, vocal percussion
- Spanish—tambourine, castanets, triangle, snare drum, bass drum, crash cymbals
- Middle Eastern—riq, doumbek, frame drums, finger cymbals
- Balinese (gamelan)—tuned gongs, metal instruments (pipes, cans, brake drums, etc.) in sets of 5 to 10
- Chinese—different types of gongs, tom-toms, wind chimes, temple bowls, woodblocks, templeblocks
- Indian—tabla

Sample Setups

This appendix provides a variety of sample instrument lists, setup diagrams, and instrument keys. These diagrams represent some of the many ways to set up each group of instruments. Specific placement of some instruments may change depending on the writing in the particular piece, the size and shape of the instruments available, and the performer's preference.

There is no standard method of drawing percussion setup diagrams. The composer should feel free to draw diagrams in the fashion he or she feels best represents the setup.

If the part is conceived for a specific setup, then it is helpful to include a diagram at the beginning of the score and percussion part. If the part was written without a visual image of the setup in mind, then a diagram should be only included, if at all, after the piece has been worked out by the performer.

In many of these examples, the setups are rather simple and a diagram in the score is not necessary. The diagrams are included here to give the composer an idea of how a percussionist might set up these instruments and how the setup relates to the staff notation.

All of these setups would likely include a trap table or two. A trap table is a small table (or music stand, laid flat and covered with a towel) on which beaters and small instruments are placed. Placement of trap tables and music stands, although often important, is not necessary to show in setup diagrams. Trap tables and music stands may be included, if at all, after the piece has been worked out by the performer.

The "X" indicates the position(s) of the performer. Multiple "X"s mean multiple player positions, not multiple players. The audience is located at the top of the page unless otherwise indicated. When the instruments are numbered, no. 1 is the highest pitch. Instruments are not drawn to scale.

Beater needs are described only for setups where the composer may need to leave time for the performer to make a switch. Otherwise, the composer can assume the percussionist will make appropriate beater choices without complication.

Example 1

Setup (figure B.1a)
Notation (figure B.lb)

    suspended cymbal
    2 bongos
    2 timbales
    bass drum

Figure B.1a

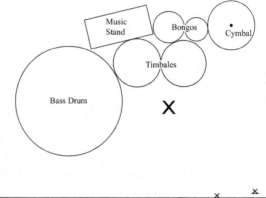

Figure B.1b

For bass drum notes that need to be especially big at loud dynamics or especially warm at soft dynamics, the player would pick up a bass drum beater if there has been a small amount of time allotted to do so.

Example 2

Setup (figure B.2a)
Notation (figure B.2b)

Figure B.2a

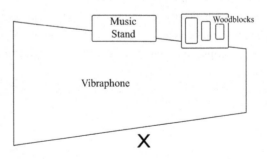

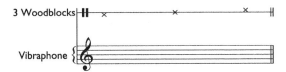

3 woodblocks
vibraphone

The woodblocks would likely be mounted on a trap table.

Example 3

Setup (figure B.3a)
Alternate setup (figure B.3b)

2 octaves of crotales
snare drum
triangle
sleighbells
tambourine
pair of maracas
slapstick
guiro

The small hand-held instruments are usually picked up and played by themselves. If this is the case, these instruments would rest on a trap table. The triangle could be clipped to the music stand. The placement of small instruments does not need to be included in a setup diagram if they are played alone, especially in a setup this small. The two octaves of crotales can be placed next to each other (see figure B.3a) or stacked with the lowest octave closer to the player (figure B.3b). The latter is a more compact and centered setup but requires the player to think of the keyboard in an unusual way. This arrangement also makes it difficult to bow the notes on the inside of the stacked instruments. The composer would likely notate this setup on one staff with indications of instrument switches. If two instruments are used together or in quick succession, two staves should be used. It would be unnecessary to include a setup diagram for a work like this.

Ideally, the player would use plastic or brass mallet for the crotales, sticks for the snare drum, and a triangle beater for the triangle. Concessions could be made if necessary, such as playing the snare drum with plastic mallets or the crotales with triangle beaters. The guiro would be scraped with the triangle beater or the shaft of a crotale mallet.

Figure B.3a

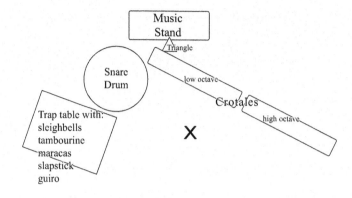

Figure B.3b

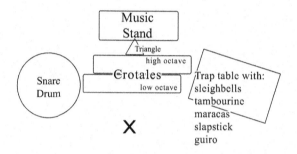

Example 4

Setup (figure B.4a)
Notation (figure B.4b)

> 2 woodblocks
> 3 cowbells
> 2 tom-toms
> vibraphone

For a simple part, just music stand A would be used for the whole setup. If there are complicated passages on both the vibraphone and non-keyboard instruments, then stands B and C may be preferred. This is entirely the player's preference, but the composer may want to supply two copies of the part. The woodblocks and cowbells would likely be mounted on a trap table.

The pitch relationships suggested by this notation should not be assumed. The toms would likely be lower in pitch that the woodblocks and cowbells, but the woodblocks may be within the same pitch range as the cowbells. If the woodblocks and cowbells were used separately, this would not be a problem, but if the relative pitch relationships of these instruments is important, the composer should specify the arrangement (e.g., "woodblocks should be pitched higher that the cowbells").

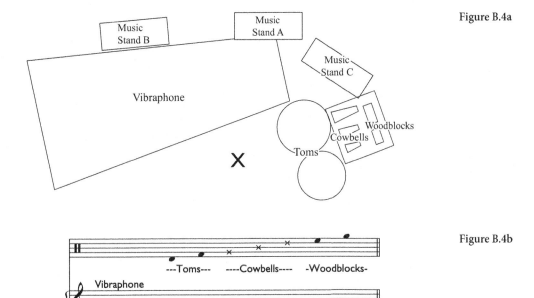

Figure B.4a

Figure B.4b

Example 5

Setup (figure B.5a)
Notation (figure B.5b)
Alternate notation (figure B.5c)

5 tin cans
2 bongos
3 tom-toms
2 timpani

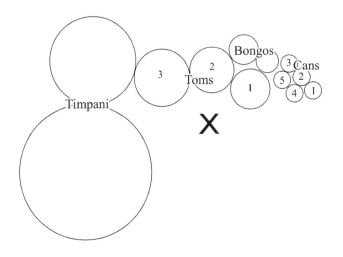

Figure B.5a

If the timpani have the same pitches throughout, they can be notated as indeterminately pitched instruments with the pitches indicated in the instrument list (figure B.5b; see also figure 3.17). If the timpani pitches are manipulated during the piece, the notation shown in figure B.5c is more appropriate.

Figure B.5b

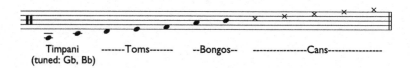

Figure B.5c

Example 6

Setup (figure B.6)

glockenspiel
vibraphone
triangle

Since the triangle is so small, it can be placed just about anywhere. Here, it is clipped to the music stand.

Figure B.6

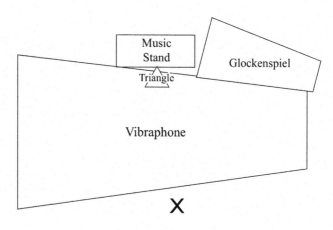

If the writing is sparse, the vibes and glock could be notated on the same staff and differentiated with the written instrument name and with note stem directions. Otherwise, two separate staves should be used—glockenspiel above vibraphone.

Ideally, the player would use cord mallets for the vibraphone, plastic mallets for the glockenspiel, and a triangle beater for the triangle. Time must be allotted for the performer to switch mallets. The performer could hold two cord mallets and two plastic mallets (one in each hand); this would facilitate two mallet passages on the vibraphone and glockenspiel without the need to switch mallets, but four-note chords would not be not possible (see Beater Tricks in chapter 4).

Example 7

Setup (figure B.7a)
Notation (figure B.7b)

> high octave of crotales
> glockenspiel
> 3 suspended cymbals
> 3 triangles
> bongo

Although only one bongo is required, both are present because bongos are attached in pairs. The triangles would hang from a stand.

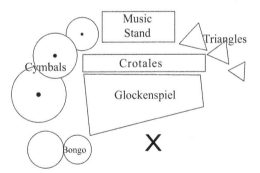

Figure B.7a

Depending on how they are used, the glockenspiel and crotales could be notated on the same staff or as shown in figure B.7b. The bongo would likely be used on its own, so a representation in the notation of its placement in the setup is unnecessary.

Figure B.7b

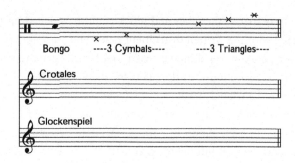

The plastic or brass mallets the player would use for crotales and glockenspiel could work on the triangles and cymbals, but the sound would be clunky. If there is time to switch, the performer may choose triangle beaters for the triangles and cymbals.

Example 8

Setup (figure B.8a)
Notation (figure B.8b)
Alternate notation (figure B.8c)

  5 metal pipes
  5 tom-toms
  pedal bass drum

Figure B.8a

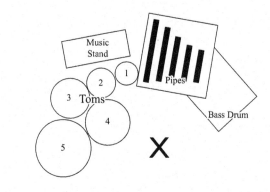

Figure B.8b

Figure B.8c

Example 9

Setup (figure B.9a)
Notation (figure B.9b)
Alternate notation (figure B.9c)

  2 bongos (with hands)
  2 congas (with hands)
  hi-hat

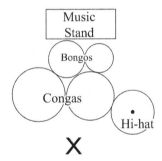

Figure B.9a

Different sounds on the hand drums could be notated using different lines (figure B.9b) or with symbols beneath the note (figure B.9c).

Figure B.9b

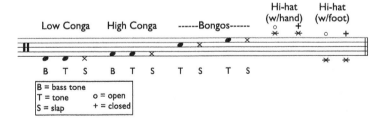

Figure B.9c

Example 10

Setup (figure B.10a)
Alternate setup (figure B.10b)
Notation (figure B.10c)

2 cowbells
2 bongos
3 tom-toms
2 suspended cymbals
china cymbal
pedal bass drum
tam-tam

With a large tam-tam, a low stand behind the player would probably be used (figure B.10a). If a small tam-tam were used, it could be mounted higher, above the bass drum (figure B.10b).

Figure B.10a

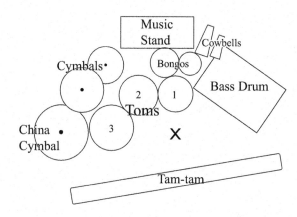

Figure B.10b

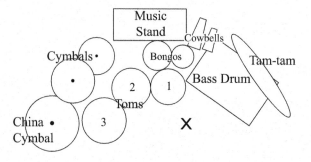

Figure B.10c

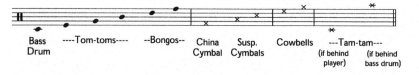

Example 11

Setup (figure B.11a)
Notation (figure B.11b)
Alternate setup (figure B.11c)

    marimba
    vibraphone
    4 tom-toms
    bass drum
    2 suspended cymbals
    tam-tam

If all the instruments are used together, figure B.11a is one possible setup. The bass drum is located to the right of the toms (it would normally be on the left) so the toms can be located closer to the mallet instruments. If the bass drum was on the other side, the toms would be very far from the rest of the action. It will be only a small task for the player to adjust to playing the part with the bass drum on the "wrong" side.

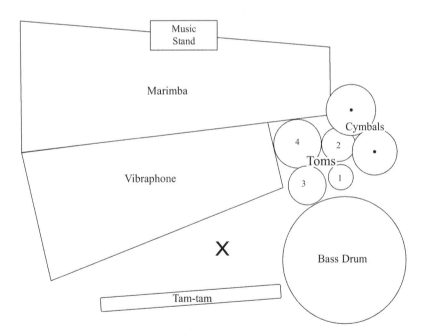

Figure B.11a

With the same list of instruments, if the non-keyboard instruments are primarily used only around the vibraphone—with the marimba used separately—then the setup might look as shown in figure B.11c. In this case, the vibraphone and marimba could share a staff with written instructions "marimba" or "vibraphone" where needed.

Figure B.11b

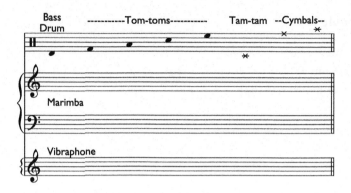

Figure B.11c

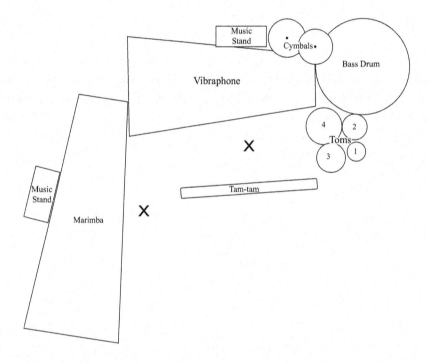

The vibraphone mallets appropriate for the keyboard instruments, toms, and cymbals would get a bright, thin sound out of the bass drum and tam-tam. A short amount of time should be allotted for the performer to switch before important bass drum or tam-tam notes. A tam-tam beater could be hung from the stand for quick access.

Example 12

Setup (figure B.12a)
Notation (figure B.12b)

vibraphone
glockenspiel

xylophone
triangle
5 templeblocks
tubular bells
3 temple bowls on a timpano

This is just one of many possible ways to set up these instruments. If the glockenspiel is used with the vibraphone and the tubular bells with the xylophone, then the glockenspiel and tubular bells would be switched. If there are quick passages between both the glockenspiel and the vibraphone and the glockenspiel and the xylophone, the glockenspiel might be put in the middle, or two glockenspiels may be required. If the player must move quickly between the bowls and the vibes, then the timpano would be placed on the other side. All large setups will have many variations. The damper pedal of the tubular bells, in the setup shown in figure B.12a, is not reachable and would be preset to always let the chimes ring.

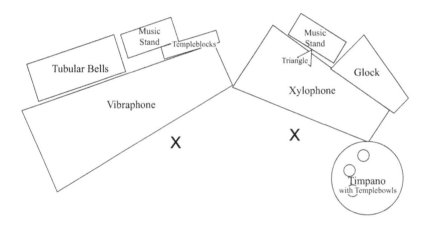

Figure B.12a

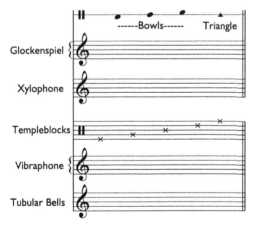

Figure B.12b

Hard rubber or plastic mallets would be used for most of the instruments on the right side of the setup; triangle beaters would be used for the triangle. Cord mallets would be used for all the instruments of the left side, although chime hammers would be required for any exposed or loud playing on the tubular bells.

Example 13

Setup (figure B.13a)
Notation (figure B.13b)

marimba
vibraphone
glockenspiel
5 tom-toms
bass drum
2 suspended cymbals
tam-tam
maracas
claves

Again, this is a set of instruments with many possible setups. The maracas and claves would be placed on a trap table with sticks and mallets. Depending on player preference, this table may be behind the player, next to the glockenspiel, next to the toms, and so on. The glockenspiel in this configuration would likely be used for isolated notes and simple figures; for a more involved glock part, or one that is tightly integrated with the other instruments, the glockenspiel may be relocated to where the toms currently live, pushing the non-keyboard instruments farther upstage.

Figure B.13a

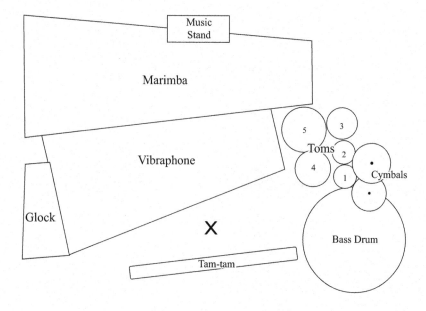

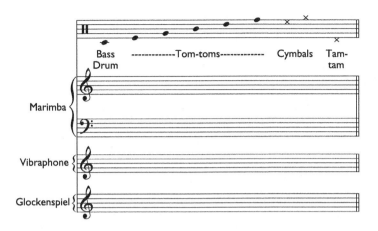

The performer would need to switch to a bass drum beater or tam-tam beater for important notes on those instruments. The tam-tam beater could be hung from the stand for easy access.

Example 14

Setup (figure B.14a)
Original notation (figure B.14b)
Alternate notation (figure B.14c)

This is the setup for Shawn Crouch's *Suspended Contact,* written for the Yesaroun' Duo (Eric Hewitt and Samuel Solomon).

    vibraphone
    3 nipple gongs (no specific pitches)
    2 crystal glasses
    3 frying pans
    3 cowbells
    2 woodblocks
    pedal bass drum
    3 tom-toms
    snare drum
    hi-hat
    2 suspended cymbals
    large tam-tam
    triangle

The gongs hang from a rack over the vibraphone; the triangle hangs from a music stand. The vibraphone, bass drum, and hi-hat have pedals, so footwork—as well as the direction the player is facing—must be considered. Pedals can be played with the heel of the foot, so the player can play a pedal instrument even when facing the other way.

Figure B.14a

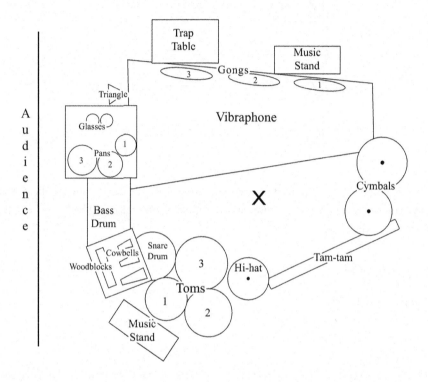

This setup surrounds the player entirely so there is no clean way to notate it. Figure B.14b shows the notation used, which Crouch and I designed before the piece was written. The gongs are notated without pitch specification. In hindsight, for reasons specific to the writing in the piece, the notation shown in figure B.14c may have been more appropriate; however, either notation is effective and functional.

Figure B.14b

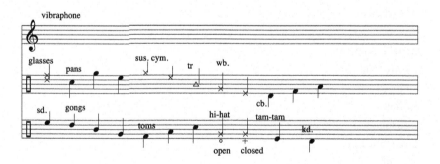

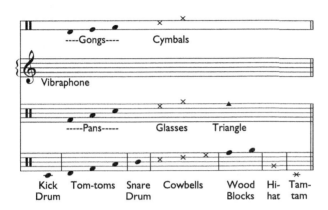

Figure B.14c

With large setups like this one, it may be appropriate to alter the notation for different sections of the piece. For example, *Suspended Contact* features an extended passage for the suspended cymbals and hi-hat, during which those instruments could be consolidated onto one staff. As long as they are clearly labeled, these types of adjustments can and should be made.

Beaters for the piece are specified throughout, making use of the head and shaft of cord mallets, sticks, and knitting needles. Crouch and I worked out the beater plan in preparation for the first performance, balancing Crouch's requests for specific timbral changes with the feasibility of making the beater switches.

Example 15

Instrument key (figure B.15a)
Inital setups (figure B.15b)
Reworked setup (figure B.15c)
Complete ensemble setup (figure B.15d)

Figure B.15a is the instrument key for Steven Mackey's *Micro-Concerto* for percussion and five players, written for the New York New Music Ensemble (NYNME). The solo part was written with the assistance of percussionist Daniel Druckman. In preparation for this piece, Druckman provided Mackey with a number of instruments with which he could experiment, so prior to and during the composition process, Mackey was able to design his own sounds, playing techniques, and setup.

Mackey originally conceived these as two separate setups, but after working out the notation and diagrams, he realized that they might be consolidated (for example, by having the Asian drum in Station 2 be the medium tom in Station 1). While composing, he was able to set up and experiment with the instruments in Station 1; he did not, however, have access to all of the instruments for Station 2 and could only guess at its exact arrangement. Figure B.15b shows the rough diagram on which the notation was based, drawn with the knowledge that some adjustments would be necessary once Druckman started working with the score.

Figure B.15a

Station 1: Percussion Map

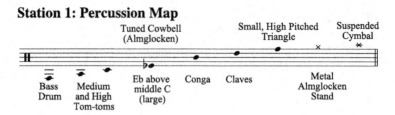

Station 2: Percussion Map

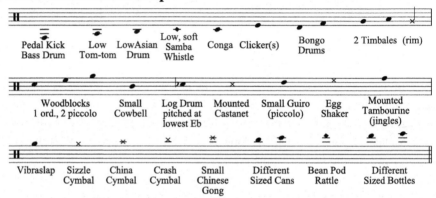

•Low Asian Drum should be pitched much lower than Bongos and a bit higher than low tom-tom.

•Conga when struck with hand uses three types of attacks: tone (t) normal resonant palm strike, bass (b) heel of hand in center for low bass notes, slap (s) for crisp high pitched snap.

•Clickers are toy noise makers sold in toy stores and party supply houses. They make sound when pressed and again when released. Typically, the "release" is pitched slightly lower than the "press." There is no notational distinction made between clickers in right or left hands. Occasionally the distinction is made between press (P) and release (R). If not indicated, it is up to the performer; obviously two Ps or two Rs in a row indicates alternating hands.

•Small Cowbell should be pitched above regular wood block. "Clinky," not resonant.

•The bean pod rattle should have the smallest possible bean pods, so that the sound is more of a soft "crackle" than "rattle."

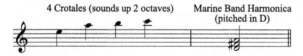

Figure B.15b

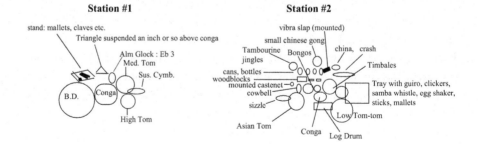

Ultimately, the two stations were consolidated; the low tom-tom and lower drum of the timbales in Station 2 became the medium and high tom-toms in Station 1. Many other instruments were rearranged as well, especially in Station 2. Station 1, the setup which Mackey had while composing, remained almost entirely intact. Figure B.15c shows the setup Druckman designed.

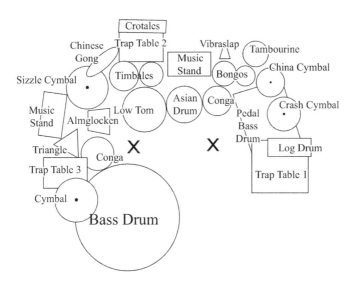

Figure B.15c

Most of the small instruments are mounted either on a stand or on a trap table; the few that must be held to be played are the claves, samba whistle, clickers, egg shaker, bean pod rattle, and harmonica. The crash cymbal is a suspended crash cymbal, not a pair of crash cymbals. The samba whistle, clickers, cowbell, castanet, guiro, and egg shaker rest on trap table 1; the cans, bottles, and woodblocks rest on trap table 2; and the claves and bean pod rattle rest on trap table 3.

During the transition from the original to the final setup, Mackey and Druckman worked together to tweak both the setup and some of the more complicated passages to fit each other. As a result, this setup is closely linked with the writing but seemingly not so with the notation. Much of the music uses only small groups of instruments at a time, so an intuitive notation which represents the entire setup as one instrument (like those in many other examples in this appendix) is not necessary. The entire setup for the *Micro-Concerto* is shown in figure B.15d.

The piece is in five movements and the soloist uses the instruments as follows:

Movement 1: Station 1
Movement 2: vibraphone
Movement 3: Station 2
Movement 4: marimba
Movement 5: both Stations 1 and 2

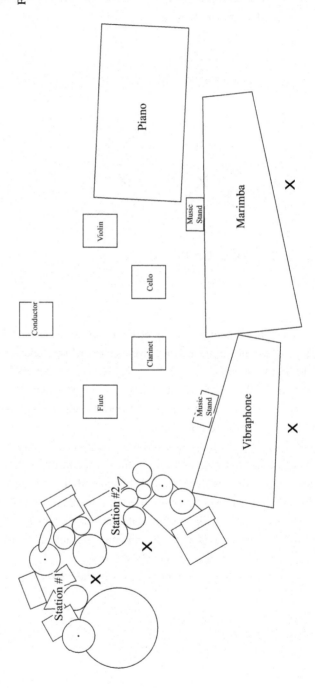

Figure B.15d

The vibraphone movement is played with the flute and the marimba with the cello, so those instruments are set up near each other to achieve the proper instrument pairings. The fourth and fifth movements are *attacca*, so there is a rather quick switch between the marimba and Stations 1 and 2; however, this switch is not so fast that it is unreasonable to observe the instrument pairings. If the performer had less time to make the switch, the position of the marimba and vibraphone would have to be reversed.

Extended Techniques

The techniques of percussion playing are so numerous that it may seem inappropriate to refer to any as "extended." Collected here are many of the common techniques that stray from traditional performance practice. Much of this information is cross-referenced earlier in the chapters that address the individual instruments.

When making use of these or any extended technique, the composer must:

1. Make sure there is ample time to get into and out of position to make the sound without any unwanted noise.
2. Make sure the sound, when executed in context, can achieve the desired dynamic.

The composer should always collaborate with a percussionist to confirm that the technique works in the requested musical context.

Written descriptions of less common or newly invented techniques, although necessary in the score and percussion part, are often difficult to understand. It is recommended that the composer feature video demonstrations on his or her website for clarification.

Return to a "Normal" Method of Playing

When an unusual method of playing is indicated (e.g., using a prepared instrument or playing with unusual mallets), it should be indicated when the player should stop doing this (e.g., "remove paper clip" or "return to normal beaters").

Manipulations of Timbre

🔊 Video C.a—Timbre

Timbre (or *tone color*) is the perceived sound that results from the hidden harmony present in every acoustic sound—that is, the tuning and balance of overtones (or *partials*). The arrangement of overtones is what gives each instrument its unique color. Timbre can also denote a sound's articulation and envelope.

Timbre can be described in an infinite number of ways: warm, sharp, green, sweet, dirty, and so on. For the purpose of this explanation, timbre is described only as "bright" or "dark"—that is, with more or less prominent higher overtones.

The larger the instrument, the wider the range of timbres. Just as a cello can play much lower than a violin and can also, under special conditions, produce pitches in the violin's highest range, larger percussion instruments—such as the bass drum and tam-tam—sound very low and dark and also, under special conditions, very high and bright.

With some indeterminately pitched percussion instruments, the fundamental is not heard at all—the sound is all overtones. In these cases, a change in timbre results in a change of the perceived pitch of the instrument.

Dynamics

louder dynamic = brighter
softer dynamic = darker

For example, when a player rolls on a cymbal or tam-tam, the pitch becomes higher as the dynamic grows, and vice versa. With sirens, the pitch becomes higher as the player blows or cranks harder. With the guiro, the pitch becomes higher as the player scrapes faster and harder. With the marimba, the sound becomes sharper as the player strikes the bar more loudly. The higher overtones are brought out as the dynamic increases.

Beaters

smaller and/or harder beaters = brighter
larger and/or softer beaters = darker

For example, felt mallets on a tom-tom sound warm and covered while snare sticks sound pointed and bright. A tam-tam struck with a triangle beater produces pitches octaves above the pitches produced with a large tam-tam beater.[1] In hand drumming, use of one finger produces a much brighter sound than use of the whole hand.

Beating Spot (Placement of Attack)

When struck closer to the part of the instrument that vibrates the least (a nodal point), the sound is brighter than the part of the instrument that vibrates the most (similar to a *sul ponticello* versus *sul tasto* effect on string instruments[2]). Specifically:

---

1. Technically, the dark sound produced with a tam-tam beater contains all of the high overtones the triangle beater produces, but these overtones are fused into the sound of the low fundamental pitches. The triangle beater produces the overtones exclusively.
2. This analogy is made with respect to bowing nearer or farther from the bridge. Because of additional differences of proximity to the resonating chamber, as well as changes of bow speed and pressure, the differences in timbre between *sul ponticello* and *sul tasto* are more subtle than simply one is "bright" and the other "dark." The analogy, however, is still a useful reference.

on drums and gongs:
    toward the edge = brighter
    toward the center = darker
on mallet instruments:
    toward the node = brighter
    toward the center = darker
on cymbals and crotales:
    toward the bell/center = brighter
    toward the edge = darker
on cowbell:
    toward the crown = brighter
    toward the lip = darker

Muting (Dampening)

If an instrument is muted while it is struck, the instrument will sound drier and more articulate. The larger and heavier the mute, the more muffling power it has. Placement of the mute affects the sound in the opposite way that placement of the beating spot does (as described above). For example:

on drums and gongs:
    mute toward the edge = darker
    mute toward the center = brighter

If an instrument is dampened slightly after it is struck, then the timbre of the ring is affected. For example, lower pitches can be taken out of the sound of a resonating tam-tam if the center of the instrument is dampened slightly. This makes the higher overtones more apparent.

Light dampening with a piece of cloth is often used to make drums drier, darker, and clearer in pitch. Light dampening is also used to clean up soft, articulate passages on timpani and other large resonant drums. Heavy dampening is commonly used with pedal bass drums whereby towels, sheets, or something similar is inserted into the drum, giving it a full but punchy sound. These types of common muting techniques do not need to be specified.

Striking Unusual Parts of an Instrument

🔊 Video C.b—Instrument Parts, Beaters, Dead Stroke, Beating Spot

The rim or shell of a drum can be struck with the shaft of a stick. (See Playing on the Rim or Shell in chapter 6 for details.) The bowl of a timpano can be struck with the head of a mallet, but this may damage the instrument. (See Timpani in chapter 6.)

The frame of a keyboard instrument or the metal stand for a cymbal or drum can be struck. These objects rarely produce good sounds, and it is often more effective to replace them with similarly functioning instruments.

The resonators of keyboard instruments can be scraped horizontally with a mallet. The resulting sound varies considerably depending on the material of the resonators, which is determined by the make and model of the instrument. Some instruments' resonators sound beautiful while others sound dull and clunky. A resonator scrape should not be done with hard plastic, wood, or metal beaters, to avoid damaging the resonators.

Unusual Use of Beaters

🌑 Video C.b—Instrument Parts, Beaters, Dead Stroke, Beating Spot

Unique effects can be achieved by using beaters not specifically designed for a given instrument. In some cases, a beater change can completely change the sound and function of an instrument.

Percussionists can, within reason, hold any combination of four mallets (e.g., a bass drum beater, two drum sticks, and a triangle beater). Specialty double-ended sticks called *flip sticks, combo sticks,* or *two-headed sticks* are commonly available; usually a drum stick is paired with a felt or yarn mallet so the player can flip the beaters over to create a totally different sound. Flipping a pair of beaters is reasonable, but flipping a set of four is not. (See chapter 4 and appendix G for details.)

The shaft or butt of a beater can be used for certain effects. For example, timpani mallets can be flipped to use the butt end like a drum stick or the shaft of a marimba mallet could strike the edge of a marimba bar for a bright, ticky color. (See The Shaft and Butt of Beaters in chapter 4 for details.)

A *rimshot* is an effect whereby the stick strikes the head and rim of a drum simultaneously. (See Sticks on Drums in chapter 6 for details.) A *marimshot* is a less common but similar effect whereby the mallet head and shaft strike a marimba bar simultaneously. (See Extended Techniques in chapter 5.)

When the edge of an instrument is struck with the shaft of a stick or mallet, the timbre is brighter when struck toward the tip of the stick than when struck toward the hand that is holding it. This is especially apparent with sticks on the rims of drums where the sound of the stick itself can be heard. The reader can observe this effect by striking the edge of a table with a pencil at different points on the pencil's shaft. (This effect is used with drum sticks on the rim of a snare drum in Neboja Zivkovic's *Pezzo da Concerto* for solo snare drum.)

Dead Stroke

🌑 Video C.b—Instrument Parts, Beaters, Dead Stroke, Beating Spot

A dead stroke is achieved by holding the mallet on the instrument after the attack to dampen the vibration. Dead strokes are commonly notated with a plus sign (+) over the note. Ringing notes in a passage with dead strokes can be indicated with a circle (○) over them; this is not necessary but can help to clarify. "D.S." or staccato dots are other common indications for dead stroke. These notations are not standard and should be explained at the top of the score and percussion part.

Dead strokes take more time to execute than normal strokes because the mallet head needs to spend more time on the instrument. Passages with dead strokes will not be effective at fast tempi.

With drum sticks, wood mallets, plastic mallets, and hard rubber mallets, dead strokes create a buzz sound as the beater bounces quickly on the instrument (like the bounce of a buzz roll). Mallets wrapped with yarn, cord, and felt have a soft layer of material to cushion the attack and eliminate the bounce. This buzz can be avoided by using wrapped mallets (e.g., instead of plastic mallets, very hard yarn or cord mallets could be used) or by wrapping a layer of masking tape or moleskin around the mallet head.

Dead strokes can be used as short notes on the marimba or vibraphone to contrast with the resonating normal strokes. (See Steven Mackey's *See Ya Thursday.*) At loud dynamics, these dead strokes can slightly lower the pitch as the mass of the mallet is temporarily added to that of the bar. On drums, dead strokes sound harsher and raise the pitch slightly as the drum head is stretched by the pressure of the stroke.

Beating Spot

◑ Video C.b—Instrument Parts, Beaters, Dead Stroke, Beating Spot

Variety of color is available on all struck instruments by adjusting the beating spot with respect to the nodal points. This is especially pronounced on timpani, where the center is a complete dead spot relative to the normal beating spot closer to the edge. (See Timpani in chapter 6.) As described earlier in Manipulations of Timbre:

on drums and gongs:
    toward the edge = brighter
    toward the center = darker
on mallet instruments:
    toward the node = brighter
    toward the center = darker
on cymbals and crotales:
    toward the bell/center = brighter
    toward the edge = darker
on cowbell:
    toward the crown = brighter
    toward the lip = darker

For this effect on drums, see the second movement of Béla Bartók's *Sonata for Two Pianos and Percussion*; John Cage's *Third Construction*; and Igor Stravinsky's *L'Histore du Soldat*. For the effect on timpani, see Elliott Carter's *Eight Pieces for Four Timpani*. For its effect on marimba, see Roger Reynolds's *Autumn Island*.

Bowing

🔊 Video C.c—Bowing, Friction Roll, Scrape

The following instruments can be bowed with a bass or cello bow: vibraphone, crotales, cymbals, gongs, crystal glasses, flexatone, marimba, xylophone, cowbells, almglocken, woodblocks, templeblocks, temple bowls, thundersheet, tubular bells, and triangle. (See Bows in chapter 4 for details.)

Friction Roll

🔊 Video C.c—Bowing, Friction Roll, Scrape

A surface can be rubbed with a finger to create a groaning sound. This technique is similar to bowing in that it rapidly re-attacks a surface to create a sustained sound. A friction roll on large drums (bass drums, timpani, and large toms) could replace the sound of a string drum. (See String Drum in chapter 9.) Deep groans can be rubbed out of walls, floors, wooden boxes, piano sound boards, and the like. On smaller drums with tighter heads, this sounds more like a very rapid tremolo.

A Superball mallet is a Superball attached to a piece of coat hanger or another slightly flexible piece of metal or wood. A Superball mallet, dragged against a surface, creates a groaning sound like that of a finger rub. The Superball may be slightly easier to use than a finger because the degree of friction tends to be more consistent. Use of either a finger or a Superball can be the performer's choice. (See George Crumb's *Idyll for the Misbegotten* and Lukas Foss's *Thirteen Ways of Looking at a Blackbird*.)

A friction roll is a quiet effect and can easily be lost in ensemble textures. Friction rolls may activate any of a number of harmonics from the rubbed instrument, so the pitches produced will be variable and unpredictable.

Scrape

🔊 Video C.c—Bowing, Friction Roll, Scrape

Cymbals and gongs can be scraped with a coin or triangle beater. The back of a keyboard mallet can work on cymbals, but not very well; a fingernail can work, but only at extremely soft dynamics. To notate a scrape, simply write "scrape" over the note. The length of the note indicates the length of the scrape, not the length of the sustain. A quick scrape with a crescendo is easiest and most effective, but longer scrapes are possible. It is assumed that the scrape will be left to ring unless otherwise indicated. (See the second movement of Joseph Schwantner's *Percussion Concerto* and Ryan Streber's *Cold Pastoral*.)

A scrape is sometimes called a cymbal or tam-tam glissando because there is a glissando of overtones. A quick stroke with a crescendo results in a glissando upward. (See the Sacrificial Dance in Stravinsky's *Rite of Spring*.)

A scrape is commonly executed on drums when the player holds brushes. (See Brushes in chapter 4.) The brush scrape can add variety of length to the otherwise short sound of a drum strike. (See John Cage's *Second Construction*.)

In all cases, a scrape tremolo is possible by rapidly scraping back and forth.

Cymbals and gongs are also capable of a scream (or *screech*). A scream is a technique whereby a stick is held perpendicular to the cymbal or gong and the tip or butt is dragged across the instrument's face. This produces a sound similar to bowing the instrument, but it is even more shrill and abrasive.

Prepared Instruments

🔊 Video C.d—Preparations

The snare drum, tambourine, ocean drum, and sizzle cymbal are instruments that have preparations by definition. The snares of snare drums and field drums add a snappy buzz to what otherwise would be a tom-tom. Tambourines are frame drums outfitted with several small cymbals called "jingles" that ring along with articulations of the drum. In the case of orchestral and rock tambourines, the primary sound is that of the jingles; for many ethnic tambourines, the drum sound is most prominent with the jingles only contributing random ornamentation. An ocean drum is a two-headed frame drum; the space between the heads is filled with small metal ball bearings that can rattle along with drum articulations or be swirled around for a sustained sound. A sizzle cymbal has small holes around the outside edge that are filled with metal rivets; when the cymbal is struck, the rivets bounce up and down inside the holes, contributing a sizzling sound.

For resonant metal instruments like cymbals and gongs, a sizzle effect can be created by attaching a coin, paper clip, or thin metal chain; this is similar to the traditional sizzle cymbal. A manual sizzle can be achieved by holding a triangle beater or coin against the instrument; in this case, the sizzle can be added and taken away while the instrument is resonating.

The same is true of resonant metal keyboard instruments, vibraphone, crotales, glockenspiel, and tubular bells. Coins, paper clips, and other such items can be taped to individual bars to sizzle when that note is struck. These preparations slightly dampen the bar; smaller bars, like those on glockenspiels, crotales, and the upper register of vibraphone, are most susceptible to this problem. On the vibraphone and marimba, aluminum foil can also be placed over the top of the resonators of individual notes for an interesting buzzing effect. (See Jay Alan Yim's *Jam Karet*.)

Various bells, shakers, rattles, or jingles can be found attached to drums in African traditional music. This effect can easily be recreated on standard percussion instruments. Drums are the most eligible for preparation in this way, either with bells or rattles attached to the side of the drum or even with small objects (e.g., bells, shakers, a coin, paper clip, ball bearings, etc.) resting on the head. At loud dynamics, objects resting on the drum head will likely bounce off onto the floor; this is especially so with large and resonant drums like timpani and bass drum. Objects can be secured to the head with tape to rattle at louder dynamics without falling off, but this will muffle the head. Taped or not, any object resting on the head of a drum will dampen the head to some degree.

There are unique types of preparations for timpani. Crotales, temple bowls, or an upside-down cymbal can be placed on a timpano head and struck, rolled on, or bowed while the percussionist pedals up and down. A thumb piano can also be played while resting on a timpano. These preparations produce haunting effects. In each case, the overtones of the timpano head resonate sympathetically with the pitches produced by the instrument resting on it; the moving pedal gives the impression that these pitches are glissando-ing. The effects are very soft and will not be noticed if the pedal moves up and down too slowly. The specific pitch of the drum head will not be heard. (See Per Nørgård's *I Ching* and George Crumb's *Music for a Summer Evening*.)

Playing too many crotales on a timpano is unwieldy and passages will be difficult to execute; it is best to use no more than six notes in these situations. If quick passages or passages with many notes are needed, it is more appropriate to use a regular set of crotales on a stand.

The player's hands, arms, feet, or mallets can be prepared with bells or rattles to add ambient sounds to the player's normal motions. Bells that attach to a player's wrists or ankles are common. (See the ankle rattles in James Wood's *Village Burial with Fire*, and the wrist bells for marimba players in Sofia Gubaidulina's *In the Beginning There Was Rhythm* and Adam Silverman's *Naked and on Fire*.)

Pitch Bending

🔊 Video C.e—Pitch Bend, Vibrato, Adding Mass

Timpani, roto-toms, flexatones, and slide whistles have mechanisms that can bend the pitch.

Indeterminately pitched instruments like cymbals, tam-tams, guiros, string drums, cuicas, sirens, and wind machines produce a pitch or pitch spectrum that becomes higher with an increase of dynamic and lower with a decrease of dynamic. Friction rolls on drums exhibit a similar effect.

Some gongs, most notably Chinese opera gongs, naturally produce a pitch bend when struck. Small opera gongs (6 to 10 inches, 15–24 cm) bend upward and larger gongs (10 to 14 inches, 24–35.5 cm) bend downward.

On all drums, the head can be depressed with a fist, elbow, or stick to stretch the head and raise the pitch.

Individual notes of a marimba, vibraphone, xylophone, and glockenspiel can be bent downward by sliding and pressing a hard plastic or rubber mallet into the center of the bar. (See Extended Techniques in chapter 5 for details.)

Resonant metal instruments like gongs, crotales, tubular bells, and triangles can be lowered into a tub of water to bend the pitch downward. (See Water in chapter 7 for details.)

A pitch-bend effect can be achieved by playing instruments like cymbals, crotales, or temple bowls that rest on the head of a timpano. The overtones of the head of the timpano resonate sympathetically with the pitch of the instrument resting on it. When the pedal of the timpano is manipulated, it gives the impression that the pitch of the instrument resting on it is bending. (See Prepared Instruments earlier in this appendix.)

A pitch-bend effect can be achieved by manipulating the resonating chamber between two cymbals. If a hi-hat is slowly closed while rolling softly on the top cymbal with sticks, the pitches of the overtones become gradually lower as the cymbals become closer to each other; this is a subtle and quiet effect used with amplification in Peter Eötvös's *Shadows*. The same effect could be achieved by moving a pair of ringing hand crash cymbals toward or away from one another; this is done with Chinese hand cymbals in Lei Liang's *Dialectal Percussions*.

A pitch-bend effect can be achieved by blending an instrument's sound with that of another instrument capable of glissando. In his *Music for a Summer Evening*, George Crumb asks the performer to whistle along with the vibraphone and glissando (with the whistle) from note to note. This sounds as if a portamento effect is achieved by the vibraphone.

Vibrato

◑ Video C.e—Pitch Bend, Vibrato, Adding Mass

Percussion vibrato is a pulsing vibrato (like flute vibrato) and not a pitch-bending vibrato. Vibrato achieved by using some of the above pitch-bending techniques is not common and would be rather awkward to execute.

Vibrato on vibraphone is common through use of its motor. Mouth vibrato, another vibraphone specific technique, is achieved by rapidly opening and closing one's mouth while holding it over a ringing bar. (See chapter 5 for details.)

Triangle vibrato can be achieved by shaking the instrument back and forth after it has been struck. This can only be done when the triangle is held, not when it is mounted. Glockenspiel vibrato is created by waving a hand up and down over the struck note. These are soft, subtle effects.

Rolls in percussion can act expressively as vibrato does for other instruments. A player can achieve a vibrato-like effect by manipulating the type and speed of rolls. Specifics of roll speed and type are rarely prescribed by the composer; an *espressivo* marking is enough to indicate this type of execution.

Adding Mass

◉ Video C.e—Pitch Bend, Vibrato, Adding Mass

The pitch of an instrument can be lowered by adding mass to the resonating body. In all cases, added mass will dampen the resonance of the instrument. The more mass added, the more dampening will occur.

As mentioned earlier in Pitch Bending, a player can bend the pitch of a marimba, vibraphone, xylophone, or glockenspiel note by pressing and sliding a hard plastic mallet into the center of the bar. This adds the mass of the mallet head to the bar and thus lowers the pitch (see chapter 5).

Also mentioned earlier, metal instruments can be lowered into a tub of water to lower the pitch. The mass of the water is added to the resonating instrument. (See Water in chapter 7.)

A bottle or glass filled with water resonates at a lower pitch than the empty vessel when struck, bowed, or rubbed. As more water is added, the pitch becomes lower and the instrument becomes more dampened. (See George Crumb's *Black Angels*.) A bottle played by blowing over the opening will be affected oppositely: adding water shrinks the resonating chamber and raises the pitch.

Little bits of clay can be applied to an instrument to lower the pitch. This is used directly in back of the nipple to tune nipple gongs, in the center of the drum head on some hand drums, and on the edge of the marimba, vibraphone, or xylophone bars when microtonal tuning is required. In addition to lowering the pitch, the clay dampens the instrument. With hand drums and nipple gongs, the dampening of the clay serves an additional purpose: it dampens the higher overtones and clarifies the fundamental pitch.

Dampening an instrument in a normal fashion may result in a pitch drop. Normally, the cloth, body part, tape, or other that is dampening the instrument is too loosely applied to create this effect. If the instrument is held tightly, however—for example, by a hand—then there will be a noticeable difference between the dampened and undampened pitch; of course, the dampened pitch will only sound for a short moment before the dampening takes full effect. The reader can observe this subtle effect with a drinking glass: strike the glass with a pencil then strike it again while grasping it tightly with the other hand; a slight pitch difference will be observed.

Sympathetic Resonance

◉ Video C.f—Sympathetic Resonance, Clusters, Harmonics

Certain resonant instruments respond in sympathy to other sounding instruments. This can be used as a special effect, but in some cases it can cause problems.

Metal instruments tend to sing along with other loud sounds. This sympathetic resonance is soft and will only be noticed in the silence after a sound is made. For example, in a silence after a loud orchestra passage, those sitting around a tam-tam will notice it resonating at one or several of the pitches previously present in the orchestra. Cymbals and tam-tams resonate at a wide number of pitches and are especially susceptible to this effect. The vibraphone and tubular bells with pedals down quietly hum pitches that are loudly introduced to them from an outside source. Amplification can help bring out the subtle resonance in these instruments. This is the same effect that is commonly used with sympathetically resonating piano strings.

Two timpani tuned in unison will ring sympathetically with one another. By striking one drum loudly and then muffling it, one can hear the sympathetic resonance of the other drum. This effect is subtle, and a glissando on the drum not struck can be used to make the sympathetic resonance more noticeable. (See Elliott Carter's *Adagio* from *Eight Pieces for Timpani.*) (See Timpani in chapter 6 for details.)

Timpani can also be used as resonators for other non-percussion instruments that are played into the heads of the drums while the pedal is adjusted (with trumpets in Jefferson Friedman's *Sacred Heart: Explosion,* and trombones in Christopher Rouse's *Seeing*).

With the prepared instruments described here, the rattling or buzzing sound achieved by placing an item (coin, paper clip, tin foil, rattle, tambourine, sleighbells, etc.) on an instrument is a function of sympathetic resonance. In the case of prepared timpani, the harmonics of the drum head resonate sympathetically with the resonance of the crotales, temple bowls, or cymbal. (See Prepared Instruments earlier in this appendix.)

Sympathetic resonance can be a problem in the case of unwanted additional vibrations. Some instruments, like the bass drum, produce many pitches that correspond to those in the hardware used in a setup or to those in objects in the room (heating ducts, etc.) and can set off many rattles and buzzes when played. This should not be a problem in concert halls and with properly cared-for instruments and hardware.

Sometimes an instrument itself can respond unfavorably to outside stimuli, as is often the case with the snare drum. When a snare drum is used in a setup or ensemble, the unwanted sounds of vibrating snares are almost always a problem. On the other hand, the snare's sympathetic buzzing can be an effect to enhance a wind or brass sound or that of another percussion instrument. (See chapter 6 for more information.)

Clusters

◖ Video C.f—Sympathetic Resonance, Clusters, Harmonics

Clusters can be produced by striking a keyboard instrument with a dowel lengthwise. Clusters are most effective on the vibraphone and tubular bells where the notes can ring freely and sustain the cluster sound. (See Extended Techniques in chapter 5 for more information.)

Harmonics

◉ Video C.f—Sympathetic Resonance, Clusters, Harmonics

On timpani, harmonics can be produced by pressing a finger or mallet against the drumhead about halfway between the center and edge and then striking toward the edge. This sounds the harmonic an octave above the fundamental. It is a subtle effect, and a moment of preparation is necessary to get the finger or mallet into position. (See Elliott Carter's *Eight Pieces for Four Timpani.*)

In the low register of the vibraphone and marimba (C5 and below), a harmonic two octaves above the pitch of a bar can be produced by slightly dampening the center of the bar (with a finger or mallet), striking toward the node, and then quickly removing the dampening. From C2 to A2 on the marimba, a harmonic three octaves and a major third above the pitch of the bar is prominent. Harmonics are far more successful on the vibraphone, where the pitch can be left to resonate alone. Vibraphone harmonics can also be bowed. Harmonics are somewhat unpredictable and are difficult to produce with consistency. (See George Crumb's *Madrigal I* and Christopher Deane's *Mourning Dove Sonnet.*)

The composer should be aware that on a five-octave marimba, the notes in the lowest octave have strong and clear harmonics; three octaves and a major third above (a major 24th) are especially apparent. If a minor tenth (or minor 17th, minor 24th, etc.) is struck, the dissonance between that interval and the overtone is very audible; it sounds almost as if all three notes had been struck. This applies to 11ths, 18ths, and so on, as well.

Pitch Specification

There are a handful of examples in the repertoire where pitch specification is requested for instruments that are normally indeterminately pitched. This practice is more or less reasonable, successful, and necessary depending on the instrument.

It should be noted that, for many of the non-keyboard instruments listed below, specified pitches are best used in small numbers—no more than a set of five. The type of music that composers tend to write using pitches—that is, melodic material—does not work as well on these instruments. Besides its being potentially logistically or financially restrictive, forcing a non-keyboard instrument to act as keyboard instrument often results in clunky and unclear music. Composers should remember that these instruments are capable of significant musical contributions when used in ways that take advantage of their unique strengths.

Always Reasonable

The following instruments are determinately pitched and commonly available. It is always reasonable to request specific pitches for these instruments.

vibraphone
marimba
xylophone
glockenspiel
chimes
crotales
steel drums
timpani
roto-toms*
flexatone*
crystal glasses*
slide whistle*
thumb piano*

*Roto-toms and crystal classes with specific pitches should be requested in reasonable numbers. Three or four is easy; 33 would be clumsy and unwieldy. Thumb pianos vary in size but are able to accommodate at least seven fixed pitches. Roto-tom, crystal glass, and thumb piano pitches must be preset; roto-toms may be retuned during a piece with a small amount of time. Only simple melodies are reasonable on the flexatone and slide whistle.

Reasonable But Not Always Available

The following instruments are usually determinately pitched but are rarely available in full chromatic sets. It is reasonable to request specific pitches for these instruments, but requested pitches may not always be available.

almglocken
nipple gongs
church handbells

Reasonable in Small Numbers

The following instruments are usually indeterminately pitched, but they are easy to tune. It is reasonable to request fixed pitches for these instruments in small numbers (e.g., two tuned congas, not a chromatic octave of tuned congas).

bongos*
congas
timbales
tom-toms
tenor drum
boobams*

*See the tuned bongos in Steve Reich's *Drumming* and the tuned boobams in Christopher Rouse's *Ku-Ka-Ilimoku*.

Reasonable But Unclear

The following instruments are usually indeterminately pitched, but they are easy to tune. It is reasonable to request fixed pitches for these instruments in small numbers; however, the pitches are unclear and may be difficult to discern.

snare drum
field drum
concert bass drum
pedal bass drum

Somewhat Reasonable

The following instruments are usually indeterminately pitched, but they are sometimes tunable. It is somewhat reasonable to request specific fixed pitches for these instruments in small numbers.

frame drum
djembe
doumbek
ethnic tambourines

Somewhat Reasonable But Expensive or Time Consuming

The following instruments are usually indeterminately pitched, and it is not difficult—but can be expensive or time consuming—to find items with specific pitches. It is somewhat reasonable to request specific pitches for these instruments in small numbers.

temple bowls*
metal pipes*
mixing bowls*
tin cans
pots and pans
bell plates*
glass bottles*
ceramic rice bowls*
flower pots
wooden planks and boxes

*With the exception of the temple bowls, all of these are re-purposed objects found in hardware and home goods stores, kitchens, and junk yards. Sifting through a shelf of rice bowls at a dollar store may yield one approximately tuned to a specific pitch, but temple bowls must be professionally manufactured as a musical instrument. Tuned temple bowls do exist (see Gyorgy Ligeti's *Síppal, dobbal, nádihegedűvel*), but they are uncommon. The pitch of mixing bowls, glass bottles, and rice bowls can be tuned lower by adding water, but the water will dampen the instrument. (See Water in appendix C). The tools to cut metal pipes to specific pitches are not difficult to acquire, but the process is time-consuming. (See Paul Lansky's *Threads* and Adam Silverman's *Naked and on Fire*.) Cutting bell plates to pitch requires professional machinery.

Not Recommended But Possible Through Playing Techniques

The following instruments are usually indeterminately pitched, but pitch can be manipulated by playing technique. It is not recommended, but it is possible to request specific pitches for these instruments.

cuica*
prayer stones*
sirens*

*Cuica and prayer stones are instruments capable of simple limited variations in pitch, but to play them accurately in tune is difficult. Usually these instruments are used for relative pitches—high and low, or high, medium, and low—or for more speech-song style pitch contours. Cuica is capable of two or three different pitches within the drum's harmonic spectrum plus small variations around each of those pitches. Cuicas may be tuned to adjust the harmonic spectrum, but the tuning will be fixed while it is played. Prayer stones are capable of specific pitches only when using the player's mouth as a resonating chamber; it is the pitch of the mouth, not that of the stones, that is manipulated. Sirens produce a whine, the pitch of which glissandos up and down with changes in dynamic; the player can control the pitches of the top and bottom of the pitch sweeps and even hover within a whole step of a single pitch.

Not Recommended But May Be Possible

The following instruments are usually indeterminately pitched, and it is difficult but not impossible to find items with specific pitches. It is not recommended but possible to request specific pitches for these instruments in small numbers.

triangle
finger cymbals
brake drums
small handbells
sleighbells
cowbells (see almglocken)
anvil
small gongs (see nipple gongs)
claves*
woodblocks
templeblocks*
log drums
conch shell*
whistles (except slide whistle)
string drum

*With a conch shell, pitch control within about a whole tone is achievable by moving the hand into the "bell" of the shell. Steve Reich requests tuned claves in his *Music for Pieces of Wood* and other works; claves with these pitches (A5, B5, C♯6 D♯6, and D♯7) are occasionally available. Templeblocks with specific pitches are requested for Louis Andriessen's *Woodpecker,* a solo work for marimba and templeblocks; the blocks must be specially made, and as a result, this work is rarely performed. If pitch specification of a wood instrument like a clave, woodblock, or templeblock is needed, single pitches from a xylophone or marimba might be a better option.

Not Recommended But May Be Possible, Though Unusual

The following instruments are usually indeterminately pitched, but isolated pitches may be available or achievable through playing techniques. It is awkward, unusual, and not recommended, but possible to request specific pitches for these instruments.

mark tree
metal wind chimes
medium and large bamboo wind chimes
glass wind chimes
bell tree

Not Reasonable

The following instruments are usually indeterminately pitched, it would be very difficult to find items with specific pitches, and these instruments sound rather unclear pitches. It is not reasonable to request specific pitches for these instruments.

medium to large tam-tams
suspended cymbals
spring coil
castanets
cajón

Unnecessary

The following instruments are usually indeterminately pitched and sound unclear pitches. It is unnecessary to request specific pitches for these instruments.

hi-hat
hand crash cymbals
thundersheet
rims of drums
Mahler hammer
cabasa
maracas
shakers
rainstick
guiro
washboard
ratchet
rute

sandpaper blocks
slapstick
stones
tambourine (jingles)
vibraslap
wind machine
small bamboo wind chimes

Dynamics

There are many variables that influence the dynamic at which an instrument sounds, and there are also many variables that influence how a performer interprets a written dynamic. For these reasons, precise balance is difficult to prescribe before the music is played by an ensemble, and dynamics are often the least reliable markings in a new score. The following charts are a tool with which the composer can more accurately balance percussion sounds in an ensemble to create effective orchestrations and well-blended sound combinations.

Just as *fortissimo* on a tuba is different from *fortissimo* on a harp, the written/sounding dynamic relationship can be different on different percussion instruments. These charts assume a one-to-one relationship between the written and sounding dynamics of a six-foot grand piano (i.e., a written dynamic of *piano* will sound at *piano,* and *fortissimo* will sound at *fortissimo*). The six-foot grand's dynamic is used as a yardstick to describe the sounding dynamic of percussion instruments interpreting the same written dynamic; for example, if a pianist plays music marked at *ff* on a six-foot grand piano, then a percussionist playing music marked at *ff* on snare drum with snare sticks will produce a sound louder than the piano (see chart).

Of course, in performance percussionists reinterpret dynamics with respect to musical considerations; the dynamics listed here are out-of-context dynamics—dynamics that would be produced if the percussionist were not playing a piece of music and not playing with anyone else.

Also listed are the maximum and minimum dynamics under normal playing conditions with the most common beater. For this, *ffff* and *pppp* are the assumed maximum and minimum dynamics for the six-foot grand. These are approximate, general dynamic boundaries that can be broken. In some cases, the maximum and minimum dynamics would be played on two different instruments (such as one large and one small ratchet), rather than played softer or louder on the same instrument.

These charts present the most usual sounds. It is assumed that the instrument, playing conditions, and beaters are the most common and usual as well. For example, a player could use brushes on a frame drum but probably would not. For all beater possibilities, see appendix G.

"Medium soft beater" means the yarn or felt mallet appropriate for that instrument. For the marimba, it means yarn mallets; for the bass drum, it means felt bass drum beaters. "Hard beater" means plastic, hard rubber, or metal beaters appropriate for that instrument. For the glockenspiel, it means plastic mallets; for the triangle, it means a triangle beater. The others are self-explanatory.

Instruments struck with beaters

written dynamic	medium soft beater		snare drum sticks		hard beater		hands		brushes		min dynamic	max dynamic
	p	*ff*	*p*	*ff*	*p*	*ff*	*p*	*ff*	*p*	*ff*		
six-foot grand piano	*p*	*ff*	*p*	*ff*	*p*	*ff*	*p*	*ff*	*p*	*ff*	*pppp*	*ffff*
marimba	*p*	*ff*	—	—	*mp*	*ff*	*pp*	*mp*	*pp*	*mp*	*n*	*fff*
vibraphone	*p*	*ff*	—	—	—	—	*pp*	*mp*	*pp*	*mp*	*n*	*ff*
xylophone	*pp*	*f*	—	—	*mp*	*fff*	*ppp*	*p*	*ppp*	*pp*	*ppp*	*ffff*
glockenspiel	—	—	—	—	*mp*	*fff*	*ppp*	*pp*	*ppp*	*pp*	*ppp*	*ffff*
crotales	—	—	—	—	*mp*	*fff*	*ppp*	*pp*	*pp*	*pp*	*pp*	*fffff*
tubular bells	*p*	*f*	*mp*	*mf*	*p*	*ff*	*ppp*	*pp*	*ppp*	*pp*	*ppppp*	*ffff*
timpani	*pp*	*fff*	—	—	—	—	*p*	*ff*	*mp*	*f*	*n*	*fffff*
snare drum	*mp*	*fff*	*p*	*fff*	*mp*	*fff*	*pp*	*ff*	*p*	*ff*	*ppp*	*fffff*
tom-toms and other drums	*pp*	*fff*	*p*	*fff*	*p*	*fff*	*pp*	*ff*	*p*	*ff*	*ppppp*	*fffff*
frame drum	—	—	—	—	—	—	*pp*	*f*	—	—	*n*	*ff*
djembe	—	—	—	—	—	—	*p*	*fff*	—	—	*n*	*fffff*
doumbek	—	—	—	—	—	—	*p*	*ff*	—	—	*n*	*fffff*
cymbals	*pp*	*ff*	*p*	*ff*	*p*	*ff*	*pp*	*mf*	*pp*	*mf*	*n*	*fffff*
tam-tams	*pp*	*fff*	*p*	*ff*	*p*	*fff*	*pp*	*mf*	*pp*	*mf*	*n*	*ffffff*

continued

Instruments struck with beaters (*Continued*)

	medium soft beater		snare drum sticks		hard beater		hands		brushes			
nipple gongs	p	ff	p	ff	p	ff	pp	mp	pp	mp	n	ffff
Chinese opera gongs	p	fff	mp	fff	mp	fff	pp	f	pp	mf	n	fffff
triangle	–	–	–	–	p	ff	–	–	ppp	mp	pp	fff
temple bowls/mixing bowls	p	f	p	ff	p	ff	p	mf	pp	mf	n	fff
cowbells/almglocken	p	ff	mp	fff	mp	fff	pp	mf	pp	mf	pppp	fffff
brake drums	pp	f	mp	ff	mp	ffff	pp	mp	pp	mp	n	ffffff
metal pipes	pp	mf	p	f	mp	fff	pp	pp	ppp	pp	n	ffff
spring coil	pp	mp	p	f	mp	f	–	–	pppp	p	n	fff
ribbon crasher	p	ff	p	ff	p	ff	p	f	ppp	f	ppp	fff
thundersheet	p	ff	p	ff	p	ffff	pp	fff	pp	mf	n	ffff
steel drums	p	f	–	–	–	–	p	mf	–	–	n	fff
bell tree	–	–	–	–	mp	ff	–	–	pp	mp	pp	fff
wood blocks/temple blocks	p	ff	p	fff	mp	fff	pp	mf	ppp	mp	ppp	ffff
log drums	p	ff	p	ff	p	fff	pp	mp	ppp	mf	pppp	fff
wood planks	p	f	p	f	p	ff	pp	mp	ppp	p	pppp	fff
wood boxes	p	ff	mp	fff	mp	fff	pp	mf	pp	mp	ppppp	fffff
crystal glasses	pp	mf	–	–	–	–	ppp	mp	ppp	p	pppp	mf
tambourine	mp	ff	mp	ff	mp	ff	mp	fff	mp	mf	pp	ffff

Instruments not normally struck with beaters

written dynamic	p	$f\!f$	min dynamic	max dynamic
six-foot grand piano	p	$f\!f$	$pppp$	$f\!f\!f\!f$
	no beater			
castanets	mp	$f\!f$	pp	$f\!f\!f\!f\!f$
maracas/shakers	mp	f	ppp	$f\!f$
guiro	p	$f\!f$	ppp	$f\!f\!f$
washboard	mp	$f\!f\!f$	pp	$f\!f\!f\!f\!f\!f$
claves	p	$f\!f$	$pppp$	$f\!f\!f$
cabasa	mp	f	p	$f\!f$
ratchet	mf	$f\!f$	mp	$f\!f\!f$
mark tree	mp	mf	p	mf
wind chimes	mp	f	p	$f\!f$
finger cymbals	p	f	$pppp$	$f\!f$
slapstick	mp	$f\!f\!f$	pp	$f\!f\!f\!f\!f$
vibraslap	mf	$f\!f$	mp	$f\!f$
sleighbells	p	f	ppp	f
sandpaper blocks	p	mf	$pppp$	f
whistles	mf	$f\!f$	p	$f\!f\!f\!f$
sirens	mp	$f\!f\!f$	mp	$f\!f\!f\!f\!f$
conch shell	mf	$f\!f\!f$	mf	$f\!f\!f\!f\!f$
wind machine	mp	f	p	$f\!f\!f$
rainstick	p	mf	$pppp$	mf
flexatone	mf	$f\!f$	p	$f\!f\!f$
string drum	mp	f	pp	$f\!f\!f$
cuica	p	f	$pppp$	$f\!f$
friction roll/superball mallets	pp	mf	$pppp$	f

Register

This appendix catalogues the ranges of nearly all the instruments discussed in this book—instruments of both determinate and indeterminate pitch, as shown in the series of figures shown below. The actual ranges of instruments of determinate pitch are notated with regular noteheads. The approximate ranges of instruments of indeterminate pitch are notated with square noteheads. Ranges for indeterminately pitched instruments are conservative, representing the most commonly available instruments under normal playing conditions. The ranges for cymbals, triangles, and thundersheets represent the spectrum from the lowest fundamental pitches to the clearest overtones present at loud dynamics. These are sounding, not written ranges for xylophone, glockenspiel, and crotales.

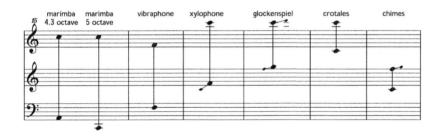

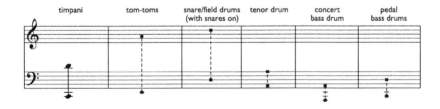

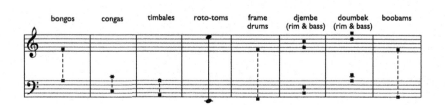

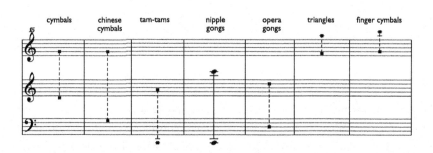

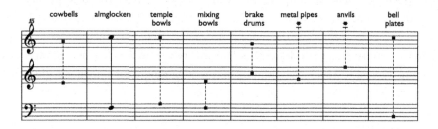

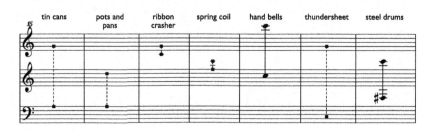

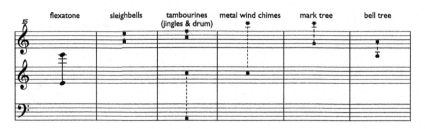

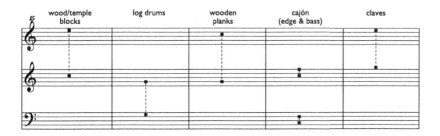

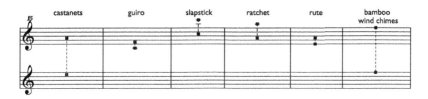

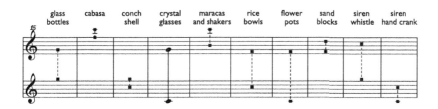

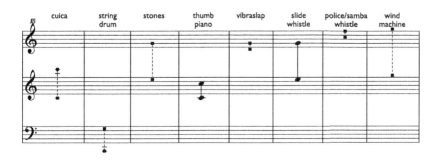

Beaters

The following table explains which beaters are most appropriate and/or possible on various instruments. This information will be valuable to composers writing for setups involving instruments that require different mallets. For example, a composer writing for crotales, marimba, and tom-toms can use this chart to see that time must be allotted for the player to switch between the mallets used for the marimba and those used for the crotales, but both mallets can be used successfully on the toms. (See chapter 4 for more information.)

Note: Numbers in the table are as follows:

1—best, most appropriate, most common sound
2—acceptable, but not ideal
3—acceptable, an unusual sound, a special effect
4—can be used, but sound will be of poor quality
5—can be used, but may damage the instrument
6—not acceptable

The instruments listed are those that one might strike with a stick or mallet. Claves, in this case, would be mounted.

Table of Beater Usage

	yarn/cord mallets (marimba/vibe mallets)	snare sticks	felt mallets (timpani mallets)	rubber mallets	wood mallets	plastic mallets (xylo/glock mallets)	brushes
marimba	1	5	2	1	5 (2 in upper register)	5 (2 in upper register)	3
xylophone	4 (2 w/very hard mallets)	5	4	1	1	1	3
vibraphone	1	3	2	2	3	5	3
glockenspiel/crotales	6 (4 w/extremely hard mallets)	4	4	4 (2 w/hard mallets)	2	1	3
tubular bells	2	3	2	2	2	2	3
timpani	4 (2 @loud dynamics)	5	1	2	2	5	2
tom toms/snare drum	2	1	1	1	1	1	1
bass drum	2	2	1	2	1	2	2
bongos/congas	2	1	1	1	1	2	2
wood blocks	2	1	2	1	1	1	3
temple blocks	1	1	2	1	1	1	3
log drums	1	2	2	1	2	5	3
boxes/plank	1	1	2	1	1	1	4

cajón	5 (2 w/soft mallets)	5	2	5 (2 @very soft dynamics)	5	5	3
machine castanets	2	2	2	2	2	5	2
claves	6 (4 w/very hard mallets)	4	6 (4 w/hard mallets)	4 (2 w/hard mallets)	1	1	6
cymbals	1	1	1	1	1	1	1
gongs	2 (1 on small gongs)	3	2	2	3	3	3
temple bowls	1	1	1	1	1	1	3
triangle	3	4	3	4	4	2	3
cowbells	1	1	2	1	1	1	3
brake drums/anvils	2	2	2	1	1	1	3
pipes/spring coil	4 (2 w/very hard mallets)	2	4	1	1	1	3
bell plates	1	1	2	1	2	1	3
thundersheet	2	2	2	2	2	2	3
steel drums	5	6	5	5 (1 w/soft mallets)	6	6	3
crystal glasses	1	1	2	1	1	1	3
tambourine	2	2	2	2	2	2	2

	brass mallets	hands	triangle beater	bass drum beater	gong beater	chime hammers	rute
marimba	6	4	6	6 (2 in lower register)	6	6	5
xylophone	6	4	6	6	6	6	3
vibraphone	6	4	3	6 (2 in lower register)	6	6	3
glockenspiel/crotales	1	4	2	6	6	6	3
tubular bells	3	4	3	4	6	1	3
timpani	6	2	6	4	6	6	3
tom toms/snare drum	6	2	5	4	6	6	3
bass drum	6	2	5	1	2	2	3
bongos/congas	6	1	5	4	6	6	3
wood blocks	6	2	2	6	6	6	3
temple blocks	6	2	2	6	6	6	3
log drums	6	2	5	4	6	6	3
boxes/plank	6	2	5	2	4	2	3
cajón	6	1	6	2	6	6	3

machine castanets	6	1	2	6	6	6	3
claves	6	6	2	6	6	6	6
cymbals	2	2	2	4	6	4	3
gongs	3	2	3	1	1	2	3
temple bowls	2	2	2	6	6	6	3
triangle	2	6	1	6	6	6	3
cowbells	2	2	2	6	6	6	3
brake drums/anvils	1	4	2	6	6	1	3
pipes/spring coil	1	4	2	6	6	1	3
bell plates	1	4	2	2	1	1	3
thundersheet	2	1	2	1	1	1	3
steel drums	6	2	6	6	6	6	5
crystal glasses	6	2	5	6	6	6	3
tambourine	6	1	5	4	6	6	3

Percussion Family Tree

As described in The Dysfunctional Family in chapter 1, the percussion repertoire is riddled with issues related to wrongly assumed equivalencies between percussion instruments. This is not a surprise, as the common methods of categorization inside the percussion family—wood/metal/skin, idiophone/areophone/membranophone, hit/scrape/shake, pitched/unpitched, and so on—are overly simple and incapable of capturing the sophistication of the relationships existing in this very large collection of instruments and sounds. Composers, without extensive listening and experimentation, are essentially combining instruments in the dark.

The following Percussion Family Tree sheds some light on these relationships. Like a traditional family tree, this tree presents the relationships between instruments and explains how, why, and to what degree they are different from one another. Four criteria have been used to determine the similarities and/or differences with respect to their compositional function:

    I. Pitch clarity
    II. Register
    III. Length of sustain
    IV. Sound production

Before presenting the Percussion Family Tree, however, this appendix offers the following explanatory figures for the individual variables.

Pitch Clarity Chart

Figure H.1: "Det." means the instrument is determinately pitched—that is, it is used with pitch specification. "Indet." and unmarked instruments are indeterminately pitched instruments—that is, they are used without pitch specification.

Note-Length Chart

Figure H.2: Arrows indicate the range of instruments with variable sustain. All Group 2, 3, and 4 instruments can be dampened to have minimal sustain (Group 1). Mark tree can only be dampened to be as short as Group 2. All instruments can be "sustained" with tremolo to sound as long as Group 4.

Figure H.1
Pitch clarity

Group One	**Group Two**	**Group Three**
Clear Pitch	Somewhat Clear Pitch	Less Clear Pitch
vibraphone (Det.)	steel drums (Det.)	tom-toms
marimba (Det.)	nipple gongs (Det. or Indet.)	roto-toms, low (Det. or Indet.)
xylophone (Det.)	timpani (Det.)	tenor drum
glockenspiel (Det.)	thumb piano (Det.)	djembe
tubular bells (Det.)	bongos, congas, timbales	ethnic tambourines
crotales (Det.)	frame drum, doumbek	triangle
almglocken (Det. or Indet.)	roto-toms, high (Det. or Indet.)	sleighbells
flexatone (Det. or Indet.)	boobams, (Det. or Indet.)	wood boxes
temple bowls	cowbells	tin cans
metal pipes	anvil	medium and large tam-tam
agogo bells	small gongs	mark tree
brake drums	wood blocks, temple blocks	glass or shell wind chimes
mixing bowls	log drums	med./lg. bamboo wind chimes
pots and pans	wooden planks	bell tree
finger cymbals	claves	string drum
bell plates (Det. or Indet.)	ceramic rice bowls	friction rolled instruments
small handbells	church bells	
church handbells (Det.)	glass bottles	
crystal glasses (Det. or Indet.)	whistles	
conch shell	cuica	
sirens	bowed cymbals and gongs	
	metal wind chimes	

Group Four	**Group Five**	
Nearly Unclear Pitch	Unclear Pitch	
snare drum	hihat	guiro, washboard
field drum	hand crash cymbals	ratchet
concert bass drum	ribbon crasher	rute
pedal bass drum	thundersheet	sandpaper blocks
suspended cymbals	rims of drums	slapstick
very large tam-tam	Mahler hammer	stones
castanets	cabasa	tambourine
cajón	maracas	vibraslap
spring coil	shakers	wind machine
	rainstick	small bamboo wind chimes

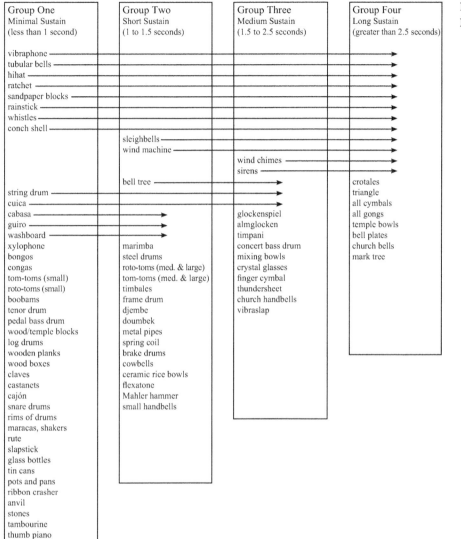

Figure H.2
Note length

Register Chart

Figure H.3: This is a low-resolution version of the multi-part figure in appendix F.

Sound Production Chart

Figure H.4: This is the only figure that shows discrete groups rather than a scale (from clear to unclear, long to short, or low to high). Instruments are often categorized by wood, metal, or skin; that method is not always accurate. The categories shown in figure H.4 illuminate more of those similarities that are functionally effective.

Idiophones are instruments that produce sound through vibration of their entire body. *Membranophones* are drums. *Friction instruments* produce sustained sounds

Figure H.3 Register

Group One
Treble 15ma (top of the piano keyboard)

glockenspiel
crotales
xylophone
claves
woodblocks
castanets
triangle
brake drums
suspended cymbals
metal pipes
spring coil
finger cymbals
anvil
bell plates (small)
glass bottles
small handbells
mark tree
glass/shell wind chimes
bell tree
cabasa
maracas
shakers
rainstick
ratchet
rute
sandpaper blocks
slapstick
sleighbells
tambourine
whistles

Group Two
Treble

marimba
vibraphone
tubular bells
steel drums
tom-toms (small)
roto-toms (small)
snare drum
bongos, congas
frame drum (small & med.)
djembe (rim tone)
doumbek (rim tone)
rim of drums
log drums
woodblocks, templeblocks
wooden planks, boxes
cymbals
tam-tams (small)
opera gongs
nipple gongs
bell gongs (small)
bell plates (medium)
cowbells, angleblock
church handbells
flexatone
temple bowls
mixing bowls
pots and pans
tin cans
ribbon crasher
ceramic rice bowls
crystal glasses
guiro, washboard
conch shell
thumb piano
sirens
cuica
stones
metal/bamboo wind chimes
vibraslap
wind machine

Group Three
Bass

marimba
timpani
tom-toms (med. & large)
roto-toms (med. & large)
field drum
tenor drum
frame drum (large)
djembe (bass tone)
doumbek (bass tone)
pedal bass drum
boobams
log drums
cajon
tam-tams (med. & large)
nipple gongs (med. & large)
bell plates (large)
church bells
thundersheet
string drum
Mahler hammer

Group Four
Bass 8vb (bottom of the piano keyboard)

concert bass drum
very large tam-tam

Figure H.4
Sound production

Group One
Struck Idiophones

marimba	mark tree
vibraphone	small handbells
xylophone	church handbells
glockenspiel	church bells
crotales	steel drums
tubular bells	woodblocks, templeblocks
cymbals	log drum
gongs	wood planks, boxes
triangle	Mahler hammer
finger cymbals	cajón
cowbells	claves
brake drums	castanets
anvil	rute
metal pipes	slapstick
bell plates	rim of drums
spring coil	ceramic rice bowls
temple bowls	crystal glasses
mixing bowls	glass bottles
pots and pans	thumb piano
tin cans	stones
thundersheet	coconuts
sleighbells	flexatone
bell tree	tambourine
wind chimes	

Group Two
Shaken and Rattled Idiophones

maracas	tambourine
shakers	small handbells
rainstick	wind chimes
vibraslap	mark tree
sleighbells	

Group Three
Scraped Idiophones

guiro	ratchet
washboard	wind machine
cabasa	bell tree
sandpaper blocks	

Group Four
Struck Membranophones

timpani	timbales
concert bass drum	frame drums
pedal bass drum	djembe
tom-toms	doumbek
roto-toms	snare drum (snares)
tenor drum	field drum (snares)
bongos	ethnic tambourines (jingles)
congas	

Group Five
Friction Instruments

bowed instruments
string drum
cuica
crystal glasses
wind machine

Group Six
Aerophones

conch shell
whistles
sirens

when bowed or rubbed. *Aerophones* produce sound with a stream of blowing air. The tambourine, sleighbells, wind chimes, mark tree, bell tree, handbells, and wind machine appear in multiple groups.

The struck, shaken, and scraped idiophones are more like each other than like the instruments in the other categories. Friction instruments and areophones are similar to each other because they both produce sustained tones.

The Percussion Family Tree

Figure H.6: The horizontal bottom line of the graph (X axis) represents note length. The vertical side line (Y axis) represents register. The pitch clarity is represented by shading (as showing in Figure H.5).

Figure H.5
Pitch clarity
shading

Clear Pitch
Somewhat Clear Pitch
Less Clear Pitch
Nearly Unclear Pitch
Unclear Pitch

Note 1: "Det." means the instrument is determinately pitched—that is, it is used with pitch specification. "Indet." and unmarked instruments are indeterminately pitched instruments—that is, they are used with without pitch specification.
Note 2: Sound production is indicated by abbreviation, as follows: StI = struck idiophones; ShI = shaken and rattled idiophones; ScI = scraped idiophones; M = struck membraophones; F = friction instruments; A = aerophones. The idiophone groups will be more similar to each other than to the M, F, or A groups.
Note 3: "Sm.," "med.," and "lg." mean small, medium, and large.
Note 4: Arrows indicate range of instruments with variable sustain.

Using the Family Tree

Of the four variables—pitch clarity, register, note length, and sound production—note the following. If two instruments share:

> four of the four variables, it is very likely a homogeneous-sounding combination.
> three of the four variables with one neighboring category, it is probably
> homogeneous and very likely a good blend.
> two of the four variables with two neighboring, it may be homogeneous but is
> probably a good blend.

And so on. As a point of reference, the combination of violin and cello is considered homogeneous sounding; the combination of bass clarinet and cello is considered a good blend.

Beater choice, beating spot, degree of dampening, and dynamic can significantly affect some of the variables, as follows:
Harder beaters:

less clear pitch
brighter color or higher pitch
louder dynamic

Playing toward the node:

less clear pitch
brighter color or higher pitch
softer dynamic

Addition of damping:

more clear pitch (light dampening)
less clear pitch (heavy dampening)
shorter sustain
softer dynamic

Louder dynamic:

less clear pitch
brighter color or higher pitch

The opposite treatments—soft beaters, playing away from the node, removal of dampening, and softer dynamics—have opposite effects. The Percussion Family Tree represents a dynamic of *mf* and "normal" beaters, beating spots, and degrees of dampening.

Treble 15ma   **Treble**

Stl crotales (det.)
Stl triangle
St/Shl mark tree
Stl suspended cymbals
Stl hand crash cymbals
Stl small gongs/tams
Stl church bells
Stl nipple gongs (det. or indet.)
(F only)
Stl temple bowls

Stl glockenspiel (det.)
St/Shl handbells (det. or indet.)
Stl finger cymbals
St/Shl wind chimes, sm.
Sr/Shl bamboo wind chimes, sm.
Shl vibraslap
Stl/F crystal glasses (det. or indet.)
A sirens
Stl almglocken (det. or indet.)
Stl mixing bowls
Stl handbells (det.)
Stl bell plates (det. or indet.)

Stl brake drums
Stl metal pipes
St/Shl sleighbells
Sr/Scl bell tree
Stl spring coil
Scl wind machine
Stl marimba (det.)
Stl flexatone (det. or indet.)
Stl cowbells
Stl steel drums (det.)
Stl rice bowls, flower pots

Stl xylophone (det.)
A whistles
Stl woodblocks, sm.
Stl claves
Stl anvil
Stl glass bottles
Stl castanets
Stl hihat
Shl maracas, shakers, rainstick
Scl ratchet
Scl sandpaper blocks
Scl cabasa
Scl guiro, washboard
Stl slapstick
Stl rute
St/Shl tambourine (jingles)
Stl ribbon crasher
Stl vibraphone (det.)
Stl tubular bells (det.)
A conch shell
Stl pots and pans
F cuica
Stl woodblocks, med./lg.
Stl templeblocks
Stl log drums
Stl tin cans
Stl thumb piano (det. or indet.)
M bongos, congas
M roto-toms, small (det. or indet.)

Treble

	Minimal Sustain (less than 1 second)	Short Sustain (1 to 1.5 seconds)	Medium Sustain (1.5 to 2.5 seconds)	Long Sustain (greater than 2.5 seconds)
	Stl wood drum, M tom-toms, small	M frame drum, sm./med., M djembe (rim tone), M doumbek (rim tone)	St/Shl metal wind chimes, med./lg.	Stl suspended cymbals
	Stl cajón, M snare drum (snares), M ethnic tambourines (jingles)		St/Shl bamboo wind chimes, med./lg.	
	Stl rims of drums, Stl stones	Stl thundersheet		Stl hand crash cymbals

Bass

	Minimal Sustain (less than 1 second)	Short Sustain (1 to 1.5 seconds)	Medium Sustain (1.5 to 2.5 seconds)	Long Sustain (greater than 2.5 seconds)
	Stl log drums, lg.	Stl marimba (det.)	M timpani (det.)	Stl nipple gongs (det. or indet.)
	F string drum, M tenor drum, M congas, M boobams	M timbales		Stl tam-tam, med./lg.
		M tom-toms, med./lg., M roto-toms, med./lg. (det. or indet.), M frame drum, lg., M djembe (bass tone), M doumbek (bass tone)	M bass drum, med./lg.	
	M field drum (snares), M pedal bass drum, Stl cajón	Stl Mahler hammer, Stl thundersheet		

Bass 8vb

	Minimal Sustain (less than 1 second)	Short Sustain (1 to 1.5 seconds)	Medium Sustain (1.5 to 2.5 seconds)	Long Sustain (greater than 2.5 seconds)
			M very large concert bass drum	Stl very large tam-tam

Figure H.6 Percussion Family Tree

INDEX

Page numbers for the primary entries are in boldface.

CPSIA information can be obtained
at www.ICGtesting.com
Printed in the USA
BVOW09s0758251017
498599BV00004B/15/P